FOR LIBERTY AND THE REPUBLIC

For Liberty and the Republic

The American Citizen as Soldier, 1775–1861

Ricardo A. Herrera

NEW YORK UNIVERSITY PRESS

New York and London

NEW YORK UNIVERSITY PRESS
New York and London
www.nyupress.org

References to Internet websites (URLs) were accurate at the time of writing. Neither the author nor New York University Press is responsible for URLs that may have expired or changed since the manuscript was prepared.

ISBN: 978-1-4798-1994-2

For Library of Congress Cataloging-in-Publication data, please contact the Library of Congress.

New York University Press books are printed on acid-free paper, and their binding materials are chosen for strength and durability. We strive to use environmentally responsible suppliers and materials to the greatest extent possible in publishing our books.

Manufactured in the United States of America

10 9 8 7 6 5 4 3 2 1

Also available as an ebook

For Dolora

CONTENTS

PREFACE

With the formal conclusion of the American combat mission in Afghanistan in 2014, the United States will have been at war for over a decade. Beginning with the attack and overthrow of the Taliban regime in Afghanistan in the aftermath of the 11 September 2001 attacks against New York City and Washington, DC, and the subsequent but spuriously related invasion and then ousting of the Saddamist regime in Iraq, these have been the longest continuous wars in American history. In each case United States and allied forces invaded and occupied these countries and set about trying to implant liberal democratic institutions while establishing, often belatedly, security and safety for the population. In the aftermath of these wars, whether and to what degree these sometimes halfhearted, stumbling, ill-considered, and frequently late attempts at nation building will ultimately succeed remains to be seen, as do the strategic implications of the wars. What is readily apparent, however, is the disengagement between American society and its armed forces.[1]

A professional, all-volunteer force representing something less than 1 percent of the nation's population has shouldered the burden of fighting, while the nation's political leaders have not asked the greater populace to make any sacrifices. Despite the plethora of cheap bumper-sticker sentiments expressing patriotism, hackneyed calls to support the troops, and public thanks for soldiers', sailors', airmen's, and marines' service, most Americans know little about those in uniform, and even less about military service. The wars, often well covered in the press and in cyberspace, have touched few Americans directly. The disconnection between American society and its armed forces looms large on the political, social, and economic landscape.

According to a 2011 Pew research report, over 80 percent of servicemen and women believed that American society has little or no understanding of them, their service, their challenges, nor, indeed, has much more than vague notions of previous generations' service. It seems, therefore, that an examination of soldiers' motivations and the meaning of their service is needed more than ever. Today's lack of mutual understanding by the people and their armed servants, however, is not atypical in the American experience. Except for the great national struggles like the Civil War, World War I, World War II, and the more limited Korean and Vietnam wars, Americans' connection with their armed forces has more often been the province of romantic idealizations, indifference, childish patriotic cant, or outright hostility. These attitudes have been recurrent themes throughout United States history. As lacking as Americans' knowledge of their armed forces may be, and as important as it is for citizens to develop an understanding of those in uniform is, recent events are too close to allow for a dispassionate examination of American military service and those who wear the uniform of the United States. This does not, however, preclude developing an insight into the nature or meaning of soldiering in the American experience. Indeed, in order to understand something of the present generation's service, an appreciation of the first generations of United States soldiers is in order.[2]

Military service was the vehicle by which American soldiers from the War for Independence through the Civil War demonstrated and defined their beliefs about the nature of American republicanism and how they, as citizens and soldiers, were participants in the republican experiment. This military ethos of republicanism, an ideology that was both derivative and representative of the larger body of American political beliefs and culture, illustrates American soldiers' faith in an inseparable connection between bearing arms on behalf of the United States and holding citizenship in it. Despite the undeniable existence of customs, organizations, and behaviors that were uniquely martial, the armed forces of the United States were the products of the society they represented and defended, and they cannot be examined apart from that society. Indeed, because the United States was created through war, an understanding of Revolutionary and nineteenth-century American military culture and thought brings into clearer relief some of the broader values of American society, thought, and culture.

Five broad, often overlapping, threads constituted the culture by which Americans defined and understood themselves as citizens and soldiers, the military ethos of republicanism: virtue; legitimacy; self-governance; God's will and the national mission; and glory, honor, and fame. This cultural complex informed and reinforced the connection between military service and republican citizenship. The ideas expressed by soldiers often carried multiple meanings. The distinctions between each concept were sometimes blurred or overlapping. Nonetheless, within each of the five threads of thought any number of constituent parts together formed a coherent whole. The order, conceptualization, and categorization of ideas, while not expressed as such by these soldiers, have been imposed as a way to organize and clarify their thoughts and facilitate our understanding. An examination of soldiers' records from more than forty archives in twenty-three states, encompassing a wide service, rank, chronological, regional, and documentary spectrum, revealed that the transcendent values commonly accepted by soldiers were only rarely and explicitly developed by them. To a very great degree these ideas' commonness belied the need for soldiers to expand upon them for their audiences.[3]

This study's thematic organization and methodology is explicitly derived from the continuity of the ethos. Each individual theme, just as with the greater ethos, existed as a continuum from 1775 to 1861. Except for stylistic differences and discrete historical particularities, most soldiers' letters are unified through their shared thoughts. Because of this, chronology figures little in each chapter. Because the patterns of belief remained constant, chronology has assumed secondary importance in organizing, presenting, and discussing the evidence. Dates are more important as confirmations of continuity than as markers of development. This secondary importance of chronology also accounts for the evidentiary organization within individual paragraphs and chapters. By way of example, evidence from the letter of a Continental soldier might be joined with that of a Civil War volunteer, followed by the letter of a soldier in the intervening period of time, which reinforces and speaks to the importance of the cultural and intellectual continuity of the ethos.

This work relies upon unpublished primary manuscript materials to a greater degree than on published primary sources. Most of these records are letters; orderly books, journals, and diaries make up another part of the record. Few memoirs or reminiscences were consulted. Underlying this approach is the belief that the letters and other documents written at the moment, or shortly thereafter, contain a greater degree of spontaneity and, consequently, greater authenticity and truthfulness because the authors created them in the heat of the moment and were thus unrehearsed or unembellished. Immediacy gives these documents a truer, less-rehearsed ring. Throughout, the original spellings have been largely retained. Bracketed letters have been used in the case of difficult abbreviations. Punctuation has been changed only to make confusing passages more understandable to the reader.

The records and categorizations are admittedly rationalizations, but not in the sense of excuses to assuage consciences or to justify actions or conduct. First, they are rationalizations because they helped order the intellectual lives of American soldiers. They are each soldier's effort at making sense of his military service and its connection to American republicanism, and at helping soldiers and their audiences understand the implications of their military service. Second, they are rationalizations because the order and organization this construct of ideas imposed upon these beliefs are the tools by which to understand, make sense, and order this body of thought. Taken together, these records document a pervasive multigenerational ideology. In "Ideology and the American Military Experience: A Reexamination of Early American Attitudes toward the Military," Jack C. Lane asserted that early American soldiers' belief systems were the means by which colonial soldiers responded to and made sense of war and their participation in it. Their ideology imposed order and gave greater meaning to soldiering. When thus understood, soldiers' belief systems provided them with secure psychological moorings in otherwise unfamiliar or unsettled situations. But ideology is more than a response to stress. It is also a means for the individual to order society and the world, thus enabling him to give meaning to his life and to understand his place in relation to his society and within the world. The security and surety of the military ethos of republicanism enabled American soldiers to understand their service as part of the republican experiment.[4]

Soldiers as the subjects of this study are considered in the broadest possible connotation of the word. They include officers and enlisted men of the regular army, the standing (enrolled) militia, the volunteer militia, and wartime volunteers, as well as Union and Confederate soldiers. Neither service nor regional distinctions greatly affected soldiers' acceptance of the military ethos of republicanism. Different institutions and accompanying cultures developed in each of these types of service, but, while sometimes seemingly divisive or antithetical, drew upon a common nexus of beliefs. What transpired, therefore, were variations on a shared theme.

The importance of this longer view is borne out by soldiers' records in which they and their officers looked to history, but also to the future, to influence their performance in combat. Soldiers' letters and the orders they received attest to the significance of the past as a standard for personal conduct and the future as judges upon that conduct in battle. As soldiers looked to the broader sweep of American history and they anticipated its future course, so this study looks at the broader sweep of this formative period in United States military history.

ACKNOWLEDGMENTS

This book has been a long time in coming. It and I owe much to the urgings, swift kicks, unsubtle nudges, gracious assistance, and critiques of many friends and historians. I cannot name all of those who have contributed in some way toward making this book a reality, so if I have forgotten to mention you please forgive me. I owe much to Robert Pettus Hay of Marquette University, a friend, mentor, and the finest example of a teacher. Many thanks to Mark D. McGarvie, a fellow student of Bob's, for his advice, support, and friendship. Wayne E. Lee, general editor of New York University Press's "Warfare and Culture" series, was instrumental in this work's appearance. John E. Grenier, Holly A. Mayer, and Richard Bruce Winder read through the entire manuscript and offered useful advice, most of which I took. Thank you to the anonymous readers. Their commentary and suggestions were beyond value. Thanks to Steve Lauer and Tony Carlson for reading and commenting on portions of this work, to the leadership at the U.S. Army School of Advanced Military Studies (SAMS) for its encouragement and support, and to The Hayloft at SAMS: a finer collection of colleagues does not exist. Debbie Gershenowitz, formerly of New York University Press, helped me get this project started, Clara Potter and Constance Grady have shepherded me through the process, as Dorothea S. Halliday and Willa Speiser have skillfully edited the manuscript. Peter Harrington of the Anne S.K. Brown Military Collection, Brown University Library provided the cover art. The annual meetings of the Society for Military History have been a welcoming, collegial, and convivial venue for discussions and critiques of this work with friends and fellow military historians Dave Fitzpatrick, Kurt Hackemer, Dick Kohn, Harold Selesky, John Shy, David Silbey, David Curtis Skaggs, Paul Springer, Janet Valentine, Bruce Vandervort, Sam Watson, Bob Wettemann, Kyle Zelner, and many others.

Without librarians and archival staff, this work would never have been possible. Thanks to all of them at: Alabama Department of Archives and History; American Antiquarian Society; Ancient and Honorable Artillery Company; Bancroft Library, University of California, Berkeley; Anne S.K. Brown Military Collection, Brown University Library; Boston Public Library; Center for American History, University of Texas, Austin; Charleston Library Society; Chicago Historical Society; William L. Clements Library, University of Michigan, Ann Arbor; Combined Arms Research Library, U.S. Army Command and General Staff College; The Filson Club; Georgia Historical Society; Hill Memorial Library, Louisiana State University; Historical Society of Pennsylvania; Houghton Library, Harvard University; Howard-Tilton Memorial Library, Tulane University; Henry E. Huntington Library; Illinois State Historical Library; Indiana Historical Society; Indiana State Library; Manuscript Division, Library of Congress; Maryland Historical Society; Massachusetts Historical Society; Mississippi Department of Archives and History; Missouri Historical Society; New-York Historical Society; New York Public Library; Ohio Historical Society; Raynor Memorial Library, Marquette University; South Carolina Historical Society; South Caroliniana Library, University of South Carolina; Southern Historical Collection, Wilson Library, The University of North Carolina; Special Collections, Earl Gregg Swem Library, College of William and Mary; Special Collections, United States Military Academy; Special Collections, University of Texas Arlington Library; Special Collections, University of Virginia Library; State Historical Society of Wisconsin; Tennessee State Library and Archives; Texas State Library and Archives; United States Army Military History Institute; Virginia Historical Society; and Williams Research Center of the Historic New Orleans Collection.

A Rev. John P. Raynor, S.J. Fellowship from Marquette University made the research for this project possible.

Portions of this book have previously appeared in print. Elements of the Introduction appeared as "A People and Its Soldiers: The American Citizen as Soldier, 1775–1861," *International Bibliography of Military History* 33 (2013): 9–34 (reprinted by permission of Brill). Part of chapter 3, "Free Men in Uniform: Soldierly Self-Governance," was published as "Self-Governance and the American Citizen as Soldier, 1775–1861," *The Journal of Military History* 65, no. 1 (January 2001): 21–52 (reprinted by permission of *The Journal of Military History*). Throughout the book are fragments of "Toward an American Army: U.S. Soldiers, the War of 1812, and National Identity," *Army History* 88 (Summer 2013): 42–57 (reprinted by permission of *Army History*).

Finally, thank you to Dolora Rose Herrera, Rosalie M. Herrera, and Walter and Margaret Rose for their support and faith throughout the years.

The views expressed in this book do not represent those of the United States Department of Defense, the United States Army, or any of their agencies.

Introduction

The American Citizen as Soldier and the Military Ethos of Republicanism

From 1775 to 1861, the American army was an awkward amalgam of the small regular army, the states' militias, and, in wartime, a mass of volunteers. This mixture, although complex and frequently cumbersome in practice, accorded well with the beliefs and needs of the American citizenry. Classical, Commonwealth, and American republican tradition equated citizenship with soldering, as well as a distrust of standing armies; hence the United States' greater reliance on and preference for the militia and volunteers. Americans perceived standing armies as more than potential threats to liberty. Professional soldiers were a poor commentary on the virtue and patriotism of the people and spirit of the country. Colonial Americans' experience with British soldiers in the Seven Years' War had only confirmed popular suspicions. Many thought professional soldiering to be symptomatic of popular corruption and incipient degeneracy. Nevertheless, the experience of the War for Independence had taught many Americans that a small regular army was valuable and that by restricting and securing its loyalty to the nation and its people, the army's existence might be reconciled with republican society and government. Thus, what followed was a military establishment acceptable to the larger political culture: one that was attuned and responsive to its ideology. Patterns of thought and behavior within the ethos were not, therefore, exclusive military traits, but were characteristic of the larger patterns within American political culture.[1]

So pervasive was the military ethos of republicanism that American soldiers, whether regulars, volunteers, or militiamen, believed themselves to be citizens first and foremost. Soldiers' understanding of their relationship to the republic helped define the nature of their service. Most of these men were either militiamen or volunteers, soldiers in an idealized classical republican sense. They served for short periods of time and expected to return to civilian life as quickly as possible. Most enlisted regulars served for one or two enlistments before returning to their former lives or embarking on new ones. It was only within the regular army's nineteenth-century officer corps that a core of committed professionals existed. Their numbers, however, were small. Therefore, when the republic went to war, it did so with a plenitude of volunteers and militiamen who vastly outnumbered the regulars. The sheer magnitude of volunteers' and militiamen's numbers within the ranks of wartime forces impressed upon the armies a pronounced civilian style, as historian Marcus Cunliffe observed. Indeed, as Cunliffe noted, in the republic's wars against Britain, Mexico, the Indian nations, and against itself in the Civil War, American "generals took the field at the head not of armies, but of agglomerations, each particle striving to be a law unto itself." The United States' armies were thus "affected by the whole ethos" of the "society" from which they were drawn. Volunteers, militiamen, and limited-term regulars gave American armies a distinctly civilian and republican character; their commitment to republican ideology guaranteed that American armies resonated with beliefs of American society, "its social order, and its values."[2]

In 1775 and 1861, Americans faced two great challenges. First, in 1775, Britain's North American colonies rebelled against Crown and ministerial authority, and fought to defend the traditional rights and privileges that British Americans had long identified as their constitutional liberties. With seeming singular speed, this constitutional crisis rapidly evolved into a revolution to establish an independent republic. In the course of that struggle, what began as a conservative movement to defend long-held English rights and liberties against the perceived encroachment of ministerial authority redefined the nature of the American political order and its source of sovereignty and legitimacy. The War for Independence, a colonial rebellion, was also a civil war, as well as a political revolution. Americans did not forget their revolution or their war for independence. Indeed, they went to war against one another over competing visions of that struggle's legacies. Two generations later, in 1861, Americans fought each other to establish and to defend their competing beliefs about the political nature of the republic. War, in each case, was an important transition point in United States history. National birth and survival depended on military service. The ideas under-pinning and informing American soldiers' service explained how they believed their service was an integral component of their citizenship and identity.[3]

War was a signal ingredient in Americans' creation of a national iden-tity, and it played a formative role in helping them define and under-stand what they saw as their national character. Indeed, because war was a "recurrent, almost endemic element" in early American history, it could not help but be a fundamental component in the construction of national identity. Americans remembered and celebrated the country's creation in the War for Independence. Their earliest demonstrations of what might be termed "national character" drew from Americans' shared and constructed memories of the war. Indeed early celebrations of the republic's independence were fundamentally martial in character, replete with patriotic speeches celebrating warlike valor, punctuated by artillery salutes and militia parades. A second war with Great Britain, in 1812, reinforced Americans' bellicose patriotism and the centrality of war in the nation's cultural makeup. The national anthem, a product of the War of 1812, exemplifies in popular and official culture what Marcus Cunliffe deemed a "formative martial impulse."[4]

The experience of war and military service was something shared be-tween soldiers from different states and regions, and it often transcended differences among Americans, helping them conceive of themselves as a people, however imperfectly. War and military service thus provided some necessary, even fundamental fictive elements in the construction and shaping and nature of American identity and political culture. As Jeremy Black has noted, in the tradition of American exceptionalism and the country's wars, there has been a "misleading emphasis on the volunteer military tradition and the citizen soldier." Americans' celebra-tion of this ideal was also a "closely related critique of professionalism, an emphasis that was particularly strong in the nineteenth century, and that still had echoes in the twentieth." As Americans saw their soldiers, so they saw themselves. Furthermore, as Black has contended, American political leaders and the people "have always found it hard to admit that their forces are being used for narrow selfish interests; hence, there is a high degree of rhetoric surrounding their usage." Understood in the government's public pronouncements and in popular belief, the United

States has historically eschewed "thinking or believing it is acting in a realist fashion, even when it is doing so." Culturally acceptable fictions, therefore, explain, rationalize, and justify the employment of military force and elevate the purposes of American wars.[5]

Fictions in this case are not to be construed as falsehoods but as truths of a fashion. They are the myths or principles by which people organize and understand themselves, their circumstances, and the world around them. Fictions are a fundamental element of culture, which as Michal Jan Rozbicki has pointed out, "stands on fictions," the representations of a people's reality. Having cast off the unifying element of the monarchy, a signifier of political legitimacy in the early-modern era and a unifying element within a diverse polity, Americans had to create, demonstrate, and embrace their new national identity as an independent people, a people no longer defined by their belonging to the British Empire, but to a distinctive, new state. Historian Jon Butler has argued for a mature American identity and culture by the eve of the Revolution, but this culture, while bearing many hallmarks of modern American society, was, nonetheless, understood by colonial Americans as an expression of their essential Britishness, their interpretation of British identity and conduct as expressed in the American environment, not as that of a people culturally and politically distinct from the mother country. Revolution and war created the United States. The republic and its people "owed . . . [their] existence to war." Thus it is altogether reasonable to conclude that any understanding of the American people requires understanding their military service, including the ideas underpinning and informing that service.[6]

At the beginning of this two-generation period, Americans began defining themselves as a people and as a nation in order to fix securely in their minds their place among the other peoples and nations of the world, not as subjects of the British Crown. Central to this quest for national definition and self-identification were American republicanism and citizenship. When the revolutionaries defined and understood themselves and the nature of American citizenship, they drew from a common intellectual heritage that was vibrant and meaningful and that resonated within the broader culture. In American soldiers' minds these cultural and intellectual attributes were constants that informed their service as they understood it. The durability of these ideas confirms their high degree of utility and basic truthfulness to American citizen-soldiers; their importance cannot be underestimated.[7]

Republicanism is invoked in its broadest possible aspect, holding American citizenship and how American soldiers understood themselves as members of the American polity. It is, of course, more than that. Eighteenth- and nineteenth-century republican thought in the United States spanned a continuum ranging from conservative to liberal, from the ascetic to the grasping, and everything in between. Frustrating and nebulous as this may be, this very broadness in concept is useful. It certainly was to Americans of this formative national era. By hewing to a broad rather than a narrow construction of republicanism, this framework mimics the breadth, depth, and ambiguity of republicanism as Americans conceived it in the eighteenth and nineteenth centuries. As Joyce Appleby has noted, there is "little doubt that republican and republic figured prominently, if ambiguously, in the public discourse of the eighteenth century." The very ambiguity of republicanism speaks to the plasticity and expansiveness of the concept in Americans' minds. Indeed, "Republic in fact appears as the conceptual equivalent of union in the nineteenth century and nation in the twentieth." Its meaning depended very much on the individual; it was an ideology for all seasons and all men. It was an attempt at asserting the primacy of communal values, of virtue, morality, simplicity, self-sacrifice, and frugality in the face of liberalism and its emphasis on the individual over the community, but also the reverse. Republicanism was at once the "chaste and venerable classical republicanism," but also its polar opposite, "liberal republicanism." Its central organizing concepts, "*virtue*, the *republic*, the *commonweal*," noted Daniel T. Rodgers, "were slippery and contested" even in the eighteenth and nineteenth centuries, and so it continued through the onset of the Civil War.[8]

In the 1960s, republicanism gained early-American historians' attention, and, as Appleby noted, it became through the 1980s the "most protean concept for those working on the culture of antebellum America." Although the tidal surge of the republican paradigm and synthesis has long since receded, republicanism still remains a useful concept by which to order and understand the world and culture of the American soldier. Indeed, as Robert Shalhope suggested, "Republicanism, considered as a cultural system, may well provide the most stimulating means of integrating the many insights of separate approaches into a useful reappraisal of early American society." If perhaps a bit dated or old-fashioned the system's utility remains. It provides the most coherent organizational framework and structure for grasping soldiers' beliefs as a whole. In considering mid-nineteenth-century republican belief in the northern states, Jean Baker posited a rhetorical question fit for the age: "If third-generation Americans must preserve the perfect government—if they were to be repairmen maintaining what the founders had built—why was it necessary to abandon that aspect of republicanism that depended on the public responsibilities of private citizens?" Why, indeed.[9]

Baker noted that by the 1830s it seemed that liberalism had triumphed over republicanism. America the virtuous was by then America the happy; individual fulfillment had trumped community and majority rule had triumphed over self-discipline. If, however, traditional republican discourse seemed to have largely disappeared and there were no great contests requiring republican virtue or sacrifice, the tradition continued. If not so explicitly stated as it had been in the founding era, republicanism had successfully become part and parcel of American culture and "reality." In the North, political parties and schools had become the primary repositories and transmitters of republican belief, and within these institutions their leaders celebrated the republican virtue of the founding generation while employing militarized rhetorical tropes. Among Southerners, the commitment to republican institutions remained strong. Despite the political turmoil between Democrats and Whigs in the years immediately preceding the Civil War, by 1850 white Southerners were able to agree on the need to join hands in order to protect the white political and racial order from the perceived threat of putative Northern tyrants. Their readiness and willingness to go to war to defend their vision of the republic were more amply demonstrated in 1861, as was Northerners' willingness to fight for their vision of the republic.[10]

As political and social historians shifted and broadened their horizons in the 1960s and 1970s, so too did military historians. American military historians expanded beyond the more traditional focuses on strategic, operational, tactical, institutional, and technological studies to include "New Military History," part of the larger development of "New Social History." Like new social history, new military history sought to understand the world of common people through quantifiable documentation and statistical analysis, their own records, and other sources regarding their lives. In the case of military history, scholars turned their attention to the world of enlisted men and women and ethnic and racial minorities and their experiences in military service so that they might shed light on soldiers' lives, their larger military communities, and the United States. These more expansive, critical, and extensive studies also highlighted where American society and the nation's armed forces intersected and diverged. Yet, despite the expansion of the field and the accompanying advances in knowledge, some of the works produced by the early 1980s were, according to historian Richard H. Kohn, "Myths in Need of History."[11]

Kohn suggested that historians' uncritical analyses and assumptions of American exceptionalism had led them to perpetuate little better than "stereotypical images" of American soldiers in their attempts to "discover the military essence in our character as a people." Because of these historians' notions about the singular nature of American society, they had helped perpetuate a popular, celebratory image of the American soldier as a "symbol, a political and cultural artifact for a nation diverse in culture, uncertain in unity, and concerned with proving its superiority to the rest of the world." Kohn denied that the American armed forces, "either as institutions or as collections of individuals, reflect our true character" as a people or as a nation. At first glance, Kohn's assertion rings true. The military's disciplined, uniformed, and hierarchical structure was and is anything but representative of the "decentralized, heterogeneous, individualistic, democratic society" of the United States. Upon closer reflection, however, this surface comparison does not reveal the full truth of the matter, if for no other reason than the armed forces' historic subordination to civilian control. Indeed, as General Andrew J. Goodpaster, former superintendent of the United States Military Academy, stated in a 1987 address, "Americans would not tolerate a military force that did not emanate from and reflect the breadth of American society and the ideals that animated" it. Goodpaster contended that the

American armed forces were unique. Instead of merely serving the "parent civil society," the American "military establishment" embodied the concerns, values, and fears of the society at large.[12]

In good English fashion, the Continental Congress was uneasy about the existence of a standing army and even more so about creating one. Like British Whigs, representatives to the Continental Congress feared regulars as potential tools of tyranny. Experience with the British army in America had merely compounded that fear. In order to lessen the potential threat to liberty posed by a standing army, the Continental Congress limited the initial term of enlistment to one year (later extended to three years), capped the army's initial size at about 27,000, although it likely never exceeded 25,000 soldiers throughout the war. Of even greater immediate and lasting import was the Continental Congress's appointment of George Washington as "General and Commander in chief of the Army of the United Colonies . . . , said Army for the Defence of American liberty." Congress signaled its trust in the former Virginia burgess by delegating to Washington the authority to recruit more soldiers, up to twice the number of British rankers in Boston, and giving him the right to fill officers' vacancies ranging from colonel downward. Recognizing the difficulties of communication and the need of the commander to make decisions on his own accord, Congress directed that "whereas all particulars cannot be foreseen, nor positive instructions for such emergencies . . . given," it was best to leave matters to Washington's "prudent and discreet management" and his "circumspection . . . , making it your special care in discharge of the great trust committed unto you, that the liberties of America receive no detriment." As the army's first commander, Washington set the tone of the army and helped shape its institutional culture, one that while distinct from civil society internalized its larger ethos and values.[13]

Washington was no democrat; he was a strict and even severe disciplinarian who had no truck with would-be levelers or mutineers within the Continental army or the militia. He tried desperately to create an American army in what he perceived as the image of the British army, and to a limited degree succeeded by the later years of the war. Nonetheless, Washington's strict adherence to Congress's authority signaled his deference to civilian control in much the same manner as did his regular communications with his civilian masters and the states' governors and legislatures. He tolerated or accommodated, albeit grudgingly, the often independent behavior of the states' militias.

Raising a regular establishment required that the army's allegiance, beliefs, conduct, and existence be reconciled with popular fears of standing armies. Congress, which had adopted the New England militia that besieged Boston in the spring of 1775 as the Continental army, yoked the army's loyalty to the Revolutionary and republican regimes through the Articles of War and by oaths pledging soldiers' fidelity to the revolutionary cause, with each soldier promising to "bind myself to conform, in all instances, to such rules and regulations, as are, or shall be, established for the government of the said Army." It was necessary, therefore, that the army have a broad "identification and dedication" to the "values of the society as a whole and identification with a broad segment of the society" from which it was drawn. Consequently, by virtue of creating a regular army with short enlistments, subservient to civilian control, and broadly compatible with larger norms, Americans developed a military establishment palatable to the larger political culture and responsive to its ideology. While the military's orderly structure and centralized organization did not "reflect a decentralized, heterogeneous, individualistic, democratic society," the army's existence as an instrument of the republic's policies and many of the individual beliefs impelling service certainly reflected the nature of American society. Soldiers' willingness to subscribe to the spirit of civilian control punctuated their belief in this element of the larger political culture.[14]

In their studies of American soldiers and military institutions and their relationships with the parent society and culture, including the concern over standing armies and the preservation of liberty, and even as demonstrations of manhood and masculinity, historians have broken important new ground. They have shed light on the American military experience by describing and analyzing soldiers' lives, the development of the armed forces, institutional histories of the officer corps, and the communities that formed around armies and their installations. The best of these studies have located soldiers' experiences and military institutions within the greater context and "perspective of American society and of other military systems." Since the 1990s, however, military historians have expanded beyond the realm of social history into broader cultural examinations.[15]

Examining the history of American military service through a cultural lens exposes what Wayne E. Lee has referred to as the "silent assumptions that common soldiers bring with them from society into the military." Soldiers' notions of citizenship and military mien and their concepts of people's expectations of them speak to the larger societal ideals soldiers subscribed to and that informed their understanding of themselves and their standards of conduct. Therefore, for American soldiers, the culture of the military ethos of republicanism made a "sensible and coherent order out of the myriad of differing and often contradictory ingredients" in the American experience from 1775 through 1861. It answered their "need for continuity" and order.[16]

From 1775 to 1861, American society was overwhelmingly English in its cultural, if not ethnic, derivation. From this tradition American society shaped its military values. England's late-Tudor trainbands were the progenitors of the colonial militias from which American military institutions evolved. In forming these trainbands English settlers drew upon two models. The first model, inspired by London's voluntary associations, was widely adopted in New England. In much the same fashion that London's urban density facilitated raising the city's militia companies, so too did the Puritans' propensity for settling in towns. Naturally, other factors contributed. Nonetheless, the pattern resulted in units that mustered regularly and often demonstrated an impressive degree of military knowledge and training. A prime example was Boston's Ancient and Honorable Artillery Company. Its members formed a voluntarily covenanted military association to meet the requirement for establishing and maintaining a militia for local defense. In the nineteenth century a similar organizational pattern developed throughout the United States in urbanized and town-centered locales as volunteer militia companies superseded the older enrolled militia. The second model, the enrolled militia, developed out of the county system and was common throughout British North America. Companies typically organized according to local community boundaries and exhibited few of the voluntary associative aspects present in the London or New England trainbands. In this instance the militia roll was a roster of men subject to service. These men were required to respond to local and national needs at the behest of county lieutenants and local gentry. Economics and parsimony manifested themselves in the militia's formation. Elizabeth's empty treasury and her own tightfisted nature prevented her from raising a regular army.[17]

In both of these cases, colonial military units reflected regional differences and local priorities. When raising troops for offensive or expeditionary purposes, first colonies and later the states relied upon volunteers and conscripts from the standing militia. Gradually, trainbands evolved into more formalized and regulated militias. North America's English settlers had carried with them their cultural baggage and had planted the seeds for colonial and states militias.[18]

Institutionally, and in its most idealized form, the enrolled militia embodied the notion of universal military service. Roughly speaking, all able-bodied men from sixteen to sixty were enrolled in the local militia company and were expected to attend musters or to pay fines for not complying with laws mandating such service. Depending on the laws of each colony, the personal status of obligated men ranged from freemen to indentured servants. Few men were exempt from service. Motives ranging from entertainment, adventure, social expectations, and legal requirements helped guarantee a modicum of compliance at militia assemblies. By linking status and political rights with the obligations of military duty, British colonists established the militant civic character of the American body politic.

Living on the often-violent periphery of the British Empire without a regular army for protection made colonists acutely aware of the need to develop and maintain good soldierly qualities and skills. Unlike their brethren in the mother country or so many contemporary Europeans living in states with standing armies, British colonists, often the marginalized among them, were the army. Colonists' circumstances meant that in addition to their daily lives as farmers, merchants, fishermen, tradesmen, and such they were also part-time soldiers in a nascent form of universal military service. They had transplanted their mother-country militia traditions in the colonies and introduced the "concept of the citizen-soldier" to British North America. Whereas the people armed struck a chord of fear in English and European leaders, it was a way of life, a necessity, and a demand in the New World. Consequently, colonial life joined military service, citizenship, and the rights and privileges enjoyed by English, later British, subjects in the New World. Colonials' lives also exhibited the cultural tensions and contradictions exposed by historians of republicanism. In view of that, as John Ferling noted, colonial elites "generally believed their subjects were more virtuous, enlightened, less obsequious, and more materialistic than European commoners." Moreover, creole political and military leaders, imbued with a self-confident sense of their own political and moral "virtue and acumen" and the corresponding inferiority of their opponents, believed that their brand of warfare, its motives, their soldiers, and their practices were inherently just. If wartime losses against Indian foes caused colonists to question themselves and whether they had incurred divine wrath, subsequent successes reassured them in the ultimate justness of their causes.[19]

Training-day sermons and other forms of rhetoric "concerning the defense of liberty" reinforced colonial soldiers' beliefs and were among the primary means for inspiring, reassuring, and encouraging them in the performance of their duties. Even at this early stage of development the "most striking aspect of American attitudes toward war and warriors" in the New World was "their unchanging, lockstep nature." One historian wrote that by 1775 the colonists' "violent history rendered Americans psychologically eager for conflict." Militia service, frequent wars, and the relatively recent deployment of regulars to North America deeply affected the population. The responsibilities shouldered by local communities during war contributed to the political maturation of the colonies and contributed to colonists considering the nature, shape, and formation of local and imperial institutions, governance, and themselves as a people. Understood in this context, war and soldiering were significant steps in the formation of American political culture. On a more basic level, military service was a step in the development of the American sense of self-governance. Soldiering was an entrée to the world of individual rights, responsibilities, and autonomy.[20]

Young men without a stake in society perceived that "military service was a reasonably lucrative proposition" that might provide them with the money or land grants necessary to assist them in their quests for personal political and economic autonomy. Furthermore, military service offered men the prospects of adventure, an opportunity to break free from the stifling sameness of everyday life, the expectation of personal enrichment through plundering the enemy, and the chance for the soldier to join in the age-old contest against his traditional enemies, the "papist French" and Spanish, or against more recent ones, the "barbarous Indians." Hence, for many young men "military service promised both a change from the accustomed routines and perhaps an accelerated entry into real manhood" with its emphasis on political and economic independence. In short, soldiering helped men move toward attaining their economic independence, which in turn, enabled them to participate in the political process as they demonstrated their manhood. Warfare, an element in provincial Americans' "cultural heritage," contributed to Americans' "sense of themselves as a distinct people" who had reached their political maturity and were capable of self-governance.[21]

The colonial soldiery was frequently the target of professional soldiers' barbs. According to many British regulars, Americans were undisciplined, amateurish, cowardly, and legalistic. When judged against the standards of professional European armies, it is no wonder that Americans fared so poorly in comparison to British regulars. However, when judged according to the standards and expectations of colonial society and warfare, a different picture emerges. Fred Anderson's study of Massachusetts provincials in the Seven Years' War focused on the quotidian aspects of military life: the routines of camp and march, military discipline, and their views on war "in order to gauge the effects of military service" on soldiers of the Bay Colony and established that the Yankee provincials' "apparently unsoldierly conduct" was fully in line with New England's principals and was indeed ethical and just.[22]

Willful, truculent, and obstreperous they were, but colonial soldiers' acts of mutiny and their refusal to obey orders were not due so much to cowardice or to a total want of discipline as to their belief in the "centrality of contract in popular understandings of the legitimate exercise of authority." Military officials who had failed to live up to their contractual obligations relating to food, equipment, or tenure of service nullified any expectations of obedience from the ranks. It was that simple. In this light, mutiny and disobedience were symptomatic of the deep and abiding belief in the power, legitimacy, and universal applicability of mutually binding agreements as embodied in lawful contracts. Recalcitrant soldiers were, therefore, exercising their right to self-governance in one of its most basic manifestations—the right to withhold labor following their employer's breach of contract, an act that some in the Continental army replicated when the army's paymasters and commissaries were un-able to fulfill their duties.[23]

When the Continental Congress created the Continental army in the months following the battles of Lexington and Concord, it proclaimed the new republic's self-image as much as it raised a force for self-defense, an act much in common with other newly founded countries. As S. E. Finer pointed out, for a new nation the "army symbolizes, as well as makes effective," the new country's "distinctive identity" and its self-image. This was manifestly the case in 1775. Within three months of the first engagements at Lexington and Concord, the Continental Congress adopted the army assembled around Boston, thus acknowledging the military force that embodied New England's armed opposition as the armed expression of American resistance. Because so much of the char-acteristic citizen-soldier's identity was embodied in the militia, this too must be considered a vital part of the American military equation of the army as an exemplar of national distinctiveness. The militia and the newly named Continental army were the military essence of Revolution-ary beliefs, and they expressed the distinctiveness and identity of the American cause as an army of resistance and revolution.[24]

The organization, plan, and discipline of the army in 1775 exhibited its essential character, that of a "citizen army," according to Don Hig-ginbotham. It was "composed chiefly of yeomen and artisans, the core of American society, rather than a conglomeration of flotsam and jet-sam thrown up" by European economic convulsions. Even when serving as regulars, American soldiers could not divorce themselves from the deeply ingrained strictures of civil society. A strict contractual sense of right and wrong continued among the regulars of the Continental army. Under the circumstance, it was not a "unique episode" when the Penn-sylvania Line revolted in 1781 over issues of pay and discharges due to them in their enlistment contracts. Higginbotham believes this action could "only have occurred in a country where many of the men were up-standing citizen-soldiers conscious of their rights and liberties." Revo-lutionary soldiers constituted a "republican army" that was "remarkably loyal to the civil authority and to the goals of the Revolution." Moti-vated by his understanding of republicanism and by his hope for the future, the Continental spent "his blood in his own cause, for a country in which he had a share, a country where people had more rights and liberties than anywhere else in the world."[25]

It is apparent, therefore, that the larger nexus of republican culture that linked the revolution's survival with military service also informed the nature of American military service. Charles Royster, who argued for the Continental army as the representation of "American character prevalent during the War for Independence," contended that the war was a test of Americans' virtue, and that the character of the people was the "central theme" in the struggle, as Americans considered the army and its place in the contest for independence. While war caused Americans to reflect upon themselves as a people, it also spurred individual and community action through more prosaic acts like promises of regular pay and enlistment bounties. Pay and bounties in cash or land, attractions to men without means, were more than mere economic exchanges or inducements such as men might have encountered in an exchange of cash for labor. The harsh conditions of camp life or the chance of death, disablement, or maiming from disease or the British were altogether too frequent risks for bonuses and low or infrequent pay to mitigate. After careful consideration of these possibilities it is apparent that material motives cannot have inspired more than a small handful of men to serve in the army. Larger cultural and ideological motives, including those of honor and personal repute, were truer sources of inspirations. The task of revolutionizing the soldiery and maintaining cohesion fell to the officer corps.[26]

"When all is said," wrote Don Higginbotham, "one still gets the feeling that the Continental officers' dedication to republican principles" was as sincere as that of their civilian counterparts. Higginbotham emphasized that the Continental army was a force "whose leadership was anything but divorced from society." Indeed, the vast majority of its leaders had every intention of returning to that society. Committed to the success and survival of the army and thus the revolution, Continental officers held the army together through a "mixture of threats, cajolery, and artful persuasion." Officers, inspired by the example of George Washington and his senior officers, worked to improve soldiers' living conditions and outlooks through clothing, food, and training, as well as "by explaining the issues of a struggle being fought for freedom." Officers articulated their views through the ideology of republicanism—a prescription of hope—instead of simply instilling obedience and martial behavior through fear and harsh discipline, although they often had no compunction about this as a final resort. By articulating the promise and ideas underpinning the War for Independence in common thought and words, in the phrases consonant with the broader political culture, officers both led and taught their troops.[27]

Having won their independence from Great Britain, Americans began the difficult task of securing the revolution and guiding the new republic's course, including the nature of its armed forces. In two separate works, Richard H. Kohn and Lawrence Delbert Cress examined the new nation's struggle to determine its military policy. Kohn found that the small regular army's appeal to Federalists was based on the "timeless, ordered, hierarchical" structure of armies. Talent and its reward of position and rank were more important than political "personality." For the unsure or threatened Federalist the "army represented tradition and stability in a world staggering through a wave of democratic revolution" and the aftereffects of social and political disorder. Maintaining a strong regular army officered by Federalists would allow traditional elites to distinguish themselves from the "multitude" and to help give order to the often chaotic life of the new republic. Their quest for stability and order through the agency of a standing army threatened the republic, however. The only effective counterpoise was limiting the size of the regular army and the centralizing tendencies it represented and bolstering the motley of states' militias.[28]

Concern over the army's loyalty to the nation and republicanism, noted Cress, drove the debates over the regular establishment in the early republic. Americans, from their reading of history, knew that by "their nature, military institutions held the power to destroy as well as to preserve; hence the character and composition of the military was of major importance." A standing army was necessary to defend the nation in a world full of potential threats and predatory princes. But an ideologically unsound army could just as surely become the instrument of internal oppression. Therefore, the matter raised "fundamental questions about the nature and viability of republican society." For a republic to survive and remain viable, its soldiers, indeed the institution itself, had to be representative of the greater body of beliefs held by society and act in consonance with those beliefs. Concerns such as this, coupled with the long history of the militia, led Americans to the conclusion that an active and ideologically sound citizen-soldiery could counterbalance any potential threats posed by ambitious antirepublican regulars.[29]

In 1803, the newly established military academy at West Point increased the fervor of the discussion. Academy opponents derided the institution as a threat to the republic, fearing it would become a breeding ground for incipient antidemocratic military aristocrats, an accusation that, along with polemics during the Civil War that it had been a school for treason, haunted the institution until late in the nineteenth century. Theodore J. Crackel has shown that Thomas Jefferson shared similar suspicions and intended therefore that West Point would become the chief instrument for the republican indoctrination of the army's officer corps. Instead of producing would-be dictators, the academy would educate young men of republican inclinations to introduce their political beliefs into the army, thereby transforming it into a bulwark of the Jeffersonian political order. Army officers would, in effect, become the leading agents in the politicization of the regular establishment, thus reflecting what Jefferson believed were the political beliefs of the nation. Hence, there developed a more widespread belief that the political indoctrination of the officer corps would give some form of assurance that the regulars would remain loyal to the nation and thus would not attempt to subvert the people's rights. These concerns were not manifestly present in the ranks of the militia and volunteers, who conceived themselves to be the true guarantors of the republic's liberty.[30]

American rights emerged as an international issue in early republican political discourse in the late eighteenth and early nineteenth centuries and contributed to the declaration of war against Great Britain in 1812. Set against the much larger French revolutionary and Napoleonic wars (1792–1815), American politicians protested against British impressment of American sailors and for the rights of neutral nations engaged in free trade. Free trade and sailors' rights were only part of the problem, however. Western expansion, Indian resistance against American encroachments, and British support of Indians in the Old Northwest (the present-day states of Ohio, Indiana, Illinois, Michigan, Wisconsin, and parts of Minnesota) provided for additional grievances and points of friction between the former mother country and the young republic.

Separated but a few years from the War for Independence, American soldiers echoed the beliefs voiced by their predecessors in the previous war. Their beliefs were a touchstone of cultural and intellectual constancy as Americans collectively devoted more effort and attention to western expansion and less to affairs in Europe.[31]

As the country matured and expanded westward and external threats lessened in the early nineteenth century, the states' militias declined in their importance and utility as a form of communal military service. The militias' decline, however, did not signal an end to the military ethos of republicanism. Americans with a military bent responded by joining with like-minded men in exclusive, volunteer militia companies. Within numerous communities, volunteer companies, many of which were formally incorporated into the structure of states' militias, became the craze. For these Americans, the "militia ethos was almost as viable in the nineteenth century as in the republic's dawning days." Resembling highly selective social clubs, volunteer companies frequently screened candidates and voted whether to admit or reject prospective members. Detailed constitutions specifying members' duties, uniforms, and election procedures for officers and noncommissioned officers were the norm.[32]

The volunteers' exclusivity resulted from any number of factors. For some companies it was a reaction against growing democratic practices and the perceived leveling tendencies of democracy. For others it was a way to unite and give form to political, social, or economic aspirations, democracy in action. Immigrants often formed companies to demonstrate their loyalty to the republic and to band together in common defense against rival companies. Many men joined for entertainment. All companies, however, reflected parochial concerns that fitted fully and well within the larger body of republican culture.

Despite the exclusive nature of the volunteers, these companies were, internally, among the most democratic of American institutions. In companies composed of social, ethnic, political, or economic peers and allies, all volunteers were equal. Enlisted men nominated and elected their noncommissioned and commissioned officers and company constitutions could change only through democratic processes. While the nation at large refashioned the mechanics of a democratic republic, so too did its citizen-soldiers. In spite of the conflicting and varied motives for forming or joining a volunteer company, most members were united by the desire to demonstrate their worthiness as men and as citizens. Education and periodical publishing were other arenas in which Americans demonstrated their interest in military affairs.[33]

In the popular imagination the volunteer represented, as few soldiers could, the quintessential American military character. Robert W. Johannsen wrote that "Americans perceived their volunteers as they perceived themselves: simple, unpretentious, impatient with authority, individualistic, and disdainful of class distinction." The volunteer, drawn as he was from the mass of Americans, could not help but hold such beliefs. The myth of Cincinnatus, the "image of the citizen-soldier, the individual who turned from peaceful civilian pursuits to the defense of his country" captured the "popular mind and confirmed the nation's republican mission" to spread the blessings of republican society and government globally. If the volunteer personified the militant, republican character and self-image of Americans, the war in which he served was less clear.[34]

By celebrating the volunteer, Americans celebrated the nation and the individual. War with Mexico, however, posed troubling questions about the nation, its identity, and its fidelity to the republican cultural tradition. Although many Americans, particularly northern Whigs, decried the war as an unjust conflict trumped up to serve the expansionist interests of the slaveholding South, few subjected the volunteer to their critique. Unlike the base hirelings of the regular army, many of whom were immigrant Catholics driven by poverty, the volunteer embodied the finest attributes of republican culture. Johannsen argued that the Mexican War was a signal "episode in the American quest for national identity." Americans' "egalitarian view of heroism—every man a hero, at least potentially—was reinforced by reliance on the citizen-soldier, the ultimate expression of republican virtue." Volunteers were missionaries and "pioneers, carrying the tenets of republican government and extending the bounds of American civilization" to more benighted regions, and, reluctantly, peoples. By spreading the blessings of American liberty, America's militant proselytizers were "bringing to fruition God's plan for all mankind." These soldiers, just a generation or two removed from Lexington and Yorktown, were thoroughly imbued with the spirit of "Revolutionary republicanism." A dynamic ideology, it "provided the inspiration for much of what Americans believed about themselves and their nation"[35]

Because of their self-governing and voluntary nature, militiamen and volunteers believed themselves more patriotic and more trustworthy with the republic's liberty than the regulars. These men believed in an idealized form of universal military obligation, one in which moral compulsion, not that of the state, obligated men to serve. This was the proof of good citizenship, but one in which individual rights were highly esteemed. In a variation on the myth of Cincinnatus, militiamen temporarily joined together for local defense. As soon as the threat of attack subsided or the militiaman decided he had honorably served his community, the citizen-soldier returned home. Democratically elected officers led these men, and because they were elected by their men, these sociopolitical and economic elites had to exercise their authority gently. To these volunteers and militiamen the regular was a base hireling who was unable or unwilling to exercise any degree of self-governance, in much the same fashion that militant Protestants believed that Roman Catholics subscribed without thought to Popish doctrine and the authority of princely cardinals and bishops. Slavish obedience to the military hierarchy and officers with aristocratic pretensions threatened the existence of a republican United States. Surely such men could not be entrusted with the future of the nation. Suspicions about trust and worthiness were not the province of the militia and volunteers alone.

Regulars viewed their counterparts in the militia and volunteers with concern. To some professionals these men seemed unduly concerned about their individual rights to become good soldiers of the republic. Indeed, the unwillingness of militiamen and volunteers to accept the self-abnegation demanded by military discipline caused some professionals to doubt their patriotism. As the regular army matured and developed, its communal culture subsumed many of its soldiers' more pronounced individualistic tendencies. Self-sacrifice and the needs of the community became the touchstones of republican virtue and self-worth for the Continental army and for its descendants. To many regulars the undisciplined militiamen and volunteers hardly seemed the stuff of republicanism.

James M. McCaffrey, in considering what he termed the *Army of Manifest Destiny*, discerned that the chief motives for men's enlisting were the quest for personal distinction and "glory and adventure in a foreign land." As in all wars, soldiers and political leaders hid their motives beneath a veneer of patriotic "rhetoric." In the Mexican War, they also appealed to a "perceived need to avenge the deaths of the men killed during the Texas Revolution" and during the ensuing troubles between Texas and Mexico. This heady mixture inspired the "same sort of *rage militaire* that swept across the American colonies in 1775." Glory and revenge made the war with Mexico a "crusade of sorts" for would-be republican knights-errant. The aggressive spirit of the volunteers was the very "embodiment of the concept of manifest destiny." As soldiers of the expanding republic, they were "unwilling to allow anything to stand in the way of their nation's course to greatness." McCaffrey concluded that the citizen-soldiers of the Mexican War were "not very different from the volunteer soldiers throughout American history." They too had been weaned on the tradition of revolutionary republicanism and the myth of the citizen-soldier springing to the defense of the republic.[36]

Richard Bruce Winders examined the composition and political loyalties of the army that conquered a peace in Mexico, and he uncovered the story of an "overwhelmingly Democratic" officer corps in the regular regiments raised for the war and within the body of volunteer generals. President James K. Polk believed the army was a "marriage of aristocrats and hirelings," antithetical to republican and democratic practices. When Congress created the Regiment of Mounted Rifles, today's Third Cavalry Regiment, and ten limited-term regular regiments for the war, Polk determined to "bypass the established [military] hierarchy by directly appointing men from civilian life," thus assuring himself of the new officers' loyalties. Polk followed the same practice by appointing only loyal Democrats as generals of volunteers. Mr. Polk's army was a "creature of politics" and pragmatism that would serve only as long as its tenure and purpose accorded with the popular temper and the president's wishes. Although popularly esteemed as "Young Hickory," Polk was surely the son of Jefferson when it came to his attempts at politicizing the army officer corps. Interested in politics as some army officers might have been, there were more pressing, more immediate concerns facing them in the challenges of leading, commanding, and soldiering on the frontier.[37]

Throughout this period and for much of its history, the regular army remained a small body most often posted along the frontier in company-size elements. Indeed, frontier duty, while despised by many officers, was the regular army's raison d'etre from the days of the early republic through the end of the nineteenth century. Although William B. Skelton believed, and not without cause, that frontier duty caused the army to grow "progressively more isolated, both physically and intellectually, from the mainstream of American life," other studies suggest that the army's isolation was more temporal and physical than political, intellectual, or cultural. Although the frontier army was, indeed, physically isolated, it was never divorced from its role as a political actor and agent of the federal government. In *Broadax and Bayonet: The Role of the United States Army in the Development of the Northwest, 1815–1860* and *The Sword of the Republic: The United States Army on the Frontier, 1783–1846*, Francis Paul Prucha highlighted the army as an agent of American political, social, and economic expansion and its soldiers "as the instruments of Congress and the President in vindicating American rights" as enforcers, diplomats, and administrators in the years of the early republic through 1860. The army continued this mission in the years following the conclusion of the Mexican War through those of the Civil War, the focus of Robert M. Utley's *Frontiersmen in Blue: The United States Army and the Indian, 1848–1865*. Difficulties certainly abounded as the army fulfilled, to greater or lesser success, its tasks on the frontier. Much of that success was due to the officers corps charged with executing government policy.[38]

In *Jackson's Sword: The Army Officer Corps on the American Frontier, 1810–1821* and *Peacekeepers and Conquerors: The Army Officer Corps on the American Frontier, 1821–1846*, Samuel J. Watson has written compellingly of the officer corps' commitment to republican political culture and of its service in roles beyond combat, particularly as diplomats. In addition to their diplomatic service, officers also performed invaluable work in filling in the human, floral, faunal, and geographic details of the United States' western expanses, something detailed in William Goetzmann's *Army Exploration in the West, 1803–1863*. Topographical engineers' reports, in particular, helped shape how Americans viewed the West. Closely related to officers' work and interest in science and diplomacy were their interests in painting, literature, military bands, and architecture. Indeed, Marilyn Anne Kindred's study of the officer corps as artistic patrons on the frontier makes a strong case for officers' links with American society and participation in more refined pursuits. Thus, in the realms of diplomacy, science, early ethnography, and the arts, army officers figured prominently in learned circles as contributors and as consumers. Officers' variegated work linked them closely to the eastern centers of intellectual inquiry and beyond.[39]

Despite their physical separation from major social and intellectual centers, officers maintained an active interest in American scientific, artistic, and literary life even as they performed their official duties. More important, however, was the officer corps' embrace, internalization, and practice of the "republican values" of "subordination, loyalty, and accountability" to the army's civilian masters. What becomes apparent is that the United States Army was, in Michael L. Tate's call for further research on the frontier force, a "multi-purpose" tool. Tate, in *The Frontier Army in the Settlement of the West*, Durwood Ball in *Army Regulars on the Frontier, 1848–1861*, and Robert Wooster in *The American Military Frontiers: The United States Army in the West, 1783–1900* make abundantly clear the myriad existences, functions, and roles fulfilled by the army as it extended the writ of the federal government. Physical separation might have attenuated but never broke the intellectual connection between American culture and the army or, for that matter, military service in general. Citizenship and the bearing of arms remained intimately connected, even as the nation pushed forward its western boundaries.[40]

The continuity of motives, beliefs, and actions that was so reflective of American society continued in force throughout the opening months of the Civil War. Soldiers went to war with high ideas, "when one's actions were thought to be the direct extension of one's values," but, according to Gerald F. Linderman, they returned home in 1865 "frustrated" and imbued with a "harsh disillusionment" about the cost of their battlefield sacrifices. Linderman's assessment of returning veterans' beliefs, however, has been challenged by Earl J. Hess, who argued strongly for the sustaining power of ideology during the Civil War and afterward. Arguments for the centrality of "ideology and culture as major—if not key—motivations" applied equally to the South. Over eighty years of shared history meant that the "ideas" that made and sustained the concept of American citizenship "were basic to the very definition of American nationalism" and did, perforce, affect Southerners. Republican ideology

and culture were the "common property of all Americans," not solely
the preserve of a particular section. Too many events had transpired and
too many years had passed to allow for the creation of wholly separate
ideological and cultural identities among Americans.[41]

Faith in republicanism and a sure knowledge of his place in the nation's life were basic to the identity of the American soldier. Historians
have recognized the centrality of ideology as a fundamental factor in
American military service and have noted the continuity of republican
principles from the American Revolution through the Civil War. When
the soldier contemplated his place in the republic, the meaning of his
service, and how his service was a demonstration of his citizenship, he
drew upon a common body of thought and belief to which other American soldiers subscribed: the larger construct of republican culture. The
military ethos of republicanism provided a vibrant, durable, and long-
lived set of interrelated concepts that gave order to and made sense of
Americans' military service for nearly a century. Despite the passage of
time, this ethos did not change.

This cultural imprint also manifested itself in more prosaic, if not less
important and practical matters like combat motivation and soldiers'
conduct. The elements of the ethos were sources of inspiration for soldiers and for their leaders to draw upon. Appeals to virtue, glory, honor,
or fame stand out most conspicuously as ready spurs to duty, but so
too do entreaties to the broader themes of legitimacy, self-governance,
and the nation's mission. These ideas reminded soldiers of what others
expected of them and what they expected of themselves. Soldiers, be
they regulars, volunteers, or militiamen, were not automata that simply
reacted to orders or out of fear of punishment. Indeed, when their expectations or needs were not met, it often resulted in their disillusionment with military service. More than once soldiers protested, deserted,
or mutinied in demonstration against violations of these cultural norms.

Arguing for "historical continuity," contending that American soldiers' multigenerational *mentalité* followed a pattern, is, a risky affair. It
forces one to take a broad view, especially "when invoking the republican paradigm." It is entirely reasonable to ask how, in a period of such
rapid development, there could be no change in soldierly culture or its
ideological underpinnings. Western territorial expansion, internal mi-
gration, the addition of formerly Mexican, French, and Spanish citizens

through annexation, the increase in the number of states from thirteen to thirty-four, foreign immigration, the broadening of the electorate, social reform movements, including abolitionism, and the commercial revolution were only a few of the many changes transforming American society during this period. How is it that a set of ideas could remain so enduring while so much was happening? The answer lies in the nature of culture and in the evidence itself. As Michal Jan Rozbicki noted about the nature of culture, it "tries to make a sensible and coherent order out of the myriad of differing and often contradictory ingredients that make up people's experience." Furthermore, that culture "need not be consistent" from the historian's perspective in order for it to be "real" for those whose existence it frames. Thus, these broader societal changes, while transformative to society, did not alter the connection between military service and republicanism. Soldiering was and remained an important demonstration of patriotism and was considered a proof of loyal citizenship. The ideas that helped soldiers in the American Revolution understand their service and citizenship were, at heart, the same ideas of the generation that went to war with itself in the Civil War. Accordingly, the War for Independence marks one end in an intellectual continuum that, fundamentally, underwent no constitutive change through 1861. This constancy mimics a broad pattern in the continuity of thought present in this critical time period of American history. The changes that occurred were of form and action, but not of substance or structure. American society remained faithful to previously established norms that gave surety in eras of change.[42]

Despite the great transformation wrought in the theory of sovereignty and the nearly coterminous fashioning of an American brand of republicanism during the Revolutionary era, the American character and ethos did not substantively change over these two generations. This was due not to willful ignorance, to an inability to adapt, or to irrationality; instead it derived from the basic soundness and utility of an established and accepted belief system and the elastic nature of the culture. The impact of urbanization, industrialization, and other centripetal forces affecting the fabric of American society was not yet fully felt, but they were growing. Americans' lack of awareness about broader societal or structural changes was due to the lag time between objective and perceived conditions. Soldiers' repeated references to and faith in the tenets of the military ethos of republicanism confirm the widespread acceptance and validity of this belief system and their conviction that there was a profound relevance to being an American citizen. Soldiers were keenly attuned to the rights, duties, and privileges of American citizenship. Although most of them did not spend inordinate amounts of time ruminating upon the nature of republicanism many, nonetheless, were fully cognizant of their role within the schema of the political and social order.

The American military ethos was an affirmation of republicanism. It celebrated the centrality of shared ideals and beliefs in the shaping of the American national character and the connection between bearing arms and citizenship. Because of the military's role as a defender of the Constitution, soldiers were agents of ideological promotion, defense, and preservation. Soldiers defined their character as republicans through their service. The beliefs of soldiers drew from and fit within five broad themes that can be said to constitute soldiers' understanding of republicanism. From 1775 to 1861 American military values were part of the larger ideological and philosophical constructs of American society. Understanding the military component of American republicanism sheds light on the broader landscape of American political, social, and intellectual life then and now.

1

Service, Sacrifice, and Duty

The Call of Virtue

Virtue's impress upon the ideal of the American citizen as soldier was a vital element in the military ethos of republicanism. The belief in the citizen's duty to bear arms on behalf of the common weal reinforced the citizen-soldier's conviction that he was a full member and participant in and of the "government and country" he served. His was a "unique character," imbued with an idealized vision of the nation, its promise, and of course its soldiery. Writing after the Civil War, John A. Logan, an Illinois major general of volunteers, contended that in battle, the volunteer soldier's "arm is raised for a principle, for right, for justice, for a government in which he has a personal interest and of which he is an integral part." Indeed, the soldier's character was of such importance that as early as 1775 commanders enjoined their recruiting officers to "be Very Carefull not to inlist any person Suspected of being unfriendly to the Liberties of America or any Vagabond to whom all cause are equally alike." If recruiters exercised discretion and enlisted only virtuous men to fight for the "Rights of Mankind and the Freedom of america," the republic would prosper without having had to "Resort to such Wretches" as those who served George III. Truly, it was better to "let those who wish to put Shackles on Freemen fill their Ranks and place there Confidence on Such Miscreants."[1]

Before the first shots had been exchanged between the king's troops and Massachusetts militiamen at Lexington and Concord in 1775, Americans believed, according to historian Robert Shalhope, "that what made republics great (or what ultimately destroyed them) was not force of arms but the character and spirit of the people." The people's character, their virtue on display in the public sphere, manifested itself through their restraint, public spiritedness, unadorned manners, and lack of affectations. Citizens' willing practice of these traits, their conduct in private carried over into the public arena, was the animating spirit of the republic. Virtue's ascetic and communitarian essence was thus vital in ensuring the health of the republic and in securing the common weal, which was the purpose of government. As for the citizen-soldier, following a "life of service" and sacrifice to the republic, the "patriot and Citizen," according to Charleston, South Carolina's Washington Light Infantry, could reflect upon his "fortune" with great satisfaction as he enjoyed the "trophies won from the enemies of his country."[2]

Americans incorporated virtue into their vision of themselves and accorded it a special place in the mythology that developed around military service. If myths are the tools by which a people order, perceive, and make sense of reality, they are also the cultural lenses through which a people view the world, and there is no myth "more precious to a republic . . . than the notion of the people in arms springing to the defense of their homeland." In the United States, republican mythology took on an especially powerful significance. Americans had to create a new nationality without any traditional references to monarchy or religion. A people whose national identity had sprung from revolution thus purposefully rejected the colonial past and looked to the future for self-affirmation, for the myth that would confirm the United States' place and mission in the world. What better symbol then, of the republic in arms than the American citizen as soldier. No longer a subject, but a citizen, a participant in the country's political life, the citizen-soldier "transcend[ed] mere military functionalism" and was instead a "fundamental judgment about the foundation of the state." Because of the citizen-soldier's special place in American culture, military service took on almost sacred overtones and reinforced a belief in the special nature of American citizenship.[3]

American soldiers placed great stock in their public demonstration of virtue as proof of their purity of heart and of their sincerity as republicans. In a 1777 letter to Samuel Adams, Colonel Joseph Ward deplored American soldiers' "profaneness" and ruled it to be a "growing evil in our Army" that might ultimately prove "hurtful to the Commonwealth." Britain's eighteenth-century regulars were notorious for their profanity and colorful oaths. Ward feared "if there is not more effectual care taken to prevent it we shall equal the Infidels we oppose in profanity. And in my humble opinion," he noted, "we are in more danger from our vices than from the Arms of Britain." The men, "it is a melancholy truth," followed the "impious example" set by "many Officers of rank." It was through the officers' examples of "profane language, by which vice is countenanced and virtue discouraged" in the army. Ward believed that "if no one in the future was to be honoured with promotion, of an impious character, men would take care to acquire such a character as would be most honorable and profitable; and perhaps good characters might become as plenty as bad ones *now are*." Rhode Island chaplain Enos Hitchcock echoed Ward when decrying the "vice and sensuality" of the troops, who were "lost not only to a sense of virtue, but of common modesty and decency, giving themselves up to the foulest blasphemies." Hitchcock appealed to his congregation militant "to add the more distinguished character of a virtuous, good, man" to their military character, for only "then" would they be able to "quit this stage in the full blaze of honor and receive a crown of glory."[4]

Much as the broader American society had incorporated the concept of virtue into its vision of itself well before the outbreak of war, so too had the soldiers of the republic. Military service was the provenance of the virtuous militiaman in the republican tradition. Arms, property, the franchise, social order, and political independence could not be separated without endangering the life of the republic. Armed citizens who fought for and served the interests of society would not, in all likelihood, subvert the social and political system of which they were a part. Recognizing that republics were fragile and could survive only if the people exercised constant vigilance and personal responsibility, American society broadly subscribed to the belief that the cheerful and willing shouldering of arms constituted part of a citizen's responsibility to society and to himself.

The unwillingness of citizens to share in the burdens of self-defense and in the preservation of order was an indication of moral rot and social decay. Quite naturally, therefore, American soldiers placed great stock in the public and private demonstrations of virtue as proofs of their purity of heart and of their sincerity as republicans. Soldiering was so central to early Americans' vision of themselves that historian Maarten Ultee has suggested that some members of the founding generation viewed war as a "moral test" of virtue, for the country's independence depended upon whether citizens willingly would "arm themselves and rally to the cause." If this was the case, the "recourse to arms" was the surest guarantor of public virtue. At the heart of this consideration was the virtuous militiaman or volunteer who served for no more than the simple thanks of his countrymen.[5]

Gratitude, no matter how sincere or heartfelt, was not a sufficiency. It did not pay a man, nor did it enable the United States to field an army for extended operations or even policing the coasts or frontier in times of peace. The hard reality of nationhood seemingly conspired against the idealized, virtuous republican militiaman and volunteer when the Second Continental Congress adopted New England militiamen as the Continental army and then proceeded to raise and maintain it as a regular force. The Continental army, and later United States Army, was a cause for concern for Americans. Much of the citizenry's aversion to regulars and to the institution of a standing army was premised on the conviction that regulars were antithetical to republican virtue and liberty. According to this philosophy a regular army was a potential machine for oppression. Professional soldiers "were riotous, expensive, and morally corrupt" beings serving for pay alone. Merely by existing, a regular army gave witness to "a corrupted populace and unbalanced constitution" and of a people too self-interested to defend themselves or their liberty.[6]

"A Late Captain of Infantry" understood this connection between citizenship and soldiering, and he recognized that "our good *republican* people" took a narrow understanding of the connection and its implications. When Americans "look[ed] down on the regular as a pariah," he argued, they failed to recognize that the regular's service was as important to the republic as that of the militiaman or volunteer. The professional soldier was not a loafer or a threat to liberty; he was, instead, the "faithful, humble servant of the country, of at least standard honesty as the world goes; who from love of excitement, the default of sharp wits, or inclination to lead a life of selfish aggrandisement, gives his stalwart frame, the prime of his life, and often the blood of his brave heart, in return for a contract with the government, wherein he obtains the privilege of passing a life of toil, exile, [and] privation." If that were not enough, the professional soldier risked "premature decay, at eleven dollars a month," hardly a comfortable sinecure. As citizens and soldiers, the captain argued, regulars' service was one of virtuous self-sacrifice for the greater good of the nation.[7]

Detractors of the regular army failed to see that soldiers who made a life in the army were a minority, and that those who did so understood the meaning of their service within the boundaries of the broader ethos. Fewer than half of the regular officers from 1784 through 1861, including graduates of the military academy, made the army a career. This is even lower if one takes into account the Continental army, a wartime force whose existence lasted just eight years and eight months. Most soldiers served only one or two enlistments before returning to their former occupations or starting new ones as they established their economic and political independence. Ideology and culture aside, the United States could afford its near-amateurish military establishment because there was no viable threat to the country's existence. As a result, enlisted military service was merely another job to be held before moving on to a different and more lucrative life's work. The rhetoric of republicanism fit well with short-term sacrifice.[8]

Providing for the "defense and security" of the community entailed the potential risk of one's life and endowed soldiers with tremendous physical and moral responsibility and authority. The precepts of faithful service attracted and required "altruistic men" who placed the interests of society ahead of all other considerations. They were men "concerned with serving in the best possible manner." Speaking in Mexico in 1847 on the occasion of George Washington's birthday, Lieutenant Colonel Henry S. Lane of the First Indiana Volunteer Infantry Regiment deemed that the "citizen who withholds his aid, and stops coldly to calculate the causes and chances" of his survival in "war, whatever his professions may be," surely had to be, "in his heart, a traitor." Presaging Lane's thoughts by a decade, Lieutenant Benjamin Alvord noted in 1837, that "Genuine military virtue" could not be separated "from all other kinds of moral duty." In order "to dignify and enhance the conduct of the warrior," Alvord thought all forms of military service "should be based upon the eternal foundations of justice and truth." Alvord's suggestion recognized the special ethical connection between service and republicanism.[9]

American soldiers saw a "moral significance" in the contest of arms, noted Charles Royster. Combat was the opportunity for a people to display its "character" through the voluntary shouldering of arms and willingness to sacrifice lives while expressing "national vigilance in defense of liberty." Warfare thus idealized was an "intrinsic American virtue" that announced the special nature of the republican soldier's service. Even in 1861, the sacred nature of military virtue led Captain John Scott of the Second Virginia Cavalry to declare that the "Sabbath had now been consecrated to Liberty as well as Religion" by the sacrifices of Confederate soldiers along the banks of Bull Run in Virginia. Thomas Jewett Goree, an aide-de-camp to Confederate general James Longstreet, understood his service as "I would in a religious duty, and I am not only willing, but hope that I am prepared if necessary to be sacrificed upon the altar of my country."[10]

Nineteenth-century volunteer companies set great store by the proper and virtuous conduct of their members, who willingly agreed to follow prescribed codes of conduct. Company bylaws incorporated the "virtues of citizen soldiers" acting "in a bourgeois role" as the protectors of order, society, and property. Common prohibitions against swearing and the use of alcohol reflected a reformist impulse among the members. A group of young South Carolinians "agreed to form a corps in which we could perform the duties required by our country without being exposed to the temptations arising from the use of intoxicating drinks at convivial meetings, and having our ears pained by profanity, and which alas has proved the ruin of too many" men. These men of the Moultrie Guard selected a commander who was "willing to break ground in the work of reform." One member, Thomas R. Vardell characterized temperance in drink and speech as "great principles" and the company as a "body of men endeavouring to promote these great ends" by their public example. Vardell and his compeers were not alone.[11]

Elmer E. Ellsworth's United States Zouave Cadets was one of the most popular, imitated, and restrictive volunteer companies in the late 1850s. "Principal requirements" for the cadets included "Abstinence from Drinking Saloons, Houses of Ill-Fame, Gambling Halls, and all disreputable places, under penalty of expulsion, publication in the city Papers of the offender's name, and forfeiture of uniform, etc., to the company." In a fraternal touch, the men were "required to treat all members of the company as brothers," and in "return for this you will be looked upon and treated as a brother" who will be "aided, when necessary, in sickness and misfortune, and allowed the use of the Cadets' Assembly Rooms, continuing Gymnasium, Reading and Chess Room, Piano, etc., etc., as long as your conduct proves you worthy of these advantages." Like those of other companies, Ellsworth's rules were intended to shape individual and group behavior and identities. The clublike atmosphere of the volunteer companies conferred "status and identity" on their members and their self-governing organization and rules allowed young men to "feel patriotic, and therefore democratic, and yet elevated into a romantic-genteel realm where one might talk without embarrassment of nobility, honor, chivalry," and "gallantry." Demanding and uncompromising, Ellsworth's Code of Conduct "anticipated" what Marcus Cunliffe called the "penitential national mood" of 1861.[12]

American soldiers, whether professionals or amateurs, were citizens first and foremost. Holding to the belief that "the character of a soldier is not incompatible with that of a citizen; that they may and should be blended, and the martial training and discipline of the one is a duty as sacred and indispensable as is the exercise of more pacific duties," an American soldier's military conduct was a public extension of his private persona and values. Every generation assumed the responsibility of service and sacrifice for the republic. Iowa volunteer Caleb J. Allen understood as much in 1861, when he wrote that "we can no longer live upon the deeds of our Fathers. We too must pay a price for the blessings we enjoy." Allen rejected the "idea that obtains to such an extent, that we are too enlightened a people to have necessity for resort to arms." He found that notion "absurd," for "as long as the moral sense of man permits him to do injustice it is folly to appeal to that sense for reparation."[13]

The writings of American soldiers highlight the extent to which duty and sacrifice were two inseparable components of virtue. The typical soldier "understood" his duty as a "binding moral obligation," one of "reciprocity" to his society in an unwritten contract. By attending to his duty, the soldier served a cause greater than himself. Importantly, he did so in an act of free will. From 1775 to 1783, the "American soldier, unlike British derelicts and Hessian mercenaries, faced the invaders by an act of free choice and beat them." By acting disinterestedly for the benefit of society, his service became an act of benevolence, of "unselfish love, of active concern for others," and of "eager work for the welfare of all" in society. If society was an organic whole, then that which was good for society was good for the individual.[14]

When Lieutenant George Smith Avery helped raise a company of cavalry in 1861, he told his fiancée, "I did not undertake the business with the expectation of securing an office, but for the good of the cause." Virtuous duty was not the performance of the quotidian military tasks necessary to keep an army functioning. Accomplishing these functions was but a small part of a much larger idea. By doing his duty, the soldier fulfilled expectations that had been implicitly or explicitly agreed upon by both himself and his community. He served a larger body.[15]

Sacrifice worked hand in glove with duty. It entailed the acceptance of physical, emotional, or financial risk on behalf of others. Placing one's interests in the service of a greater good affirmed both private and civic virtue. "In exchanging the Enjoyments of domestic Life for the Duties of my present honourable, but arduous Station" as commander of the Continental army, George Washington hoped to be able to "emulate the Virtue and publick Spirit" of Massachusetts, which had "sacrificed all the Comforts of social and political Life." Some believed in death and suffering as a sort of national scourging undertaken for the purification of the republic's soul. The purgative of pain, according to this line of reasoning, was the result of some social ill that had gravely upset the political order. Virtue in either public or private arenas relied on a spirit of voluntarism, a glue that held duty and sacrifice together. To act without this spirit was to act from narrow self-interest and was inimical to the good of the community.[16]

On 12 May 1775, Massachusetts militiaman Thomas Cushman laconically noted in his diary, "I went to Roxbury to serve the Cuntry." Similarly, Colonel John Whitcomb accepted a commission from the Massachusetts Provincial Congress hoping to "save this Country from Ruing." The colonel promised to "Be Ready to Do any service I am Capable of that shall Be thought Best for the Publick Good when we are Called to Gether for action." In all likelihood Cushman's "Cuntry" and Whitcomb's "Publick Good" was the province of Massachusetts. Soldiers, whether in Massachusetts or in the rest of the United States, gradually learned how to think and perceive of their new nation continentally. Brigadier General Nathanael Greene, a Rhode Islander, was "honnord" by the "Government" when he received a "command of their Troops." The sometime Quaker considered himself a public servant who owed his appointment to the "voice of the impartial Publick." Greene and his fellow revolutionaries were "Soldiers who devote[d] ourselves to arms . . . for the defence of our own" country and "for the Publick security." Chaplain Enos Hitchcock thought of his congregation at home as a "people, for whom I have cultivated a sincere affection; and in whose service I am willing to spend my Life."[17]

By 1776, at least one officer recorded having "inlisted many young Men" in his company out of "Motives purely to Serve their Country." Dr. Isaac Foster Jr., Deputy Director General of the Military Hospital, celebrated the announcement of the Declaration of Independence hopefully. He believed that it had "given great spirits to the army, so by shutting the Door against any reconciliation in the least Degree connected with dependance on great Britain, they know for what they are fighting, and are freed from the apprehension of being duped by Commissioners after having risqued their Lives in the service of their country." Realizing Foster's hopes for a greater sense of national purpose and identity, however, would take much time and effort. Problems continued within the states and their militias, which failed to "see their Danger and the duty they owe their Country and turn out with more spirit"[18]

Petitions for the formation of militia companies and covenants articulating their purposes vividly illustrated the communitarian spirit of virtue. Ninety-two residents of New Gloucester, Massachusetts in the Maine district declared that "Every Government hath a right, especially in times actual or impending Invasion, to command the PERSONAL SERVICES of ALL its Members." According to these men, the threat of invasion allowed the community's interests and needs to supersede individual rights, for in "such times no member of the Body Politic can justly withdraw himself, or decline to render, with promptitude and zeal, his utmost services in behalf of the Government, to the support of which, as a good and faithful Citizen, he is SOLEMNLY PLEDGED." New Gloucester's militiamen, "deeply impressed with the truth of these great fundamental Principles," pledged their "unity and vigor in sentiment and action" as the armed servants of their town. Connecticut men in the "town of Fairfield and Village of Blackrock" held principles familiar to the New Gloucester militia. They formed a "Company of Musquetry (Volunteers)," deeming it "the duty of every person in society to put himself in a state of defence against the enemy during the war."[19]

The sense of duty to the nation continued throughout the nineteenth century but did not necessarily indicate wholehearted loyalty to the nation over that felt toward the state. This is not to say that there was a sense of equivalency in Americans' minds between the country and the state; rather, people's emotional ties to their home states were more pronounced and heartfelt. Americans' bifurcated loyalties remained strong through 1861, but they were anything but absolute. Soldiers were well aware of the distinction between the nation and the state. Following the end of the War of 1812, Major General Jacob Jennings Brown counseled the cadets at West Point to remember "every good citizen will consider himself called upon to defend his Government and to vindicate the rights and the honor of his country, from whatsoever quarter assailed. As children of the Republic you will remember, this is your precious duty." Georgia-volunteer quartermaster Iverson Lea Graves held, "I should feel recreant to my Countrys Call if in this the time of her distress, I should withhold any service I might be able to render her" against the Creek Nation.[20]

At the presentation of a silver goblet by New York national guardsmen to Sergeant Isaac Plumb, the recipient avowed, "I am a citizen, and a citizen soldier of the republic, and that our country expects every man to do his *duty* in *peace* or *war.*" New York volunteer Kimball Hale Dimmick affirmed his belief in a debt of "service to my country." Henry Smith Lane, a Hoosier volunteer officer, had "always been opposed to the Annexation of Texas" and believed the act would lead to war with Mexico. "But," he wrote, the "deed is done and Texas is a part of the United States and I feel as much bound to fight for her as I would for Indiana, or even old Kentucky." Frederick W. Thompson, adjutant general for the state of Vermont, intoned that "Society claimed" the services of Colonel Truman B. Ransom of the Ninth United States Infantry Regiment in Mexico City. Ransom, a volunteer turned regular, and his fellow volunteers "went they forth—the strong, the brave and the free—at their country's call, and for their country's honor."[21]

When Caleb J. Allen of Iowa told his mother of his decision to enlist in 1861, he revealed what he believed to be the profound importance of being an American and what he saw as the sacred nature of the Union. The rebellion was clearly one of the "greatest crises that ever human liberty felt, and we have a duty to perform in preserving the liberties bequeathed us by our Fathers which none can ignore. Never," wrote Allen, had "men nobler or more sacred cause for which to fight, and die. And we should bless fortune that the opportunity is ours, of devoting our lives to the maintenance of that Government which our fathers purchased with theirs. To ignore our duty" to the Union and history and "drag out a miserable existance whose highest aim is selfish enjoyment is the wish" for "only those fit to be slaves." Because of this belief, he wrote, "I have enlisted in a company formed here named the Sears Rangers."[22]

This belief in the special nature of the republican experiment and the soldier's role as a defender of the nation led him to equate his own sense of individual worth with the life of his country. Dexter F. Parker admitted that in "my heart I bear no enmity to any man, but I love with intense devotion my country and if she calls for it I'll give her my life as gladly as I would water to a thirsty man." Parker's emotions were so profound that he could "but feel if I have a country worth living in, she is worth wishing our lives to preserve in tact her government, her constitution and her Union." Peter Warden knew he "could never be of more service to my country or mankind, than in lending my feeble aid to suppress the foul rebelion."[23]

Although a great many soldiers emphasized the union of states as the country from which they derived their nationality and to which they devoted their duty, this did not negate their affection or concern for their home states or local communities. Soldiers' community affiliations and affections mixed with their broader sense of state loyalty, which created a powerful emotional link with the home. After receiving his regiment's colors from the "Ladies of Soule-Chapel," Lewis Leonidas Allen, "Chaplain to our patriotic and chivalrous Louisianians" who had volunteered to fight in Mexico, confessed that he had volunteered his "feeble services" to Louisiana in an "hour when every man was called upon to go to the defence of his country." Quite simply, "I did no more than my duty." Reverend Allen characterized Louisiana's volunteers as "men possessed of the loftiest feeling, and pure motives," with each man having a "mind actuated by the most sublime and holy principle which can possibly occupy the heart of man."[24]

John Bramblett Beall, a former regular, had been "bred in the doctrine that the first allegiance of the citizen was due the State." Beall followed his conviction by enlisting in the Nineteenth Georgia Volunteers in 1861. That same year Benjamin F. Peterson told William P. Corthell to "Rest asshured" because "our Company" of the Fourth Massachusetts Volunteers "have done their duty well" and "proved themselves to be something more than fairweather Soldiers." Fighting for the Union, Peterson's thoughts, nonetheless, centered on "our *village* and *Town*." Sergeant Peterson knew that Corthell and others "cannot be otherwise than proud of them," because the men of the company, "knowing their duty" to their friends at home, "have not failed to do it." At divine services in November 1861, Chaplain Noah M. Gaylord of the Thirteenth Massachusetts Volunteers "turned to the officers and told them that these men were confided to their charge by their kindred and friends and by the state." Although the "exigency" of battle "might occur where they must sacrifice the lives of many," there was "no exigency or ocassion could give them the right to sacrifice or injure, either by precept or by example, the moral life" of a soldier. Gaylord reminded the officers that the "influence surrounding them from their New England homes must be kept pure and undefiled." Captain William O. Crutcher, a "soldier of the Confederate Army battling for the glorious cause of the South," expanded upon his localism when he called his region his new country.[25]

There were, of course, some men who did not do well by their states. Writing from Mexico in 1847, North Carolina's Colonel Robert Treat Paine complained to his wife, Lavinia, that "not one officer in my regiment . . . undertakes either to carry out in his own conduct or to enforce obedience among his men" and "I sometimes sit down and curse them all, officers and men." When Paine's officers complained that he was "wanting in respect to them," he informed them he could not "treat with respect any one who neglects the duties imposed on him, more especially when a neglect of those duties will brook discredit on our State." As time went on, Paine grew "more and more disgusted with the Volunteer service." He remained solely because of the "strongest feeling of duty to the public." Volunteers bridled at military discipline and often proved to be surly and uncooperative soldiers. They acted out of a conviction that their right to self-governance was immutable and, therefore, not subject to military dictates. They wanted to be soldiers, but on their own terms. "I cannot discharge my duty as I think it should be discharged without offending many," reported Paine. While out riding, "I was very near being mobbed in the Miss[issippi] Camp" that day by soldiers who were "headed by their officers." Colonel Paine remained mounted and "laughed at them, they were much excited," but he was as "cool as a cucumber and sat quietly until the mob dispersed." The colonel believed that Major General John E. Wool and all the "officers of the other regiments are perfectly outraged at the conduct" of the Mississippians. Reckoning them a "most rowdy set," Paine thought their presence would do "great injury to our brigade." Paine was not alone. Henry S. Lane of Indiana noted much same the sort of misconduct and indiscipline in his regiment while in northern Mexico in 1846. American volunteer virtue spread far and wide.[26]

Captain John Bratton was frustrated when, he observed, "All the companies" in the Sixth South Carolina Infantry "except mine are making efforts to get into the C.S. Service, and will probably succeed in doing so." Bratton believed that the performance of military duty ought to be derived from a basic impulse of communal obligation and that a man so inspired had little or no need of prompting. The man in need of group pressure or great persuasion did not have within him the sincerity of conviction or purity of mind required of a virtuous and dutiful republican soldier. Thus Bratton disapproved of the "means" recruiters "used to get up the volunteering excitement." Recruiters were "going around to all the tents calling on the different officers for speeches" in order to "get up a sensation against those who do not enter the service." Bratton did not "believe in this way of bringing outside pressure to bear on a company." If Bratton's men "would not go" forward "when the question was put to their calm judgment, he preferred that they "would not" do it out of "fear of outsiders."[27]

Captain Bratton's disappointment deepened "when the mustering officer came three Chesterfield companies stepped out strong and full,[but] not a single fairfield company" did so. Bratton "appealed" to his company, the Fairfield Fencibles, to "come up in this hour of need, and send a thrill of joy through the heart of our noble district, but only "twenty five of them responded." Despondent and "sick with disgust," the South Carolinian "concluded that I was not fit to lead the company or else it was not fit to follow me. I tried to do my duty to my country as an officer," but "I have failed to meet the requirements of the position." A few days later, Bratton felt "free and light" because of an impending furlough and the prospect of enlistment as a private in the Sixth South Carolina. Bratton's keenly felt sense of duty may have paid off for him. He eventually rose to the rank of brigadier general in the Confederate army.[28]

Lieutenant David Gregg McIntosh faced a situation similar to that of Bratton's with his company of the First South Carolina Volunteers. In the early spring of 1861, McIntosh received orders "directing" that the "Regiment should at once proceed to Virginia." Since the men had "enlisted in the service of the State" of South Carolina, "there was some doubt about the right to order it out of" that state. To circumvent this dilemma, mustering officials made an "appeal to the Regiment to volunteer for that purpose." Orderly Sergeant John Harrington "read the call and the order, the Captain stood fast," and McIntosh "and little less than half the company followed." Military service and war had contributed to the growth of American nationalism and, in some cases, to the acceptance of the federal republic as the single focus of loyalty. However, it would take a civil war and a long period of recovery and reconciliation to bring about an end to Americans' bifurcated loyalty.[29]

The deep seriousness of duty became more apparent to soldiers as the secession crisis approached its climax and turned to open rebellion. The irony, distress, and deeply felt sense of duty was reflected in the letters left by John S. R. Miller, a sergeant of the Tenth Infantry Regiment who later became a Confederate captain. A veteran of the Mormon War (1857–1858), Miller considered the use of military force to compel the Latter Day Saints to recognize federal authority wholly justified. He believed that the federal "Government has made but little by their war and should yet exterminate or drive without its jurisdiction every hoary headed sinner in the Terr[itor]y who professes his belief in Mormonism, then destroy the buildings and improvements and leave the country to the crows and wolves of which there is no end." Writing to his mother, Miller emphatically stated that the Mormons "must be taught their duty with an iron hand or they will never learn it." However, when news of North Carolina's secession reached Miller he concluded, "I am placed in a peculiar position; as a soldier I must bear allegiance to the Federal Government. I have sworn to serve the *United States* against all her enemies and opposers whatsoever, if called upon I might be compelled to battle against my own friends and relations and unless I am free of the Army, although it would be bitter indeed, I will not swerve from the path of duty." Miller, despite the unpleasant nature of the decision he faced, chose to follow the course of duty he believed consonant with the oath he had taken as a regular and awaited his discharge from federal service before entering the Confederate army.[30]

When Brigadier General Albert Sidney Johnston learned of the secession of his adopted state of Texas in April 1861, he believed that it was "my duty to conform" to "her will and that I ought to forward *my resignation* to the President." Johnston believed that his course of duty belonged with Texas, but that "until" he had been "properly relieved," he had overriding "obligations to the government as an officer." A sense of personal honor demanded that Johnston, and men like him, continue serving "faithfully," while doing "nothing inconsistent with" the dictates of virtuous duty or that which "would embarrass" them in the "proper discharge of" their military "duty."[31]

Writing to his father in April 1861, Ulysses S. Grant contended that "every one must be for or against his country and show his colors too, by his every act." After "having been educated" at the military academy "for such an emergency, at the expense of the Government," he wrote, "I feel it that it has upon me superior claims, such claims as no ordinary motives of self-interest can surmount." John E. Anderson of Massachusetts realized "our individual independence has departed," and now "we belong to Uncle Samuel without any reserve."[32]

Shortly after the battle of First Bull Run, Major James B. Walton of New Orleans's Washington Artillery explained that he continued to serve "supported by the same consciousness of right and duty, as when I consented to leave" New Orleans in "defense of my country." Soldiers who believed their cause was "good" often went to war with a "stout heart," asking family and friends to "keep up your spirits and don't fret." Common sentiments included the "duty which I owe to my God my country and my friends" and a "full determination to stand or fall in harness untill the term of my enlistment had expired. If it is likely I shall fall, well and good, my *Country* needs the sacrifice and I submit, I *would not leave* the service had I an honorable discharge in my pocket and ready to start home." William Anderson, a captain of the Fourth South Carolina Volunteers, was "willing to suffer any disapointment or Privation for the good of our contry." In part, Anderson felt compelled to remain in service because of the "confidence which my fellow Citizens have reposed in me, in placing me in the high position which I now occupy" as captain. Duty "Call[ed] upon" Anderson "not to retract until our liberty is accomplished."[33]

Not all soldiers were enthusiastic about or even in agreement over the reasons for which they served. Many believed American society lacked virtue, was ungrateful, or had dismissed its soldiers with indifference or disdain. Some men hated the discipline and rigor of army life; others had serious reservations about the causes in which they were engaged. More than a few were simply homesick, as were some Continental army officers in 1776. Colonel Israel Shreve of the Second New Jersey Continentals missed his wife Polly and had a "Great Desire once more to Return" home. But on reflection, "knowing I Owe my Service to my Country," Shreve was "Ancious to Conquer" the British soon so that he might return home to Polly. On "Cold Nights" William Henshaw, lieutenant colonel of the Twelfth Continentals, was "sensible of the want of" his wife Phebe as "a Bed fellow" and longed for the "satisfaction of having" her by his side. Expecting an "Engagement with our unnatural enemies," Henshaw hoped "every Man will be animated by the consideration of the Glorious Cause he is engag'd in, to behave Valiantly and Soldier like." Captain Otho Holland Williams, a Maryland Continental, recalled the "pleasure of enjoying the Conversation and presence of my Brothers, sisters and other friends" and wished "most heartily for the time when I may again Indulge myself with the happiness of meeting them." Williams noted that although "My duty to my Country requires that I sho[uld] be as Active and Vigilant as possible in my present station," he could not "think it reasonable to sacrifice ev'ry social Pleasure and Domestic enjoyment for more than twelve months." Presumably, duty and pleasure were not always mutually exclusive.[34]

Pleasure, however, rarely attends virtuous service. Angry Continentals, frustrated by congressional parsimony and seeming indifference to their health and welfare on the part of both Congress and the people, considered themselves the "unsupported slaves" in the service of a "nation who have by Law robed the Widow and the Fatherless." If only, lamented Major General Alexander McDougall, soldiers' sacrifices were "necessary to Protect a people in the enjoyment of Liberty, who were sensible of it and disposed to bear an equal share of the Burden." Samuel Blachley Webb "hope[d] devoutly the War is nearly over," and vowed that the "next time I enter the lists of an Army, of Republican States, I

wish I may be a CORPORAL," so as to avoid having to deal with disingenuous politicians and an ungrateful public. Webb, colonel of the Third
Connecticut Continentals, "believe[d] we shall soon get clear of the War
with the British myrmidions, but if we (America) deserve liberty, I am
Damnably mistaken." Webb predicted that "we poor Dogs shall retire
with broken Constitutions and Empty purses" because the "Cursed Sin
of Ingratitude has taken such deep hold of our *Virtuous* Countrymen."[35]

Colonel Sharp Delany echoed McDougall's and Webb's sentiments to
call "some people" in the country to a "very severe Account to restore
that Republican Virtue, which in the beginning of this Contest was our
only support and which can only carry us through" to independence.
Soldiers such as these held that the example of their "conduct" would
"be handed down to the latest ages, as a model of Virtue, perseverance
and bravery," especially when measured against the "smallness of their
numbers, and the unparalleld hardships and excess of difficulties that
they have encountered in the defence of this Country from her *coldest*
to her *hottest sun*." Unfortunately, Delany argued, the same could not be
said of the "leaders of *faction and party* who possessed neither the virtue or fortitude to meet the Enemy in the field." In a moment of anger,
a Major Smith accused his fellow Americans of "murthering them, and
their familes" and asked why "Don't Every Lover of his Country oppose
this fatal mischief, The deepest and most subtil plan of our Enemies
was never Equal to this, to Effect the Ruin of our Country." Toward the
end of the War for Independence, Colonel Timothy Pickering, quartermaster general of the Continental army, reflected bitterly on the army's
treatment by Congress. Pickering concluded, and "justly, that they," the
Continentals, had been "ill used by their country." Worst of all, the men
had "been dismissed abruptly—without money, and even (what it was
easy to give) without thanks" for their services. Pickering's bitterness
revealed not only his sense of sacrifice on behalf of the greater good but
also his concern for the common soldiers, his understanding of the army
as a community held together by shared values and conduct. Within the
Continental army, especially within the officer corps, there developed
a "sense of solidarity" and corporate identity in response to the shared
ideology, hardship, suffering, losses, and victories. By end of the war,
however, officers and soldiers alike had developed the belief that "an
ungrateful society" had abused them. Soldiers' sense of alienation rein-

forced their corporate identity. Alienation and corporate identity not-withstanding, the bonds of family and friends formed powerful ties that helped soldiers maintain their connection to the larger society.[36]

Family and friends were powerful bonds that impelled service yet also made service difficult. The desire to remain at home was powerful, for, as Colonel W. H. L. Wallace noted in 1861, "duty and inclination some times clash[ed]." It was not uncommon for soldiers to reveal the "sincere truth that I had Rather continue at home with my dear parents and Rela-tives." Fears for the safety of wives and "Darling Infants unprotected in a savage world" caused "high millatary sperits [to] falls below par" in Captain James Callaway's company of Missouri Rangers in 1814. Some soldiers wished they were "going to school or teaching." If the desire to return home was strong, duty was more powerful. Failure to complete a term of service honorably brought personal and familial shame.[37]

In writing to their loved ones, soldiers revealed the intimate connec-tion between soldiering and an idealized masculine image. Their willing sacrifice of familial comforts in order to serve the greater good but also to fulfill their own and others' expectations of manly conduct spoke to what political theorist R. Claire Snyder termed an "ideal [that] fuses military service and participatory citizenship as well as citizenship and masculinity." Soldiering was thus the highest form of "participatory citi-zenship," much as it was one of the highest forms of manhood. It helped fuse the individual man, his conduct, and his identity with his fellow sol-diers and within the greater political body. Soldiering reinforced a man's identity and membership within republican society by serving that so-ciety; hence the individual man's worth was measured by his participa-tion in the life of the republic. Differing notions over masculine conduct existed according to Americans' class, status, race, and region. Scholars of gendered identity in early and nineteenth-century American history have discerned regional variations on the theme of manhood and mas-culine identity, and although these variations did exist they spoke more to the textures and nuances of masculinity as an aggregate in American culture.[38]

A man who deserted his comrades and neighbors could not be trusted. He was self-serving, and therefore without virtue. Captain Cal-laway was "almost readdy to resign" his militia "commission, but a mo-ments reflection with respect to the situation of my country together with this consideration that their is a number of men that has joined the service that would not if any other person commanded makes me quit such thoughts." Hopes for "Glorious" campaigns, the reassurances that "the American Cause will ultimately prevail," or "Believing that I am on a Just and Righteous Cause" bolstered morale and helped assuage emotions. Daniel B. Holmes, an Illinois volunteer in 1861, knew that it was "necessary that I should be here" and therefore had "no reason to complain." Holmes's thoughts resonated with those of Major William McCauley, a North Carolina militiaman serving against the Creek Indians in 1814. McCauley believed that when "my Country Calls I must obey."[39]

Wives and families were important to a soldier's decision to serve. Rebecca Pickering "consented" to her husband Timothy's service during the Revolution with that "good sense and prudence which mark[ed] all" her "actions." Wives' support comforted and reassured soldiers in their service. Mary Pillow's letter to her husband, Gideon, "breathed a spirit of tenderness and directed affections" that caused the Tennessean to "reproach myself for leaving under a *sense of duty to my country.*" Brigadier General Pillow set aside his emotions, because "If I had consulted my feelings my Dear, you know I should never have left you" to fight in the Mexican War. Pillow asked his wife to be "cheerful" during his absence and "patiently *await* the arrival of the happy hour when your Husband can return to the endearments of his family after having *honorably* discharged his duty to his country." North Carolinian John Avery Benbury longed to "return to my Darling, to clasp her in my arms, and press her close and tight to my breast, to feel her arms around my neck and her head upon my bosom." But until that happy moment, Captain Benbury was willing to "sacrifice all those pleasures now, for my country wants me." Confederate Major General Edmund Kirby Smith reassured his wife that "I do cherish the remembrance of your virtues, the sweet recollection of your love, it sustains me and bears me up in this Seperation, it cheers me in the discharge of my duties, and nerves me to greater sacrifices than I have even yet been called upon to make for my countries good."[40]

Elodie Todd's support and encouragement was central to Nathaniel Henry Rhodes Dawson's service as captain of Alabama's Magnolia Cadets. As Dawson courted Todd, the sister of Mary Todd Lincoln, he "rejoice[d] to know that" she thought of him in the "path of *duty,*" and that she did not want him "idle at this time, when the enemy has invaded our borders." Todd's encouragement, Dawson believed, would, after the conclusion of the war, cause her "face [to] glow with pride at knowing that" her "husband has faced dangers and hardships and made sacrifices in the cause of his country." He plainly believed "I *owe duties to you and my little girls* that are *paramount* to all others." Todd reminded Dawson that his service as a soldier was needed if the Confederacy was to achieve independence. Feeling remiss, Dawson wrote, "I must endeavor to do as you have enjoined me to behave, like a true Southern soldier." He was "afraid that duty will compel many of us to continue in the service, and I know you want me to do my duty, my whole duty." Dawson's year-long absence and contemplated reenlistment affected Todd. She hoped that "such a step would not be necessary for you to take again." Moreover, she thought "one year" in the army was "quite enough for one man to serve," but she had "nothing else to say as doubtless" Dawson considered it his "duty to do so and would not be satisfied to remain at home." Todd was not happy that she "must be *secondary*" to her "*country*." Initially, she had hoped that Dawson would "go and serve a short time," for she "would not for any consideration marry a man who would not go and fight for his country and endeavour by his courage and sword to maintain his rights and liberties." Eventually, Nathaniel and Elodie reconciled their differences in favor of continued service in the army.[41]

Soldiers found their separation from loved ones a painful experience. Support from home helped ease the pain and helped soldiers concentrate on more immediate tasks at hand. In this way, women and children played an important role in the maintenance of virtuous military duty. William Anderson relied upon the moral support of his wife, Creek, and the understanding of his family for moral and emotional support. As "Much as" Captain Anderson and his wife "wish[ed] to be together," he felt "assured" that his she "would be the last one to throw any obstacle in the way of my serving." The Confederacy had a pressing need for soldiers, "But my Dear Creek," wrote Anderson, "this is not a time for us to consult our Personal feelings. We must take a wider view of the subject, and the confidence which my fellow Citizens have reposed in me" as captain "calls upon me not to retract until our liberty is accomplished." William H. Dunham had misgivings about leaving his family in Ohio in

1861, noting that at times he felt "that I may have done wrong in leaving my family for the battle field." Yet Dunham and others soldiered on.[42]

Major James Griffin of Hampton's Legion "thought more about" his wife, Leila, and his "darling little children than" he had "at any time before." Griffin, a Confederate officer, thought that "it does indeed seem to have been an age since I left you. Were it not for the conscientious feeling that I am doing my duty by serving my country, I could not stand it." The major did not know if he was "sorry" for having "volunteered." He did know, however, that if "I were at home, I could not be satisfied and here I feel that my sacrifice is great indeed." Griffin had left his family for his "country," and he "earnestly hope[d] and believe[d] that the God of us all will take good care of my family." John W. Dodd reflected wistfully on his decision to enlist in 1861, noting that "Those only who were happily situated and secure in the love of each other, who feel the loss of each other's society and mourn the absence of each other, are alone capable of appreciating the sacrifice which is made when the call of honor or duty, force a separation." Soldiering, family, and republican citizenship were intertwined, for "the man qualified for a soldier is not the one who leaves a home he is glad to leave, for the same qualities which make the patriot make the wise father, the tender husband and the constant friend."[43]

Lieutenant Thomas Thomson Taylor, an 1861 Ohio volunteer, accepted the prevailing belief that men alone were fit for soldiering and for battle. He did, however, attach great significance to the supportive role played by republican women. "Our Fathers made our Country," he wrote, and "we, their children, are to save it. Females are unable to do duty on the field, men alone are permitted to make sacrifices." Excluded from combat, women, like Taylor's wife Antoinette, were "compelled to display their patriotism in another sphere, to make their sacrifices at the domestic shrine, to gird the armor on husband, son and brother and with smiles bid them to defend their country's standard and their country's honor." Moral support from home mattered a great deal for the soldier. "How noble, how patriotic such conduct, how great the sacrifice" made by soldiers and women, "God alone can tell."[44]

God alone may have been able to judge the worth of soldiers' sacrifices, but soldiers were in no need of divine guidance when it came to judging the government, their superiors, or one another, or in freely expressing their opinions. Dissatisfied soldiers aired their views through their letters home, to newspapers (often anonymously or under pseudonyms), or to sympathetic peers, mentors, or politicians. These soldiers did not see that any inherent contradiction arose by their participation in the fractious arena of politics while acting as the conscientious servants of the republic. Members of a participatory republic could not keep silent on matters of personal or national importance. Rhetoric was often heated and made the army, the volunteers, and the militia look like a debating society or hopelessly fractured club. Running feuds between senior officers, such as those between generals Winfield Scott and Edmund P. Gaines or between colonels David E. Twiggs and William J. Worth over seniority and brevet rank, might last for years or poison the command structure of the army in the field. Within the volunteer regiments, electioneering often resulted in strained relations within companies and between officers. On the whole, however, soldiers performed their duty while working around these dissatisfactions and internecine feuds. For the majority of soldiers their sense of obligation overrode their discontent and they continued to perform their duty.[45]

Colonel William Edwards, an artillerist of the Massachusetts militia, reminded his men that "whatever may have been the original cause of the War in which the Gen[era]l Gov[ernme]nt tho[ugh]t it proper to engage" in 1812, it was "enough for us to know that our State is invaded by an enemy who can make no distinction between those who were the authors of the War and those inhabitants who have uniformly opposed it." Major General Winfield Scott, in an "address of a warrior to warriors," made clear his discomfort over Indian removal in 1838. Scott reassured the Cherokees that the "desire of every one of us" in the army is to "execute our painful duty in mercy." Captain Robert Anderson, facing the prospect of service against the Seminoles, lamented the policy of "keeping a small force in Florida." In Anderson's opinion, the policy had resulted in a "constant drain on the treasury at a loss of life and reputation without corresponding benefit to the Nation." According to Anderson, "no troops ever performed more laborious and thankless service than has our small suffering Florida army. They deserve credit and thanks," but instead "they obtain abuse and taunts from the pens and mouths of those who live in idleness and rule as bar room orators." Unionist Selby Stephen Fish soldiered for over a year despite "the *Slavery* of American soldiery." He did so "under the stern necissity" of war and was "willing and anxious to do my part for the welfare of my native land."[46]

Outside Camargo, Mexico, Private William Alexander McClintock of the Second Kentucky Mounted Volunteers reflected on the "Valleys of the Rio de Grand and San Juan" that "were spread out at my feet." Initially, as McClintock "stood and surveyed" the scene his "heart swelled with emotions of pride and joy." The Kentuckian's satisfaction in his "country" and "her chivalry and prowes" in war mixed with the personal "pride and Joy" he experienced from having "overcome the distance, danger, and disease" of the march. He "now stood ready to invade the very homes of our insidious and obstinate foe." Emotions of "regret, remorse, and pity soon arouse unbidden to chase away" his "exulting delight." McClintock "regretted the cause—the depravity, the cupidity of mankind, which has brought thousands" of men to "this bourne." He wondered how it was that "we should be engaged in a sanguinary war, with a nation for whom we could feel no emotions save that of pity." Professional soldiers like Captain Joseph H. Lamotte wished the "cause in which we are now to embark were a better one" so that "I might go into it with a zeal becoming so important a subject." He thought the United States had "grasped at large possessions and braved a power disorganized, weak, and therefore not to be feared." But, he observed, "We are now on our way to Mexico and laying all scruples aside I hope always to be found where duty calls me."[47]

Philip St. George Cooke, colonel of the Second Dragoons, thought his rank and power "unenviable" as he struggled "against obstacles and the oppressive sense of responsibility!" Policing the frontier and chasing Indians did not bring to mind "the exalted consciousness of well-used power, warming and ennobling the mind." Cooke found himself "overpowered and depressed by a struggle against disheartening difficulties, which he *knows* his government and his fellow-citizens will not and cannot appreciate." Scruples aside, frontier soldiering denied Cooke "even the pomp and circumstance of arms" which attended wars between Western nations. When Cooke did have his chance at a "civilized foe" in the Civil War, he found himself chasing, but never catching, "glory" or his Confederate son-in-law, James Ewell Brown Stuart.[48]

Despite mediocre leadership and management and complaints of poor treatment, virtuous soldiers continued in service. Major John Francis Hamtramck of the newly created United States Army confided to Lieutenant Colonel Nicholas Fish in 1785 that "nothing but a real intention to Serve the public has induced me to Continue So long at" West Point, a lonely, dreary, gray, and foreboding place in winter. Loyal officers who felt "indignant" at real and perceived mistreatment refused to "debase themselves by any insubordinate conduct." Certainly, "as individuals and as Gentlemen," noted Major General Jacob Jennings Brown, they could "give vent to their honest feelings, but, as soldiers, they always recollected" what was "due their Government and Country."[49]

Newly enlisted soldiers were often shocked by military life. Northern and Southern men were often taken aback when they entered service in 1861. Many had come to the army expecting adventure, glory, and even refinement, but instead found demanding and seemingly arbitrary discipline. Recruits soon discovered that a "soldiers life is a hard one." Private William H. Ker of Mississippi's Jeff Davis Legion freely complained of his officers' abuse and maltreatment of troops, attributing this to artificial distinctions of rank. Although Ker did not elaborate on his officers' offenses, he believed they had "used and treated" the men as "*stepping-stones* by which they were to mount from one high position to another." When Company A of the legion "left home, there was not a *man* in it—I should have said *private*—who was not anxious to sustain the reputation we had, by doing his *duty*, no matter what it was or how unused he may have been to such things, and who was not willing to undergo every hardship," and if by "doing so he could serve his country or deserve the praise of 'those at home.'" Believing in the importance of duty, Ker persevered. Mason Gordon, a trooper in the Albemarle Light Horse, thought "military discipline" was "rather revolting," although he was "willing . . . to undergo all hardships and privations in the cause of my country." Five months later, Gordon still found life in the army "a miserable one" devoid of "refining influences." Gordon consoled himself by remembering that "the cause we are engaged in makes it bearable and ought to make it exalting." Dexter F. Parker found nothing endearing about the army and was baffled by his receipt of a commission. He found that "beside this physical depression, I am badly perplexed in regard to my recent appointment" to a lieutenancy in "the army, for I need hardly say to you that the military *profession* has no charms for me and only the stern convictions of duty have led me" into the service.[50]

Many soldiers, particularly regulars, dreaded the onset of civil war in 1861. In an 1861 speech to the Sons of Temperance celebrating George Washington's birthday, James Ewell Brown Stuart contemplated the future of Union and that of the regular army's officer corps. Stuart conceded "we can not even in the hour of festivity banish from our minds the fear that the time may shortly come when we will occupy the anomalous position of an Army without a country, and if we are to change our avocations of life, if instead of the rugged path of glory, we are to pursue the tortuous windings of the civilian it will not be less the path of honor and of duty." In the secession winter of that year, Captain Roger Jones reported that he and the other regulars defending the armory at Harpers Ferry were "determined to do our duty." Jones undertook this duty with great reluctance. For while he was "resigned or prepared for whatever may come," he thought it was a "most painful idea to have to fight against one's countrymen" and "would not willingly do it, but situated" as Jones was, he could not "avoid it with honor."[51]

Captain George Gordon Meade found the "unnatural contest" between Americans manifestly wrong, and "cordially unite[d] with" Joshua Barney in "earnest prayers that a merciful Providence would so guide the rulers on both sides, as to terminate" the war. Meade thought the rebellion wrong, but as for "myself, I have ever held it to be my duty to uphold and maintain the Constitution and resist the disruption of this government." Major William Chapman of the Second Infantry hoped to remain in New Mexico "until the fall." He thought "perhaps it would be as well, for I might thereby escape the most disagreeable duty that ever devolved upon an officer, that of drawing his sword against his fellow Countrymen." Considering the "present attitude of our National affairs," he wrote, "I think the best place for an officer of the Army is in the heart of an Indian Country, where orders cannot reach him." Chapman informed his wife, Annie, "I shall hold on to my commission as long as Maryland clings to the Union, or until circumstances force me to resign" from the army.[52]

David H. Pierson, a member of Louisiana's secession convention, voted against the Ordnance of Secession in 1861. Secession, he believed, would be "violative of every natural feeling and impulse," and to "rise up against the Government in which we live and under whose care we are protected" was sinful. Although the representative from Winn Parish opposed secession, his overriding sense of duty to defend "our common country and homes" against "invasion and annihilation" led him to enlist in the Third Louisiana on 17 May 1861. Pierson reassured his father that he was not "acting under any excitement whatever but have resolved to go after a calm and thoughtful deliberation as to all the duties, responsibilities, and danger which I am likely to encounter in the enterprise."[53]

Virtuous duty demanded altruism, and eschewed narrow self-interest. Nonetheless, soldiers could benefit personally from the performance of duty despite the theme of disinterestedness that coursed through republican rhetoric. Duty to oneself was not undertaken for tangible reward or personal distinction, but for the purpose of improving the individual character and the moral spirit of the soldier. Duty undertaken in the cause of character improvement would allow "tranquil joy in constant streams [to] form round our hearts and raise the genuine transport of the Soul; for conscious worth outweighs the wealth of worlds," wrote Colonel Joseph Ward. Suppressing the desire to serve one's self-interest while acting for one's personal development was difficult, but worth the effort. Ward held that succumbing to a "narrow Soul, whose views are confined to its little self, is a greater curse than we ought to wish the vilest foe," for it resulted in the "*Poverty of the Soul*," which was the "doom of every little and inglorious mind."[54]

The assumption that soldiers were capable of suppressing or acting beyond the range of their self-interest drew upon men's ability to govern themselves, and it placed much of the onus for individual discipline and conduct upon the soldiers themselves. General orders in the Fifth Virginia Continentals enjoined soldiers to "Pay the Strictest attention to their Duty and Exert them Selves to Learn that Discipline so Necessary to their own Honour and Safety." Commanders reminded their men "that they will behave with Decency to their Fellow Citizens Whose Persons and Property they were ordained to Protect and Defend; and that they will not by any unworthy Conduct Disgrace the Honourable Profession of a Soldier."[55]

William W. Tompkins, a militia captain and the editorialist of the *New York Military Magazine* announced that "my duty to myself, not to my country," would not be "fulfilled until I should have exerted myself to acquire practical knowledge of the duties of a soldier." Furthermore, he held that his "doctrine ever has been that every able-bodied citizen should cultivate his mind in military science" as it was "our duty as citizens." Sergeant James L. Converse of the Sixth Wisconsin thought that if he were to die as a soldier, he at least had had "the satisfaction of believing I spent my last days in doing my duty to my self my country and I hope to my God." Henry Lord Page King, a Confederate officer, continually reminded his sister of his need to perform a "duty" to "himself, his family, and his country."[56]

Not every soldier met the high standards of virtuous conduct. In the summer of 1775, Colonel John Patton's commander heard with "astonishment the very frequent applications that are made as well by officers as soldiers for Furloughs." He reminded his soldiers that "Brave Men Who are engaged in the noble cause of Liberty, should never think of remission from the Camp whilst the Enemy is in sight." While campaigning in South Carolina and Georgia, Colonel Otho Holland Williams of the First Maryland Continentals decried the degraded state of public affairs and dearth of civic virtue. Backcountry militias terrorized the region and led him to think that there "are [but] a few Virtuous, good men in this state [South Carolina] and in Georgia." According to Williams the "great majority of the people is composed of the most unprincipled, abandon'd Vicious Vagrants that ever inhabited the Earth. The Daily deliberate murders committed by pretended Whiggs and reputed Tories (men who are actually neither one thing nor the other in principle) are too numerous and too shocking to relate." Instead of principled soldiers, Williams found "Licentiousness" in the "Clans and Denominations of Villains." Men, it appeared, who only wished to "Desolate this Country, Impoverish all who attempt to live by other means and destroy the strength and resources of the Country which ought to be collected and United against the common Enemy."[57]

Private Peter Juty was unwilling or unable to suppress his narrow self-interest in order to perform his duty. Juty deserted, was captured, tried, found guilty, and sentenced to be shot on 21 May 1778. Major General Robert Howe declared the condemned man guilty of violating every "moral sanction" and of betraying the "cause of freedom, the darling rights and privileges, both of the present and succeeding generations, which soldiers were ordained particular to secure and protect." He held Juty and his act in such contempt that he concluded that "No sense, therefore, of public or private virtue, no sentiment of honor or religion, can possibly actuate the bosom of that wretch who can have enough to perpetuate a crime in which felony, perjury and treason, to the United States of America, are complicated."[58]

Enlisted men were not the sole violators of republican coda. Captain John Taylor of the First Virginia Continentals believed that there was a "superior merit in not resigning when not promoted in place of a less worthy man." Continental army officers were a notoriously prickly lot when it came to matters of honor and slights, real or imagined. In officers' attempts at asserting their pretensions to gentility and their right to command, they revealed the often-precarious foundations of their social and economic standings and their own insecurities about their status. It was altogether likely that the greater the insistence on individual honor, the greater the likelihood of its unstable foundations. Therefore, by remaining in service "every one will agree that your continuance in commission would be the most noble disinterestedness." Officers who avoided the "rust of self-interest and ambition" would "furbish up the breast-plate-of Honor, so as to make it shine with" extraordinary "Lustre." Taylor derived inspiration from the "Roman Examples of virtue and honor," and found them to be "striking and brilliant." Some officers sorely needed these reminders. Lieutenant Francis Collins, a regular army artillerist, found that Major General William Orlando Butler, a Kentucky volunteer commanding a division in Mexico, was devoid of a sense of a sense of duty. Upon receiving confirmation of his nomination as the Democratic candidate for vice-president, Butler "immediately left the army to shift for itself, thinking undoubtedly that the health and comfort of an expectant Vice President were of more consequence than the lives of a few hundred vile soldiers, whom the country no longer had any need of" while they were in Mexico. Collins thought Butler behaved "like the politician he" was, not the "soldier" he pretended to be. Butler's example stood out as the measure to be shunned.[59]

The most fundamental "conception of a good soldier, wrote philosopher Sidney Axinn, "is that of an individual who agrees to sacrifice his . . . own life, if necessary, for the welfare of others." What greater evidence could a solider give of his disinterested nature, his willingness to forego self-interest in an act of private or public virtue, and his dedication to the republican ideal than through his willingness to sacrifice his wealth, happiness, or life? Soldiering out of "'love of Country' and defense of 'real Liberty' gave American war-making a disinterested, self-sacrificing purpose." Hence the "highest virtue required the greatest risk," which was the "willingness to sacrifice one's life, voluntarily, for the public good." For examples of virtuous self-sacrifice and inspiration, Americans had only to look to their past. Robert F. W. Allston, onetime lieutenant of artillery and adjutant general of South Carolina, commended to the people of Georgetown, South Carolina, George Washington as a model for emulation in an 1841 speech. Allston cited Washington's "firm, virtuous" nature, his "pure, disinterested" motives, and his "generous self devotion" to liberty. "No people," Allston intoned, "are deserving of Liberty, nor can they long enjoy it, who are unmindful of the perils, privations and heroism of those who achieved it, and none can long preserve its privileges, who in defence of them when threaten'd, are not able and willing to encounter the same perils, endure the same privations and exhibit the like heroism."[60]

John Whitcomb, a successful lawyer and newly minted colonel of colonial Massachusetts's militia, thought himself "unequal to such a service." But upon reflection, when Whitcomb considered that "our enemies Here have had the Cheef Posts of Hon[o]r and Profits in this Goverment and are now striving to Take all the Essential part of Goverment from the Voice of the People so that they may Take their Preperty as they plese and make them slaves," the lawyer found himself deeply "move[d]" by "Concern and Resentment." Whitcomb was "willing to Contribute my Property or Hazard my Life if there is a Call in Providence for it." Furthermore, he noted, "I have lost at least at the rate of £250 a Year, and this purely from Patriotic Principles."[61]

Revolutionaries reminded one another that "these times Require great Sacrifices to be made," and that "the Blood and Treasure of the Choicest and best Spirits of this land is but a triffling Consideration." "Were I possesed of an ample fortune," mused Timothy Pickering, "I should spend of it with pleasure in the public cause." George Washington believed that no "set of Men in the United States (considered as a body)" had "made the same sacrifices of their Interest in support of the common cause as the Officers of the American army," and that "nothing but a love of their Country, of honor and a desire of seeing their labors crowned with success could possibly induce them to continue one moment in Service." Anthony Wayne knew "Our Soldiery are not devoid of reasoning faculties, nor Callous to the first feelings of Nature. They have now served their Country for near five years with fidelity, poorly clothed badly fed, and worse paid." Indeed, of the "last Articles," wrote Wayne, "They have not seen a single paper Dollar in the way of pay for near twelve months." George Weedon recognized that as "Debilitated as our Troops are from the exceeding hard service" in the field, "Their Zeal for the Country does not abate." Although the Continentals "suffer[ed] greatly for want of shoes and other necessaries they seem determined to surmount our Difficulties and turn hardships into Diversion."[62]

As late as 1861, soldiers reminded their family and friends that "I am not fighting for money" but for principle. Others wrote of their "sacrifice of personal interest" despite having an "office full of business and a hundred clients depending on my labor for the maintenance of their rights." But if local leaders and "those situated as I am do not go who will?" Who indeed?[63]

For soldiers of the Continental army and for the citizenry, pay, especially in the form of enlistment bonuses and service pensions, was a vexatious issue. The very idea of soldiering for pay seemed to contradict the self-sacrifice called for in a virtuous soldier. Only mercenaries, men devoid of the communitarian and self-sacrificing spirit so vital to virtue, demanded money for their service. Conveniently, republican rhetoric glossed over the parliamentary largesse that allowed for the raising of provincial regiments in the Seven Years' War. As for pensions, they smacked of the corrupting British practice of sinecures. This was not the case, however. Charles Royster noted that Henry Lee, and those of like mind, realized a "virtuous willingness to fight" would not be sufficient to raise and maintain a respectable army. Lee and others recognized that the length of the war and warfare's increasing complexity demanded skilled, long-service soldiers. Militiamen and short-term volunteers would not do, because without "training and continuous service, well-meaning citizens could lose both their cause and their lives." Continental soldiers recognized that "professionalism would not alienate them from their families or the republic."[64]

The devotion of Continental officers to "republican principles," noted Don Higginbotham, "was as strong as that of most political leaders." These frequently vain and argumentative political men had a real "concern for the public good, for the practice of virtue, and the notion of sacrifice." The communitarian impulse within American republicanism led officers to expect all citizens to sacrifice something of themselves for the good of the republic, yet the "officers, carrying such principles into daily practice, looked around them and saw far too much 'idleness and dissipation' in the cities, an inordinate desire for profits and riches on the part of hordes of merchants and farmers." Colonel Philip Van Cortlandt's experience was common among Continental officers. He reported that he was "loosing ground fast" and was forced to "live like a Vagabond," but that at same time he had to maintain his outward appearance as an officer. Van Cortlandt thought it was "more than my Patriotism can put up with at this Day." In a pique of frustration and anger, he recalled that "there was a time I would have fed on bread and water as I have done and was content. The reason, my Country I thought Virtuous and Approved my Services, [but] now, I find it the reverse." He saw "men living in Luxury," participating in the "Distructions of Every thing Virtuous," whose "Grand Object is gain and living in high life." It was depressing to reflect "on future Events." Officers who had sacrificed their private fortunes in the cause of revolution suffered financial hardships. Those who contemplated leaving the "Service" wondered if they had "enough" savings to "make some provision to Support" themselves "thro life." If, however, they continued serving until the war's end, it might be a great "Folly, A Sweet Consolation truly, that my great patriotism, should reduce me to Bigiry."[65]

Revolutionaries contended that the "Soldier, who in Freedom's Cause has borne all the ills misery had in store and braved death in every form, should share the sweets of life in every clime" of the new nation they had helped to create. In their eyes, the Continental deserved some material reward for his many sacrifices as a soldier of the new republic. Soldiers, poorly and irregularly paid, continually bereft of proper supplies, and chancing encounters with injury or death, had had no time to prepare themselves for the future. They feared lives of "poverty," dependence, and charity. Colonel Joseph Ward asked rhetorically, "Shall he earn scanty bread by hard fatigue, whose unwearied hand hath purchased happiness for thousands, and paid the price of Freedom with his blood?" Revolutionary soldiers, perhaps self-servingly, believed they deserved a reward as public recognition for having faithfully done their duty. Pensions and bonuses were badges of status and public proofs of the virtue and service of the soldier. Ward wondered, "Shall the sordid mind that never rose above the love of gold nor spent an hour to bless mankind, riot in the sweets of life, and hold the reins of State, while the Sons of Honour beg their way through life in the Land that borrows lustre from their names—in that land their virtue and their valour won? Forbid it Honour!" If, however, Congress and the people were so cruel as to ignore the sacrifices and contributions made by the army, veterans counseled, "Our joys shall rise from a source beyond the reach of fortune or the smile of mortals, from conscious Virtue, which envy cannot reach or malice wound or time or chance destroy."[66]

Discussions, promises, reductions, and retractions by Congress of officers' half-pay made Ward and other officers "sincerely sorry that they ever made us the Promise of it." Had it not been for the officers of the army, they believed, "The Country would then have gone to *Hell* . . . (a political one at least)." Samuel Tenny, surgeon of the Second Rhode Island Continentals, wanted to know what "Actions can demand more Gratitude than those by which Millions are rescued from Tyranny and Misery?" Colonel Philip Van Cortlandt, commander of the Second New York Continentals, had pronounced similar concerns. Van Cortlandt feared that he and his compatriots would be "thought useless beings" who would then "receive similar treatment the Old pack Horses did on the western Expedition" in Pennsylvania's Wyoming Valley. What the New Yorker found "truly Mortifying" was that the "foremost of this Class I am Difending have made Fortunes at our Expence."[67]

Continental soldiers believed that they alone had sacrificed their interests for the republic. In a theme that echoed long after these soldiers' passing, the public had not done its part. Devalued and irregular pay, shrunken and shoddy supplies, congressional promises and retractions of pensions, bonuses, and land, and high-living civilians convinced Continentals that the citizenry was corrupt and had forgotten and snubbed the army. In soldiers' hearts, they knew there was a grievous lack of public virtue on the part of a people unwilling to sacrifice self-interest. Continentals responded with protests, petitions, and mutinies. Soldiers had signed contractual agreements in the form of enlistment papers. They had met and were meeting their contractual obligations, but the country had abrogated its obligations. Soldiers' protests were, therefore, not the repudiation of beliefs but the recognition of and reaction to broken contracts by a distinctly unvirtuous people. "If the revolution depended on money as the only motive—or even the main motive—for facing the British," wrote Charles Royster, "it would have failed quickly." The Continental army depended on the voluntarism of men willing to make "sacrifices in public service" for a "righteous cause." Revolutionary soldiers were "anxious to defend American liberty, convinced that such service showed one's virtue. Their records and "witnesses agreed that nothing except this conviction, not even the most stringent discipline, would have kept them on duty when clothing, food, and pay dwindled or gave out." Indeed, "only a fool would remain a soldier for reasons of immediate material interest."[68]

The loss of life or limb was the ultimate act of virtuous sacrifice for any republican soldier. In battle, noted Robert Middlekauff, the soldier faced in "stark form . . . one of the classic problems free men face: choosing between rival claims of public responsibility and private wishes, or in eighteenth-century terms choosing between virtue—devotion to public trust—and personal liberty." Nathanael Greene was "willing to spend and be spent in so Righteous a Cause" as independence from Britain. Greene admitted to his brother Christopher, "Chearfully would I risque my Life for the Salvation of my Country." Combat tested the depth of a man's fidelity to others, and "virtue demanded that men give up their liberties and perhaps even their lives for others." Colonel Edmund Kirby thought as much, when he reported to his sister, Frances Kirby Smith, the death of her son Ephraim "at *Molino del Rey*, at the foot of Chapultepec" in Mexico City. Kirby noted that his nephew was a "noble brave fellow" who had "sacrificed his life to a sense of duty, in an exhibition of daring courage and gallantry unsurpassed on any occasion."[69]

Connecticut's John O'Brien was not "sorry" about his decision to enlist in 1861, although he found his "soldier's life is a harder one than I would choose, and no one need envy their lot." Looking forward to the day when "this rebellion is put down," O'Brien predicted he and other soldiers "will all be glad to lay down the sword and musket and go back to the workshop. Some of us may come home with a pair of wooden legs, or might do things that would be more patriotic." In O'Brien's estimation, the soldier's highest demonstration of patriotism was "leaving their bodies on a victorious and well fought field," because "their graves would always seem a warning to those who wish to overthrow one of the best governments that has ever been formed by the hand of man"[70]

When writing about the sacrifice of life soldiers often followed a simple dialectical formula. Writers presented two irreconcilable extremes, thus leaving the reader with a choice between victory or death. Phrasing their thoughts in this manner, writers made plain the seriousness with which they approached the idea of virtuous sacrifice. Beyond this, writers attempted to convey their passion, their maturity, and their worthiness as members of a republican soldiery.

Major Nicholas Fish rejoiced to "command Men whose Hearts are filled with a generous Emulation of excelling each other in the strictest Discipline whose Judgement enable them to discern the Justice of our most righteous Cause, and whose Motive is not mercenary (as with most soldiers)." This New York Continental refused to believe that any "American (that is not a disgrace to the Name) can brook the Thought of being dependant upon a Power that both exhausted its Strength and Treasure in endeavouring to subjugate and make us Slaves!" Fish announced "I would rather fight to my Knees in Blood, than see these flourishing Colonies dependent upon that tho' once flourishing and renowned, now degraded, sullied and infamous Britain." The First New Hampshire's Lieutenant Colonel Henry Dearborn waxed poetically as he celebrated the October 1777 victory at Saratoga:

AMERICAN SOULS ARE TOO VALIANT TO YIELD

A host of brave patriots with hearts that beat high
Rush'd onwards to conquer or die or die
led on by commanders the Heirs of bright fame
he saw skill and discipline ever must bend
Where glory and freedom and virtue contend

the hearts of our heroes new and one inspir'd
hopes the sad hearts of the timmerous fir'd
by virtues voice

Shur when slaves with bold freemen in combat engag'd
vain, ever will be their rage their rage

then to Glory you gallant Americans fly
Hark Washington calls you to victory! Plain
A Chief in whose each excellence reigns
Guided by him
We'll beat British Nero's
and triumph like heroes

Or die[71]

When George Smith Avery left Illinois in 1861 touting "Liberty or Death!" he hoped "never to return until this terrible contest between freedom and anarchy shall have been brought to an end." Avery "regard[ed] the rights of an American citizen dearer than life itself," and he "resolved to die rather than have one of those rights taken away." The "noble" Seventh South Carolina, according to David Wyatt Aiken, "long[ed] for the time when we will get a chance at the Hessians" from the North. He swore, "We will conquer or die, nothing else will satisfy us." Lieutenant Colonel William Preston Johnston, a Southern-sympathizing Kentuckian, knew the "path of duty is hard to tread" but was willing to accept any "sacrifice of any personal consideration" for Confederate success. The Kentucky colonel knew his sacrifices would be "more than repaid by his own consciousness of right." He preferred to be a "poor exile, fighting in the ranks of the Confederate Army, than the sleek and supple slave of power, in any home, with all that the soul-bought gold of Lincoln could supply."[72]

Some soldiers announced their willingness to trade their lives for their respective causes. Theodore Talbot, a lieutenant of the Fort Sumter garrison, placed his life in peril, "*voluntarily*," he added to "defend that Flag which too many traitors both north and south would gladly see trampled in the dust." Edward Murphy was "willing to sacrifice all to get Independent of the whining Yankees," while others espoused their willingness to "fall for the cause of Liberty and Independence." Along with the violent and often bloodthirsty imagery of battle, a good number of these soldiers reflected upon death as an ennobling experience or with a remarkable sense of stoicism. It was an "honor to fight and die if needs be in defence of the union." An Ohio college student, John R. Hunt Jr., reassured his father, "I am prepared to meet what will come, as I left home and all its endearment for the purpose of defending the stars and stripes." Hunt's "willing[ness] to suffer most anything in behalf of that star-spangled banner" may very well have had the opposite effect for his concerned father.[73]

Soldiers resigned themselves to a "verry hard life it is true, but nothing can be too hard, no sacrifice too great or death in its most horrid and ghastly forms can have no terror" to patriots while "fighting for the Land of my birth and for those at home." Some accepted that if it is to "be my destiny to die young, there is no death that I would prefer than to die in the defence of my Country, Liberty and honour." Some soldiers considered the lessons of history and concluded that the "price of human freedom has ever been human life," and if "we prize the latter higher, then the other cannot be ours." En route to join the Confederate army, Rufus W. Cater was ready to "sacrifice my life if necessary in the cause of our independence."[74]

John Henry Stibbs wrote that if "my life is needed for the defense of My Country I am ready to give it" in the cause of union and to do it "freely, for I think it is my *duty* to act in this matter." Stibbs's words spoke for countless numbers of Union volunteers in the first rush of enlistment in 1861. After taking a "solemn oath to support and protect the Constitution" and to "show ourselves faithful to her, against all her enemies and opposers," J. Mason Henry did not "think" there was a man in the Bay State Artillery "who would not lay down his life on the battle field if need be, before he would see a star effaced or a stripe obliterated." The young gunner's passion was further kindled by news of Colonel Elmer Ellsworth's death on 24 May 1861. Clearly moved, Henry announced, "'Revenge for his death' is now our motto" in the battery, and we will carry the war to the death." Should the Confederacy "not yield to our power," he thought, "then our millions upon million that are ready to lay down their lives if it must be before one star or a stripe of the American Flag is polluted" by treason.[75]

Not all deaths in war validated sacrifice. Some, like that of Virginian "Charles Weaver a fine young fellow only twenty years old, from Martinsburg," were wasteful. Weaver was "accidentally mortally wounded." His comrades thought the death "very sad," and that to "see one young so attractive, and so fullest of the highest hopes and anticipations, brought this suddenly to death's door, without an opportunity to signalize his devotion to the cause in which we are embarked, or to meet his fate upon the battle field in defence of his native state" a tragedy. The circumstances of Weaver's death compounded the misfortune of the event. Instead of receiving the wound from an "enemy," he "die[d] by the hand of a friend."[76]

American soldiers' reflections on the death and suffering they endured in service suggest a belief in the country's need to undergo a form of national scourging in order that Americans might atone for past sins or correct their course. To them, war, because of the sure chance of great suffering on a national scale, was akin to a penitential rite undertaken by society in the form of the soldiers it sent forth into battle. Marcus Cunliffe described the mid-nineteenth-century development as a "penitential national mood." Sectionalism engendered divisiveness in national discourse and cast a pall over the nation. To soldiers it seemed the republic had fallen far short of its promise, and that war was the only means by which the nation could expiate itself of its ills.[77]

"The mass of ordinary Americans," according to Earl J. Hess, "tended to associate Christianity with the gloom of Calvinism." Thus, soldiers accepted without question the basic premise of redemption through sacrifice. "The warrior hero embodied all that was good in the nation," and his sacrifice would purify the United States. The soldier's death "became something of a ritual purification, a symbol of the regeneration of American society." "Times change constantly for the worse," or so thought Lieutenant Robert Anderson in 1840. "Nothing," he believed, but a "long and hot war" with another country would unite the nation and "save us from disunion and demoralization." Anderson accepted the "regenerative potential of the warrior hero's death." He lamented the lack of "national character or feeling," and looked forward to the "time to come when we may stand boldly up and proclaim 'I am an American citizen.'"[78]

For Charles B. Fox of Massachusetts, civil war was not a total loss, but was, instead, a chance for national redemption. "That wars are always accompanied by cruelty and horror," Fox freely admitted, but "there are many ugly sores in the body politic which would be healed" by war. Fox had no doubt that the "good resulting" from civil war would "more than counterbalance the evils from the other case." Confiding to his diary, Fox noted "We still believe in the justice of our cause, but it does seem as if we must go through the fire ere we become the pure gold."[79]

2

Preserving, Defending, and Creating the Political Order

Legitimacy

Legitimacy was both conservative and forward looking. In its first role, legitimacy was conservative. The preservation and defense of the political and social order upheld the legitimate disposition of republican society, and in doing so soldiers were the agents of conservatism. Nearly every soldier considered himself a defender of traditional social and political rights and privileges, the republic, or of the Constitution, thereby elevating his purpose from simple defense into a principled act. These military agents of conservatism conceived of themselves and the army as the inheritors of a sacred trust, one that they had a responsibility to safeguard. Their writings incorporated idealized images of the ancient Greek *poleis*, the Roman republic, their colonial forebears, the Revolutionary generation, the Constitution, and other powerful metaphors that conjured evocative representations of soldiers' beliefs. Their strong sense of a vital personal and communal history compelled them to make the past a touchstone for their world view and made American soldiers "determined to Defend [the] Rights and privaleges" they considered "so just."[1]

Defending the republic meant preserving its past as that past existed within living institutions like government and culture. Importantly, it meant following the example set by the Revolutionary generation, which as Charles Royster noted, had "explicitly deprived citizens and soldiers" of any "opportunity for moral abdication by asserting that the founding and survival of the nation were a public responsibility." Citizens in uniform were, therefore, the conservators of liberty and the republic. In peace, they reinforced the republican order by quelling social disorder and through their public displays of ceremony and their success in battle "accomplish[ed] society's purposes by protecting republican self-government." Soldiers took inspirations from their past to serve when "liberty seemed threatened."[2]

The liberty that American soldiers asserted was their right as citizens to participate publicly and freely in the affairs of government. This liberty was both personal and political. One could not exist without the other. By exercising their political liberty, citizens acted as the agents who safeguarded "personal liberty and private rights" from encroachment by the state or the mob. Americans' personal liberty, their natural rights as bounded by laws established by their elected representatives, was society's correlative of natural rights. Citizens' natural rights could only be proscribed through legislation that reflected the will of the people. These laws binding natural rights existed to maintain a proper balance between governmental and social forces, which, if unchecked, would produce an imbalance of power leading to either a state of tyranny or of anarchy. Accordingly, laws performed the delicate task of minimally checking the rights of individuals while at the same time giving the state enough power to govern and to protect those individuals in the exercise of their natural rights. Citizen-soldiers understood that liberty was a delicate thing; soldiers realized it needed vigilant tending and guarding if it was to survive against the encroachments of power or disorder. This was why the men of Whitney's Regiment, "we the subscribers," decided to "solemnly and severally Engage and inlest our selves as soldiers in the masachusets service for the preservation of the Leberties of america" during the Whiskey Rebellion of 1794.[3]

Legitimacy in its progressive guise looked forward to creating a new political reality. Soldiers had directly participated in the creation of the republic through revolution in the eighteenth century and were now proof of the republic as a legitimate member of the community of nations. The army and the militia, in effect, served as badges of status and as proofs of the United States as a legitimate political entity. These forces demonstrated the nation's ability to defend itself, a direct link to conservatism, and of the republic's ability to enforce its will or impose it on others. Military service also worked in a more mundane but no less important way. Soldiering was a means to establish and demonstrate the political legitimacy of ethnic and racial minorities, their membership in the broader society, and their ability to participate in the life of the republic. This was especially so for immigrants and a small number of free blacks.

Immigrants and free blacks believed that military service would confirm to the native-born population their worthiness and ability to assume active roles in the life of the republic. By demonstrating their fitness for republican life through soldiering, these groups hoped to prove that they were legitimate participants in the American experiment. So, while the sustainment of communal norms and harmony was the goal of "many volunteer militia companies," those groups with the greatest desire to enter American society and gain acceptance by the native-born used military service as a public demonstration of their good citizenship, their ability, and their desire to assume an active and responsible role in society.[4]

The means by which soldiers preserved, demonstrated, or entered the republican order varied. A few men, like Nathanael Greene, recognized the distinctive role played by the militia. Greene advised Governor Thomas Jefferson that militiamen constituted a "great bulwark of civil liberty." But because the militia served local interests and was, by nature, poorly trained, Greene counseled that "they are not [to be] depended upon as a principal" force in war. As Greene noted, the militia was a thin reed upon which to defend liberty. Lieutenant Christopher Van Deventer of the Second Artillery, a close observer of military affairs, thought otherwise, however, about this bulwark of the republic. Writing in 1810, Van Deventer saw danger in relying on the militia as a "system of defense." If the citizenry seriously devoted its time to military affairs it would neglect "internal improvements," destroy the "domestic oeconomy," and open the nation to "external attack." He feared that "such reliances have always been . . . the forerunner of slavery." Van Deventer instead argued for a strong regular army to free citizens for more industrious pursuits and to prevent the militarization of society. For a regular officer, Van Deventer's view was rare, although it resonated, if discordantly, with American fears of standing armies. Yet, in this case it was fear of a militarized society that concerned the lieutenant. Van Deventer need not have worried, however. The position and condition of the states' militias were changing.[5]

Popular adherence to compulsory militia duty waned in the closing years of the eighteenth century and continued throughout the nineteenth century. Unequal military burdens among the citizenry and receding threats from Indians and European powers contributed to the demise of the popularly constituted militia. But as the obligatory system fell aside and "waned, volunteering waxed" as exclusive volunteer com-

panies arose in the early nineteenth century. State governments happily enrolled enthusiastic volunteers as elements of the states' militias.
Volunteer companies helped fill militia ranks and performed the functions of the lapsing enrolled militia, including patrolling slave beats in
the Southern states and riot control in urban areas. Additionally, they
answered a public desire for dramatic public spectacle. Volunteers' displays of the "martial spirit, combined with a love of colorful uniforms,
military ceremonials, and martial music" provided a form of public entertainment as well as a reassuring demonstration of public order and
devotion to republicanism.[6]

Volunteers hoped that frequent and spectacular drills would give
them "renown and serve as a paragon of imitation to others" who might
be interested in volunteering. Observers found a "moral in this spectacle" that demonstrated the "capacity of the Republic to defend its liberty and its institutions." Indeed, it was inspiring to know "our citizens"
would "voluntarily enroll themselves in military array and Voluntarily
assume responsibilities" and military "duties." Such soldiers were "Bold,
True Hearted Men! Guardians of a trust who will never be faithless, inheritors of a freedom that must never be dissipated." Local men who
voluntarily banded together, equipped themselves at their own expense,
and elected their leaders had very real personal and financial stakes in
company affairs. Members' interests in the goings-on of the company,
its success, and its survival mirrored their philosophy of the citizen-
soldiery and its interest in national and local affairs. Volunteers believed
in "placing the Implements of War in the hands of Freemen" who had a
voice in government and a share in the nation's future, for by doing so,
"there is scarcely a possibility of their [arms] being used, but in defence
of the soil which they claim, and the Liberties which are their birthright." Adjutant General Albert Tracy of Maine thought that it was only
to an armed citizenry that a "free government legitimately look for security; to a people holding stake and interest in all for which they might
ultimately strive." Supporters referred to the militia as the nation's "sheet
anchor, our bulwark, our shield and our salvation."[7]

Volunteer duty attracted community leaders and other "men of substance" who were interested in participating directly in the means by
which "they could help defend what they owned" and in exercising some
control or direction of communal armed force. Defending property in-

terests was not the sole motive for joining, however. Volunteer militia service was also an "instrument for political communication and for [the] partisan political activity" of American society. In sparsely settled agricultural counties, few local institutions were capable of gathering together so many members of the electorate on a regular basis. Since volunteers elected their officers, the muster also provided a practical forum for aspiring and established politicians. Musters concentrated citizen-soldiers, who were voters, and the men who aimed to lead them. Militia musters were uniquely suited to the "decentralized and fragmented" interests and "political authority" that characterized much of early-nineteenth-century society. In urban locales as well, militia duty provided men with an opportunity to gather with like-minded citizens and for politicians to practice their trade.[8]

A constant theme running throughout the constitutions of urban volunteer companies was the need to maintain law and order. Few cities could field large police forces; therefore volunteers often stepped in to assist in the preservation and restoration of order and the "protection of the citizens" and their property from mobs. An 1849 riot in New York forced local officials to call on the militia to stop a mob from "assaulting the Opera House." Brigadier General John Watts De Peyster of the New York militia thought that "laws, it might almost be said, civilization, rested, and rested securely, on the broad basis, beneath which . . . gleamed the bayonets of the *Soldier-Citizens*." DePeyster, descended from an old New York family that had navigated the waters from able servants of the crown through rebellion to republicanism, went so far as to conclude that "religion, civilization, [and] freedom, have hung upon the conduct, courage, [and] fitness for the hour" of the militia. Riots and other forms of urban unrest were sometimes the events that brought about the formation of volunteer companies.[9]

The First California Guard formed on 27 July 1849 "immediately after the excitement into which the town" of San Francisco was "thrown by the capture, trial and expulsion of the notorious 'Hounds,'" a nativist gang of discharged soldiers affiliated with the Know-Nothing Party and dedicated to violence and extortion against Mexican, Spanish, Chilean, and black gold miners and immigrants. Officially named the San Francisco Society of Regulators, the Hounds expanded into robbery, the protection and extortion racket, and violence against the entire community.

With crime no longer restricted to the despised "greaser" and others of that ilk, San Francisco's leaders raised a force and chased away or jailed the Regulators. Thereafter, a number of the "most prominent citizens, dreading a recurrence" of the violence, "conceived the idea of organizing a permanent volunteer military company, to aid the legal officers in the maintenance of order and personal security." Members of the First California, "all men of ample means," established the unit as a "joint stock company" to defray the cost of uniforms and equipment and to erect an armory.[10]

Volunteers managed their companies as "exclusive private clubs" with the expectation that members would pay dues and fines as well as provide their own uniforms and weapons according to patterns decided by committees and voted on by the members of the company. Prohibitive uniforming and arming costs limited membership and resulted in units whose composition often reflected and reinforced social and economic distinctions and classes in the antebellum United States. Consequently, social and economic elites formed a goodly number of units. The "affluence" and "social prestige" of these men afforded them the time to devote to military affairs. These companies reinforced social distinctions and confirmed members' status through their military activities. Men could channel their energies and interests into organizations that protected the community and allowed them to exercise their martial fantasies as they publicly affirmed the superiority of the American citizen-soldier and the interdependent nature of soldiering and citizenship. By participating as citizen-soldiers, members "could feel patriotic, and therefore democratic, and yet elevated into a romantic-genteel realm where one might talk without embarrassment of nobility, honor, chivalry, [and] gallantry."[11]

Parades and musters played an important role as public theater. The symbolism of the uniformed militia represented the virtuous citizenry in all of its armed might and uniformed splendor. As a real and symbolic representation of law, order, and republicanism, a militia company "did not have to fight to prove its legitimacy; indeed a show of force, a marshalling of citizens in arms, seemed at times effective in maintaining order in nineteenth-century America." The experience of the War of 1812 and people's celebration of the militia under men like Andrew Jackson "gilded" the image of the virtuous freeholder springing to arms in defense of the republic. The glow shone upon the militia in the War for Independence, too, thereby endowing it with the attributes of "legitimacy and authority." The armed and uniformed citizenry embodied a vision as "both defenders and products of the republican way of life."[12]

The soldiers who "defend[ed] our Persons, familys, intrest, and Libertyes" knew they were unique. They chose to "devote" themselves to "Arms not for the invasion of other countries but the defence of our own" and for the "preservation of the rights of Human Nature, and the Liberties of America." The rights about which soldiers wrote originated in nature and in English jurisprudence. Starting with the English colonial experience, Americans conceived of their rights as the natural, "inalienable, indefeasible rights inherent in all people by virtue of their humanity, and the concrete provisions of English law." Concepts relating to the sources of sovereignty did change radically during the Revolution; those regarding rights remained fundamentally fixed.[13]

Legitimacy's conservative thrust antedated the American Revolution, but the war "established the patriotic precedent of fighting a heroic war over fundamental issues." Indeed, the ideological bent of American military service and war making touched upon almost all aspects of soldiering and continued through the Civil War. Republican soldiers were the "Sons of Freedom" who "Nobly Stepped forth" as freemen to "defend Their most Invaluable Rights and privileges." They were "Those brave men who" risked all in "defense of their Country and for the preservation of its liberty." Soldiers like Maryland's James McHenry "were not mercenaries serving temporary national interests; they came from the citizenry to defend the nation's existence." The future secretary of war left home in 1775 to "serve as a volunteer, or Surgeon, in the American Army" so that he might "defend the liberties of Americans and mankind against the enemies of both"[14]

Shortly after assuming command of the Continental army, George Washington made it clear that he served in "support of the Rights of Mankind, and the Welfare of our common Country." His "highest Ambition" as a republican soldier was to be the "happy Instrument of vindicating those Rights." Throughout the war Washington regularly reminded his men of their duty to preserve Americans' traditional rights and liberties. The Virginian railed against the "Invasions and Abuse of private property" by undisciplined men and reminded "every private soldier" of his duty to "detest and abhor such practices." Washington believed that the virtuous American soldier, "when he considers that it is for the preservation of his own Rights, Liberty and Property, and those of his Fellow Countrymen," would realize that such conduct was "unmanly and sully's the dignity of the great cause" for which he was fighting. This cultural ideal coursed through military reality when Washington railed against unscrupulous officers who pocketed men's pay and provisions or padded accounts so that they might line their own pockets. Such acts damaged the reputation of the army, which had gathered in "defence of the common Rights and Liberties of mankind." Washington advised these scurrilous creatures to reflect upon their privileged stations as the leaders of "an Army constituted for so noble a purpose, and to make haste with their corrections."[15]

When Americans decided to "take up Arms in defence of our Rights and Priviledges," they cast themselves as an obedient people who were unjustly oppressed by the "heavy and tyrannical Hand of Power." Militia covenants made plain their case *"To all Christian People believing in, and relying on, that God to whom our Enemies have at last forced us to appeal."* Revolutionaries "declare[d] to the world that we from the heart disavow every thought of Rebellion to his Majesty" George III or "opposition to Legal Authority." In truth, these soldiers believed they had been "deprived of that Legal Authority whose dictates we ever with pleasure obey." Parliament, through its suspension of colonial rights, had "Driven" loyal subjects to the "last necessity": taking up arms in "defence" of their "Lives and Liberties." The motives that impelled Americans to form an army were just and universal. It was important for the revolutionaries to state that "we are not mercenaries whose views extend no farther than pay and plunder" or personal satisfaction, but "men acquainted with, and feeling the most generous fondness for the Liberties and unalienable Rights of mankind." It was a moral imperative to defend the "Rights and priviledges which the God of nature hath bestowed upon them." Any surrender of these "dear and Heavenborn Liberties" would have been an affront to that "being who delights in the Liberty and prosperity of all his Creatures." Not long after attaining their independence, Americans formalized their frame of government through the Constitution, the ultimate covenant in American political life. More than a frame of government, the Constitution was a pronouncement of

American political culture, however contentious or vague. If the Constitution gave American soldiers a tangible and enumerated representation of their rights, their embrace of the writ was due to war.[16]

Soldiers' devotion to the United States Constitution appears to have begun in earnest with the nationalist upswing at the time of the War of 1812. American soldiers still cited "the enjoyment of life, liberty, and property" as motivating factors, but to them they added the "Constitution" of the United States as the "birth right of every American Citizen." Together, these made up an "invaluable inheritance" that they had "received unimpaired" from their "Patriotic Ancestors." Patriotic intensity led Lieutenant Christopher Van Deventer to state, "I will never become a citizen of another Govern[men]t[.] My heart, by education principle and reason is unalterably bound in affection to the U[nited] States of America." Van Deventer's "ambition" was to develop the professional military "knowledge which will make my efforts useful to the perpetuation of Republican Institutions." The young artillerist hoped that "Heaven" would "grant" him "success" in his endeavors, so that he "devote" his energies to the "defense of our glorious constitution."[17]

Devotion to the "glorious constitution" or to the defense of liberty was not restricted to any one section of the nation. American cultural norms and expectations of "courage and ideals of proper behavior" were cultural norms that "transcended" localism and the "particular issues involved in the Civil War" or, indeed, any other American war of this period. An officer of the Thirteenth Massachusetts Volunteers recorded, with great regret, "that the Methodist Church [at Harper's Ferry, Virginia] was entered, and the Bible, Hymn Books and chairs taken, probably as relics" by Union soldiers. If this young officer and others like him were "fighting to restore peace to a distracted country" and were "expected to conquer a peace" then why, he wondered, "are our soldiers allowed and encouraged to hate everything from the south of the Potomac?" Violating the rights of Southerners, even of those in rebellion, was counterproductive in a "war for the preservation of the Constitution." If the nation was to be reunited, the "Constitution itself must not be violated" for any reason. Soldiers North and South could, with equal justification, lay claim to the "republican heritage of the United States." Americans were divided and united at one and the same time by their shared history and ideology. These men placed great store by their defense of "representative government, democratic practices, and public virtue." More than eighty years had passed, yet the ideals of the American Revolution still resonated. Throughout the sectional crisis and for the first year of the Civil War, Americans called upon their friends and fellow citizens to defend their political institutions, their homes, and their families.[18]

Southern soldiers feared for wives and daughters who might be "exposed to brutal outrages worse than death," conjuring the fear that their female relations might be treated by black men as so many slaveholders had treated black women, as objects for sexual predation and violence. What was good for the goose was not good for the gander. Volunteers proclaimed themselves ready to "fight side by side with my only son, my son in law, my brothers and dearest friends of every grade, in defense of our hearth stones." Confederate soldiers believed themselves "greatly outraged under the compact of Union" and that it was "right, certainly right according to the fundamental principles of our institutions, to withdraw from an oppressive Union." According to this line of reasoning, secession was an act of institutional preservation. Their letters exposed fears of Northern threats to racial relations, the social order, property rights, and local autonomy. To some, it was obvious that Northern politicians "boldly advocat[ed] a total consolidation in the gen[era]l gov[ernmen]t" and the obliteration of all "State lines" and rights. Patriotic Southerners had to defend their rights and preserve the integrity and autonomy of their states against a conspiracy "determined to overthrow republican government altogether." Despite the conviction that secession was correct, emotional attachments were difficult to sever. Soldiers remembered Independence Day celebrations, when "we wonce could celebrate this memorable day and felt proud to claim the Stars and stripes of wonce a happy and free people." Instead, it was feared, the "declaration of independence will be paraded in all the invaded localities by the infernal Lincolnites."[19]

Conservatism struck a deep chord among many Confederate soldiers. As much as secession was desire to establish a new nation, it was also the desire to preserve an old one. Southern soldiers fought to "defend their homes and their firesides against the ruthless approach of a relentless foe" bent on the subjugation of "our people." Not surprisingly, Confederate soldiers felt their former countrymen had betrayed them in order to establish a more centralized national government bent on depriving citizens of their established rights and their property in slaves. Despite evidence to the contrary, fearful perception had trumped reality. It was no matter that the Three-fifths Compromise and the Electoral College had, from 1789, given the southern states far greater national political power than warranted by their free or enfranchised populations through their overrepresentation in the House of Representatives, that eight of the sitting presidents had been slaveholders, or that Abraham Lincoln had been legally elected president and had pledged to not interfere with the institution of slavery. It mattered not: their beliefs were sincere. Lieutenant Colonel William Johnston of the Confederate First Kentucky averred that the "Northern usurpation" of government was but a stark example of "fanaticism and criminal folly, based on a mere fantasy." As far as these men were concerned, the "Revolution has been effected by our enemies" in the North, a "powerful and fanatical enemy." Confederate soldiers saw themselves as loyal republicans defending "our civilization and the operation of those rights claimed by a free people to establish their own government." Perception had become reality.[20]

True republicans were called upon to "help to save the South—to preserve Liberty Herself amongst men! And to back down and crush out the Hell inspired spirit of Abolitionism of red and black republicanism." Southern victory would secure the "blessings of civil liberty [and] the equal rights of all free white men." Southern victory would also preserve the tradition of local autonomy.[21]

Confederate soldiers strongly identified with their individual states and communities. Virginians professed "loyalty to and zeal for the welfare and prosperity of our old commonwealth" and the "honour and safety of the Old Dominion." Hannibal Paine of Middle Tennessee was "sorry to see the people in some portions of E[ast] Tenn[essee] so slow in volunteering." Paine thought their decided lack of enthusiasm "speaks but poorly for their patriotism, when their own state is menaced with invasion, and their homes threatened with fire, sword, rapine, and plunder." Louisiana's Native Guard, the city's free-black militia, declared itself "ready to take arms" as Confederate soldiers for the "defence of their homes, together with other inhabitants of this city, against any enemy who may come and disturb its tranquility." Such devotion aside, it would not do to have black soldiers in a confederacy predicated upon race-based slavery. The Confederate government refused the Native Guard's generous and patriotic offer. The spirit of conservatism, however, was not unique to Southern troops.[22]

Northern soldiers drew from the same intellectual fount, and, like their Southern enemies, fought to "preserve" what they took to be their cultural inheritance. The men who volunteered considered themselves "no better than" their revolutionary "fore fathers," under men like Washington, "who died in order to establish the laws" they were now "fighting to maintain." In Northern soldiers' minds, they knew that they were following the example of duty set in the Revolution and were fighting to save an inheritance they valued. "Maintain the honor of our flag and the dignity of our government peaceably if we can," wrote Samuel Nicoll Benjamin, "but maintain it with blood and steel if we must." Northern soldiers could not easily dismiss more than eighty years of shared history, but "however much we may feel for the south, remember that our duty is to the government of the United States. The government of our fathers." Although the "magic bond" of history which had held the nation together was "broken" and could not be mended easily, Northern soldiers knew it to be their duty to preserve the nation as best they could.[23]

Secession had to be "thoroughly crushed" to defend the Union and to prevent disunion's reoccurrence. For the typical Northern soldier, the "Confederacy represented values and ideas that were antithetical to the national heritage" and "had to be destroyed, not only to save the political union of the states but also to preserve the cultural foundations of national unity." War was "a question of self-preservation." Victory for the United States would tell "whether a republic is capable of perpetuating itself," or "whether it shall weakly submit to anarchy chaos and disintegration."[24]

Many Union soldiers shared with their Confederate counterparts a common antipathy for abolitionists and their cause. The often strident abolitionist denunciations of American society and slavery led many soldiers to conclude that the abolitionists were responsible for the war. Men from both armies cursed "all Secession, and Black Republican doctrines" with equal vehemence. They grew to "hate and despise more than ever that abolition faction who see nothing in this war but the liberation of the negroes and the humiliation of his master, be that master for or against the preservation of the Union." In 1861, emancipation simply did not enter into the argument for war among most soldiers. If emancipation came "as a result of the war," thought Lieutenant Samuel S. Elder, "then let the nigger go, but let us not make his emancipation the cause of the war." Elevating concerns for the future of bondsmen in a war for the future of the Union "would be a cheat and a fraud upon the tens of thousands who have gone to the field to vindicate a broken Constitution and uphold a falling Government."[25]

Symbols of union like the Constitution, the flag, and the federal government were powerful nationalist metaphors of the Union that succeeded in evoking strong emotional responses. Symbolism and reality were so tightly intertwined that an attack on or criticism of one became an attack on the legitimacy of the republic. A group of Massachusetts officers in Hagerstown, Maryland, left religious services early to avoid being "edified by a nauseating dose of a Secession Sermon." The Bay State men wished they could have been at home "hearing the word of God from the lips of one whos tongue had never uttered treason, and whos heart will ever cling to our glorious institutions." Perhaps because of Americans' lack of a unifying national religion, popular culture accorded almost mystical reverence to the symbols of union. Soldiers undertook "solemn oath[s] to support and protect the Constitution" and swore "to show ourselves faithful to her, against all her enemies and opposers." Unionists spoke openly of their "*one* determination" in the war, "to stand by our country, to adore the glorious old stars and stripes, and *never* see them dishonored. To be sure," it was thought, "we have seen them insulted, calmly submitted to the grossest insults, but that time has passed! Patience has ceased to be a virtue." Benjamin Grierson explained to his son Charlie that the "nice little flag Mama made for you" to carry was the "flag of liberty—The *Stars and Stripes*." Charlie's "Papa and a great many more are ready to fight so that you and many other little Boys can have a flag of that kind . . . floating over this land of Freedom."[26]

Although the United States Army would have to invade and occupy the South in order to restore the Union, Northerners saw their war as a defensive matter. The idea of defensive war ran through most Northern men's letters in 1861. Rebellion threatened union and, as Earl J. Hess has pointed out, it threatened home life. "Many men, according to Hess, "convinced themselves that saving the Union was necessary to safeguard their domestic bliss." A republic like the United States depended upon and safeguarded the personal independence of its citizenry. The ability to govern one's own home life translated into the ability to participate in the governance of the nation. The Confederacy menaced the home life and happiness of good Unionists and threatened the legitimate basis of self government. It was an evil that had to be crushed.[27]

William Harvey Lamb Wallace explained to his wife, Anne, "that in this war business I am engaged in the holy cause of defending and preserving a house made dear by your love—And although it may tear us apart for a while I hope and trust its result will be to secure . . . a home blessed by your kind affection." Men like Wallace "keenly felt the necessity of saving the home environment from the threat of an independent, aggressive slave nation." They looked forward to the time the United States would be "again a country to be proud of, when we can feel that we are safe under the protection of the old constitution, when we can lie down satisfied that the government has the power and the will to protect us in our persons, our homes, and our all." Secession and violence was "public robery" that forced soldiers into the "noble work of saving our Government" and happiness.[28]

American soldiers revered the memory of their past. They held it dear because it was an essential part of their character as citizens of the republic. Republican ancestors were points of referral from which citizens derived great inner strength, conviction, and surety of themselves as soldiers. Filiopietism fused easily with the imagery of "republican Greece or Rome." This heady intellectual mixture of direct forebears and ancient republicanism allowed soldiers to claim they defended not only the invaluable inheritance of their society and culture but also the ancient ideas that they believed had inspired their kin. The families that had "fled from the Island of great Britain Crostd the atlentick to avoid the Cruel Persecution and oppression of unrelenting British Tereny and Sought an assilean a Place of Security" in America "in order to Procure their own Liberty." Northern descendants of these families asked, in 1861, "Shall we preserve the government or can we so degenerate [all] that the Puritans suffered for?"[29]

Military commanders understood the power of oratory that drew upon the past, and they used it with great effect to motivate their men in the performance of their duties. William Henry Harrison thought "occasional military orations" to Western militiamen in 1810 would "teach them the necessity of subordination and obedience . . . by placing before them the illustrious examples of military virtue with which the history of Greece and Rome abound." Lessons from history would "impress on their minds that the temporary sacrifice of personal liberty which the military life imposes, has been cheerfully submitted to by the purest patriots, and the most zealous republicans" of classical history. As long as men understood the nature of their duty and cheerfully performed it, "liberty would have a temple" in the United States. Anthony Wayne and other American military leaders were so smitten by the ancients, that in 1792 they renamed the army the "Legion of the United States," a "designation with an attractively classical and republican tinge."[30]

It was a source of great pride to soldiers who could trace their lineal military descent from the Revolutionary generation. They were, after all, the "descendants of those progenitors, who were the desciples of WASHINGTON . . . , our departed sire to his country." Ohio militiamen facing a "band composed of Mercenaries of reluctant Canadians goaded to the field by the Bayonet and wretched naked Savages" in 1813 believed they possessed the same qualities as those of the previous generation. It was obvious to Colonel James Mills that this "Army" under his command was "composed of the same Materials" and character "which fought under the Immortal [Anthony] Wayne." Virginian Philip St. George Cocke reminded his son John to "remember that your great great grand father Daniel Barraud of WmsBurg and your great great grand father Hartwell Cocke of Surry have their names recorded with a long list of the most distinguished patriots of the American Revolution." The elder Cocke took great pride in his knowledge that his great-grandfather was a "Col. Commanding a regiment from Surry and served under Washington during the siege and at the surrender of York Town." Connection with the Revolution in its most intimate manner caused Cocke and others like him to "trust that we will show ourselves to the remotest period of time the worthy descendants of such fore-fathers!"[31]

Descendants of the Founding Fathers' generation were more than simply blood kin; they were the intellectual and cultural descendants of revolutionaries who considered it their charge to "create a Spirit of Patriotism and energy in the hearts of our fellow citizens, and to inspire the minds of our youth with a generous ambition to rival the exertions, the virtues and the patriotism of *our* Fathers who *fought* and *bled* in the establishment of the Independence and Freedom we now enjoy." Preserving the gifts of the Revolution was daunting. The generation that failed to defend the republican inheritance would discredit itself and cheapen the sacrifices of the Revolutionary generation. At times, the men who swore to protect the memory and legacy left by "by Washington and the giants of that day" wondered if they would be able to meet the challenges posed by war. A company of Massachusetts volunteers hoped they would "not be found 'summer patriots, and sunshine soldiers,' but inheritors of a spark of that fire which was kindled by our Fathers in the altar of Liberty." Soldiers were deeply impressed by the belief that they held in their "hands the destinies" of the United States as well as "her liberties."[32]

In great degree, the devotion of American soldiers to their past compelled them to make war upon one another. Much of the Civil War's tragic irony is rooted in the common heartfelt convictions of the American soldiery. "Truly," wrote a young Confederate, "we have the Spirit of 76 raised among us." Soldiers in both armies took strength from their shared heritage and were convinced of the righteousness of their respective causes. South Carolina's early rush of volunteers "touched" John W. Ervin's "heart deeply and brought" him to "tears." Scenes of "widows giving up their sons, and some their only sons to the service of the country, without a sigh, or a tear" made Ervin "think himself at Rome in her best days, when Rome was the mother of Lucretias and Cornelias and Volumnias." Ervin conceded that families may be "slaughtered down to younger sons, but thank God, your posterity and mine for generations yet to come will be able to stand" proudly "without blushing."[33]

Concern not just for the past but also for "future generations" led Erastus W. Everson to the recruiting officer. Everson, "deeply interested in our Country's welfare," did not think he would "ever" in his life "become so base a scoundrel as to sell the love of Liberty . . . to a rebel South." It was too deeply "instilled into my heart by the sacrifices of my fathers." Conserving and defending institutions, culture, and history was a prominent theme in American soldiers' writings. Soldiers also believed that military service was an engine of creation. American troops were the agents of creation and revolution, and for them "it was the experience of war with its concomitant quest for national legitimacy that served as an essential reference point in the definition of enduring republican institutions in America."[34]

Americans had conceived the United States in an act of revolution; the "country owed its existence to war." Revolutionaries fought with the assurance that "Heaven hath decreed that Tottering Empire Britain to irretrievable ruin," and they gave "thanks to God, since Providence hath so determined, America must Raise an Empire of Permanent Duration." Britain's "systematical and bloody attempt at Lexington, to enslave America thoroughly electrified" Ethan Allen of Vermont. Thereafter, Allen and others like him were "fully determined . . . to take part" in the struggle to found a new nation.[35]

Revolution explicitly countenanced "ideological war." Men who served in such a war were, by disposition, deeply interested in the imperatives and motives of the struggle and the intended consequences of their victory. Philadelphia's working-class militiamen served with a "conviction that militia participation and mobilization was a potential source of social change." The imagery and reality of working-class men shouldering muskets and deciding, in committee, the terms of their service was powerful stuff. Privates undertaking the responsibilities of political and military leadership were truly revolutionary. Even the uniform of hunting shirts indicated a distinctly democratic flavor. Uniforms bereft of badges of rank may have been indicative of the Association's desire for social and political levelling. Steven Rosswurm has concluded that "without the politicization and mobilization of the laboring poor in the militia, it seems doubtful" that Pennsylvania would have entered the "proindependence camp." Establishing independence and legitimacy by military means did not end with the peace of 1783. Americans "disputed the interpretation" of revolutionary ideology when the nation went to war with itself in 1861. They did, however, "agree on one thing: they must shed blood . . . for the sake of ideals."[36]

After winning independence, Americans had to prove to themselves and to the world their standing as a sovereign nation worthy of respect. Regulars, militiamen, and volunteers recognized the connection between themselves and the nation's repute among sovereign states. General orders issued on the eve of an invasion of Canada reminded men that the "pride and glory of this army [is] to conquer, not to destroy."

The army's "magnanimity, its forbearance, and its sacred regard of private property" would prove America's national legitimacy to observers. The people had "entrusted" their "character" and "honor" to the army's keeping.[37]

"The American army," wrote Major General Benjamin Franklin Butler, "is thus seen to be maintained for purposes the most weighty and beneficent." American soldiers would "secure from foreign powers, the faithful discharge of the duties they owe us; and . . . protect our country from those trespasses, which the proud and the powerful are so prone to commit, on the interests and honour of the weak and undefended." Civil war placed the United States in a "delicate position." Secession vitiated the premises of union and national legitimacy. Indeed, wrote Samuel Nicoll Benjamin, it "seems almost impossible to extricate ourselves without bloodshed, unless we forfeit our National honor, [and] prove to Europe, we were strong in name alone." Dedicated unionists with an eye to the republic's standing among other nations called upon each other to "look beyond the present trouble, and act for what is to happen hereafter."[38]

Many Americans believed the army and militia characterized the "distinctive identity" of the new nation and were, therefore, sensitive to perceived and real criticisms. Lieutenant George Blaney found the appointment of a French-born officer as the army's assistant engineer "beyond comprehension." Blaney was "willing to believe" Congress had intentionally "intended to insult the Corps" of Engineers because the body had not opted for "one of our own countrymen." America's ability to train and commission officers through its own institutions symbolized more than independence. It was a commentary upon the ability of the United States to raise and perpetuate native leaders and institutions and upon the country's claim to rank as a legitimate member of the world's nations. Lieutenant Blaney was clearly piqued when he asked, "Are we to be dependent on France or any other European Nation for officers? If so we had better have a Frenchman for the next President. Why not appoint an Assistant President with as much propriety? And why not give Marshall Grouchy and the whole host of Frenchmen who are overrunning the country like the Locust appointments in our Army?" Andrew Jackson's "feelings on the subject of introducing foreigners into our service" was that it ought to be forbidden by "sound policy . . . , particularly in our Engineer Corps." Jackson thought if "America cannot produce sufficient talents for its own defence, we had better resign all pretensions to self government."[39]

Nativity was a basic element in the makeup of a trustworthy patriotic citizen and soldier. How, so the logic went, could any man who had not been born and raised in the United States develop true affection for the country, its people, and their institutions? Christopher Van Deventer, a regular officer in 1813, could not "refrain from the expression of regret for the eagerness and avidity with which foreigners, vomited upon our Shores, have been welcomed by the impolitic lenity of our Laws." Admitting "Vagrant foreigners as American Citizens" was "the beginning of the approaching catastrophe, by which proud Americans will be disgraced by the most ignominious of deaths" in battle. Van Deventer believed the "American, who from affection and duty to his country, willingly yields his life to its Services and glory, must face the deepest mortification and pain, mingled" with abject "indignation, that it should be taken from him, to atone for the blood of profligate and unprincipled deserters, or abandoned traitors" in the service of the United States. Edward Fenno, captain of New Orleans's Louisiana Guards, the "only good American corps in this *famous city*," had a litany of foreign-inspired woe to relate to his family. A committee of the state legislature had summoned Fenno because he had refused to serve under the command of a French major. Although Fenno deemed the major a "very well meaning good heartfelt man" and believed him to be a "very excellent grocer," the captain believed "nature never intended him for a soldier."[40]

Captain Fenno feared the "Hon. Legislature should decide that it was proper and correct that we should serve under a foreigner" and disputed the legislature's "right" to "assume a direct authority over me." Fenno promised to "disobey" when "the *French* Major" stepped forward and "ordered" the Louisiana Guards "to parade." Captain Fenno expected "to be arrested" for his acts of disobedience and hoped his "arrest" would "be followed by the dissolution of the only American Company in New Orleans because we will not serve under an alien French Corporal." Fenno's experiences were not unique. Fears of political, social, and economic dislocation inspired by foreigners prompted native Americans to form volunteer companies. Boston's National Guard promised to "do our utmost to sustain his Excellency" Governor Henry Joseph Gardner in the "broad American platform he has taken." The nativist National Guardsmen, whose motto was "None but Americans," looked forward to Governor Gardner's "orders to disband all foreign Military Companies as a 'Red Letter Day' in the history of the citizen Soldiery of Massachusetts." This much Boston's Know-Nothing National Guard knew.[41]

At the same time that nationalists and nativists were railing against immigrants and disputing their martial and political worthiness, the foreign-born were becoming soldiers. Military service "played a part in the upward social mobility of certain disadvantaged groups in the population. In the 1840s and 1850s, for example, European immigrants were able to climb the ladder using the Army" and the volunteer militia as a "base" from which they might enter American society and prove themselves worthy republicans. Immigrants also eased their attempts at membership in society through their volunteer militia companies. Thirty-three ambitious Irish formed the New-York Hibernian Vollunteers in 1796, "a Military Corps to assist in the defence and Protection of the United States its constitution and Laws." New York's Vollunteers stipulated "that each person who is proposed to become a Member of this Company be either an Hibernian or the Son of an Hibernian." Besides proving their loyalty, the Hibernians' ethnic stipulation illustrated the importance of ethnically based organizations in creating a sense of community for newcomers.[42]

According to Robert Reinders, in "every major ante-bellum city there were volunteer ethnic companies with names like Catalanos, Jaegers, Voltigeurs, Highlanders, Hibernia Greens, or in eager identification with their new country, companies which took titles like 'American,' 'Jefferson,' 'Washington,' or names of fellow countrymen prominent in the Revolution." Immigrant militia companies helped acculturate foreigners while establishing proofs of their loyalty and "provided an ethnic refuge" to ease or retard the shock of hostility and "assimilation." Augustus P. Green's New York Irish Dragoons opted to assimilate into the native American militia. The unit shed its ethnic identification by changing its uniforms to regular army patterns, because there were "too many foreign uniforms in this City," and renamed the "troop from the Irish Dragoons to the City Horse Guards."[43]

Immigrants and laborers were not alone in their quest to establish legitimacy. New Orleans' free-black militia's history of service dated to the French and Spanish colonial regimes. Following American annexation of the Louisiana Territory, the militiamen presented a memorial and petition to Governor W. C. C. Claiborne professing their loyalty to the United States and offering their services to the new government. The representation handed to Claiborne manifested the militiamen's "belief that their personal and political freedom would be respected and that they would be treated with justice and liberality." These men, "through their memorial, sought to gain the fullest measure of citizenship under the new government and used their military record in the past and its promise for the future" to ally their interests with those of the United States. Free black loyalty to American interests was partly premised on their sense of "self-identity." James G. Hollandsworth Jr. cited the high percentage of mulatto militiamen with light skin color as evidence of racially based self-identification. Other factors included ownership of property and slaves. When Louisiana seceded, its black militia offered its services to the Confederacy. Members professed their new loyalty to the Confederacy because "many identified more closely with Southern whites than with African blacks." By volunteering, the Native Guards "expected better treatment" from the new regime.[44]

Americans soldiers were the agents of conservatism and of creation. Their actions in the cause of legitimacy ranged from grand visions of saving liberty for mankind to proving the fitness of a particular group for participation in the affairs of the republic. As conservators, soldiers transferred their affections from traditional English rights and privileges to those spelled out in the new Constitution. Throughout the process their love of personal and political liberty remained constant. In retrospect, the Revolutionary generation's defense of legitimacy was also the creation of a new legitimacy. Circumstances of American life had changed from 1775 to 1861, but the ideas underpinning protecting and establishing legitimate political systems remained constant.

3

Free Men in Uniform

Soldierly Self-Governance

American republicanism emphasized the right and responsibility of the citizen to rule himself and his society. The right of exercising nearly unlimited self-governance in virtually all aspects of life was a fundamental component of republicanism and originated inviolably in natural law. The citizenry's acceptance of this construction guaranteed that the nation's soldiers would, to different degrees, exercise their self-governing rights. The key manifestations of soldiers' self-governance were their personal independence, enlistment negotiations, petitions to superior officers, militia constitutions, and negotiations regarding military discipline.[1]

Whether implicitly understood or explicitly stated, American soldiers acted out of confidence in their ability and right to govern and direct their lives in some meaningful, however limited, manner. This construction was so pervasive that it could not help but influence the nature of military service and the imposition, acceptance, and exercise of military discipline. In these circumstances, American military discipline was not so much the unyielding application of incontrovertible regulations by superior officers as it was the result of the military hierarchy's tacit recognition and acceptance of soldiers' insistence on practicing some form of self-governance.

By the 1820s, the threats of Indian, French, Spanish, and British attacks had largely diminished or disappeared altogether, and so too had the importance of the enrolled militia as a form of communal military service. Among many Americans there was a growing view that militia service was an inequitable burden, a tax, on common men. Appearing at militia musters, and purchasing and maintaining arms and equipment were thus lost earnings and uncompensated expenses that men of middling or mean circumstances could ill afford. Interest in military affairs slackened, but did not die. Instead, a different way of responding to local military needs and to popular interest in military panoply and pageantry arose. As the republic entered the Age of Jackson, Americans' rage for voluntary association created a new forum in which good citizens could express their armed and uniformed republican virtue.[2]

For a number of communities, volunteer companies, many of which were incorporated into the states' militias, were the craze. Among many of these Americans, the "militia ethos was almost as viable in the nineteenth century as in the republic's dawning days." Acting as highly selective social clubs, volunteer companies screened candidates and voted whether to admit or to reject prospective members. Detailed constitutions specifying members' duties, uniforms, and election procedures for officers and noncommissioned officers were the norm.[3]

The volunteers' exclusivity resulted from any number of factors. For some companies and members it was a means of achieving public and personal distinction within society. Membership connoted a highly evolved sense of public duty and thus reflected well upon the organization and volunteers. For others it was a way to unite and give form to political, social, or economic aspirations. Immigrants often formed companies to demonstrate their loyalty to the republic and to band together in common defense against rival companies. Many joined for entertainment. Some understood their membership as the fulfillment of their masculine roles. All companies, however, reflected parochial concerns that were linked to the greater ethos.

Despite the exclusive nature of the volunteers, these companies were, internally, among the most democratic of American institutions. In an organization made up of social, ethnic, political, or economic peers and allies, all volunteers were equal. Enlisted men nominated and elected their noncommissioned and commissioned officers, and company constitutions could change only through democratic processes. While the nation at large refashioned the mechanics of a democratic republic, so too did its citizen-soldiers. In spite of the conflicting and varied motives for forming or joining a volunteer company, most members were united by the desire to demonstrate their worthiness as citizens and men. Moreover, education and periodical publishing were also arenas in which Americans demonstrated their interest in military affairs. State-sponsored and private schools like the Virginia Military Institute and

Alden Partridge's American Literary, Scientific, and Military Academy (now Norwich University) in Vermont and magazines such as *The Eclaireur* and the *New York Military Magazine* offer further evidence that Americans believed military affairs to be closely related to the life of the republic.[4]

Because of the self-governing and voluntary nature of their groups, militiamen and volunteers believed themselves more patriotic and worthier of being trusted with the republic's liberty than were the regulars. To many volunteers, the regular was a base hireling who was unable or unwilling to exercise any degree of self-governance. Slavish obedience to the military hierarchy and officers with aristocratic pretensions threatened the existence of a republican United States. Surely, such men could not be entrusted with the future of the nation. Many of these citizen-soldiers believed that their performance of admittedly idealized military obligations was proof of their good citizenship. Suspicions about trust and worthiness, however, were not the province of the militia and volunteers alone. Regulars also had their concerns, but theirs were about the part-time soldiers.

Regulars viewed their counterparts in the militia and volunteer forces with concern and contempt. To some professionals, these men seemed too preoccupied with their individual rights to become good soldiers. Indeed, the unwillingness of militiamen and volunteers to accept fully the self-abnegation demanded by military discipline caused some professionals to doubt their patriotism. As the regular army matured and developed, its communal culture subsumed many of its soldiers' more pronounced individualistic tendencies. Self-sacrifice and the needs of the community became the touchstones of republican virtue and self-worth.

Nonetheless, American soldiers believed themselves to be citizens first and foremost. Their service helped define their relationship to the republic. Self-governance was an indispensable component in the makeup of the republican character. Indeed, as Earl J. Hess has noted, it was "basic to the very definition of American nationalism" and was the "common" intellectual and historical "property of all Americans." Various levels of meaning existed within this thread of republicanism, but in its most fundamental sense, self-governance involved the right to govern one's own affairs on a daily basis and to exercise those individual

rights and conjoined responsibilities. The actual determination and fulfillment of those decisions by the citizen would decide the course of his
life. But beyond this atomistic concept of individualism, family, communal, voluntary-associational, state, and national self-governance were
evident in soldiers' thoughts. At the heart of these progressively more
complex levels was the individual direction of the citizen's own affairs.[5]

The necessity for order and discipline meant that soldiers temporarily surrendered much of their right to govern their lives. Because
most American soldiers chose "voluntarily [to] associate themselves,"
the decision to forgo the exercise of their rights was in and of itself an
exercise of self-governance. Samuel McGowan, a brigadier general of
the South Carolina militia, observed in 1857 that this "high military
spirit, not only in the regular army, but among the citizens of a country,
is almost the infallible test, if not the nursing-mother, of those cognate
and intermingling sentiments, love of independence, love of hearth-
stone and of home, and of the whole cluster of local attachments, which
in the aggregate constitute patriotism." McGowan attributed the close
"connexion between" military service and patriotism to the voluntary
nature of enlistments in the army and militia. Republican "institutions"
were "not imposed and endured, but chosen and admired" by the citizenry through acts of conscious choice which revealed their ability to
govern themselves. Voluntary service was an example of the "*Anglo-
Saxon's—the American's*—capacity for self-government" and they reflected both the individualistic and voluntary communal nature of the
republic.[6]

The volunteer, according to Illinois general John A. Logan, was an
"integral part of the government and country," and he "constituted its
true military power" because of his right to govern his own life and to
participate in the governance of society. Proponents of voluntary service
cited the special motivation engendered within the soldiery by American nativity. Men who had had the "happiness to be born in a land of
Freedom" and nurtured by the "blessings and advantages of civil society"
were "ready to hazard their lives and fortunes in defence of their immu-
nities." Citizen-soldiers' rights to govern their lives gave them a personal
"stake and interest in all for which they might ultimately strive." Indeed,
their political freedom had helped make the "character of a soldier" indistinguishable from "that of a citizen." Some thought a special physical

and moral power accrued to "Freemen, armed in defence of their firesides, and stimulated by a love of liberty." In any contest against a "tyrant
and his myrmidons" wrote the members of the Mechanic Phalanx in
1825, "pure republican spirit will prevail." Examples of self-governance
took many forms among soldiers.[7]

Some men were intensely interested in reforming or perfecting their
lives, and, through their example, inspiring others to imitation. Men
capable of governing their passions and conquering their weaknesses
were more virtuous and, therefore, better citizens. Temperance, a leading cause for reform in nineteenth-century America, greatly affected
some soldiers. Traditionally, militia musters had often included officers
liberally hosting their troops to rum and other strong drink after drill.
This custom, whose origins lie in colonial practices, was geared toward
insuring "officers' popularity and . . . their reelection as captains," but
by the 1830s this practice had fallen into disrepute. Temperance took a
tenuous foothold even among the traditionally hard-drinking regulars.
Men of the Third Artillery's Company D found the "use of intoxicating
liquors" to have been the "cause of nearly all military crimes, and the
source of incalculable evils" to the soldier and the army and, in particular, it had "prevented the honorable fulfilment of our sworn obligations
to our country, and our bounden duties to our God." Determined to reform their ways, the enlisted men of Company D formed a temperance
society and encouraged other soldiers to join. Lieutenant James Ewell
Brown Stuart, a frontier cavalry officer, found temperance a "cause that
so ennobles the man" in the course of his life and duties that he fostered
the establishment of a temperance society in his regiment.[8]

One of the most distinctive traits of United States soldiers was their
highly developed degree of individualism. "If we have come to V[irgini]
a to fight," wrote Louisiana's Edward Murphy in 1861, it was for "ourselves." Individual autonomy, a basic form of self-governance, was
readily apparent in many soldiers' activities. Eighteenth-century British officers had noted the seeming greed and the strict contractual and
legalistic bent of provincial soldiers. In particular, regular officers considered American assumptions regarding military professionalism and
warring utterly at odds with the British army's standards. Among other
things, British regulars noted many Americans' resistance to discipline,
their sloppy personal and camp appearance, and their readiness to quit

campaigns at their own discretion. But what seemed to be "unsoldierly conduct" was, according to historian Fred Anderson, "highly consistent, and indeed highly principled" behavior wholly consonant with a well-developed degree of individual autonomy. For a young and propertyless man "military service was a reasonably lucrative proposition, providing cash income to hasten his attainment of independence." Active service gave men the "opportunity for plunder and adventure" and the chance to "participate in the struggle" against their traditional enemies, the "papist French and the barbarous Indians." Warfare "promised both a change from the accustomed routines and perhaps an accelerated entry into real manhood." However, a young man's entry into his majority did not solely affect him; it also involved his family.[9]

Private Frank A. Hardy of the Third Ohio Volunteers explained his motives for enlisting in 1846 as he tried to console his mother about his decision. "I had pretty well served you during the years of my minority," wrote Hardy, and now "I ought to have the privilege of commanding my own person." While the young man admitted his "respect" for his parents' "authority" and for their "advice," he thought that allowing them to continue exercising parental authority would "deprive me of the full liberty to choose my own course of conduct and [I] would rather be confined in a prison" than be kept from attaining independence through military service. The first step taken toward independence began with the recruiting party.[10]

Enlistment was a contractual agreement freely entered into by soldiers and the government. Between two contracting parties equity could be achieved and maintained only by a soldier who was sure of his right and ability to govern his own life. Soldiers who contested and bargained for better terms for service were not necessarily quibbling to avoid duty or make a profit but instead revealing the "centrality of contract in popular understandings of the legitimate exercise of authority." When, during the French and Indian War, the leaders of the Old Dominion were unable to recruit men for the Virginia Regiment, they decided to pay an enlistment bounty to new soldiers. This was not an act of hiring mercenaries; it "represented the gentry's tacit recognition of the 'lesser sort' as free men who were at liberty to sell or withhold their services" or to be "soldiers when they and if they chose to be so." Thus it would seem that enlistment bounties and negotiations for terms of service cannot be written off solely as acts of narrow economic self-interest. By striking a hard bargain, these men not only demonstrated their independence but also used their service as a means to establish economic and therefore political independence following the conclusion of their service. Nearly a century later, one company of volunteers in the war against Mexico wanted active service but realized "we would not be received" into federal service "unless we were willing to go for twelve months." The men weighed their choices and decided they were "willing to do" one year's service if "we could do no better." Nevertheless, two negotiators went to "New Orleans and seeing Gen [Edmund Pendleton] Gain[e]s succeeded in getting us mustered in for six months." Bargaining and asserting individual rights did not cease at enlistment but continued for many men throughout their terms of service and took different forms.[11]

The majority of enlistment bounties and negotiations for terms of service cannot be written off as acts of narrow economic self-interest. Although some men may have enlisted for strictly economic motivations, they were a minority. Irregular, low, or depreciated pay, poor and infrequent rations and supplies, and the chance of injury or death outweighed the value of virtually any economic incentive that could be derived from military service. A soldier's potential economic return on the investment of his life was so minimal as to be a sucker's choice. Indeed, only a "fool would remain a soldier for reasons of immediate material interest." Once enlisted, soldiers' exercise of their personal liberty took other forms that asserted their personal autonomy, dignity, or sense of justice, including challenging authority.[12]

Most acts of mutiny and the refusal of some soldiers to obey orders were due not so much to cowardice or to total indiscipline as to a belief in the "centrality of contract in popular understandings of the legitimate exercise of authority." Military officials who had failed to live up to their contractual obligations relating to food, equipment, or tenure of service nullified any expectations of obedience from the ranks. In this light, mutiny and disobedience were symptomatic of a deep and abiding belief in the power, legitimacy, and universal applicability of mutually binding agreements as embodied in lawful contracts. The recalcitrant soldier was exercising his right to self-governance in one of its most basic manifestations—the right to withhold labor following his employer's breach of contract.[13]

American soldiers, particularly volunteers and militiamen, acted out their "personal liberty" by their irregular and unsteady performance on the battlefield and their general indiscipline. Battle was dangerous; when electing to fight or to run, the soldier exercised his personal liberty, his freedom to govern his life as he saw fit. The selection of whether to fight or flee was, in the words of Robert Middlekauff, one of the "classic problems free men face: choosing between rival claims of public responsibility and private wishes, or in eighteenth-century terms choosing between virtue—devotion to public trust—and personal liberty." Warfare and military service, in general, necessitated that "men give up their liberties and perhaps even their lives for others."[14]

It would seem then that some militiamen and volunteers could decide to fight or flee without much mental reservation since both choices fell within the construct of the self-governance. Surprisingly, permanent shame was only infrequently attached to their behavior; the man who would not think for himself was not fit for American society. In his frequent calls for a larger regular force, George Washington recognized American soldiers' independence when he wrote, "Men who have been free and subject to no controul cannot be reduced to order in an Instant, and the privileges and exemptions they claim and will have Influence the conduct of others." Striking a balance between the subordination called for in the army and the traditions of self-governance was a difficult task at best.[15]

Military discipline rankled many men. In the minds of some, it smacked of subservience and threatened individual and national independence. Men who voluntarily abdicated individual independence were suspected by the public of harboring disloyal or anti-republican sentiments. Thomas T. Summers of the Louisville Legion was "not altogether satisfied" with military life in 1846. Summers and his fellow Kentuckians were "not used to being bound up so tightly by military despotism (for the officers enforce every article of the law)." Ensign John Claude of the Thirteenth Infantry in the War of 1812, and a former sergeant of the same regiment, disliked military life and daily hoped for an "honorable discharge and restoration to the beloved title of private Citizen." Claude thought the "post of a Subaltern" was one of the "most unpleasant in the World" and compared it to being a "slave driver." He believed that to a "mind truly Republican, a commission in the Army is repugnant." Military hierarchy and discipline threatened individualism and the ability to think and act independently. "The habit of implicit obedience," wrote Claude, corrupted men's sense of their personal rights and liberties. Military discipline created a "soldier accustomed to blows" who soon "forgets that he ever was a free-man—Out of such materials" men created "Monarchy or Despotism." Furthermore, according to Ensign Claude, "The higher grades smack of Aristocracy, and the lower ones, if they mean to command are despotic—The general and so in succession thro' the field commissions, dismisses from the service for neglect of duty," and the "Captains and so in succession down inforce authority with the men by stripes [laid on by the lash]. I seriously believe that a war (with discipline in our ranks) of ten years would so completely change the character of Countrymen, that a monarchy would be almost the unavoidable result." Mexican War volunteer Lew Wallace considered himself and his fellow volunteers "*slaves*." The future general believed the "army is a *military despotism* as absolute as a Turkish *government!*"[16]

While volunteers and militiamen valued their own intelligence, spirit, and patriotism, few of them said as much about the regulars. Their best assessment of regulars concerned appearance and smartly performed maneuvers while on parade. Drill, however, required little thinking by the soldier. A well-drilled company called for the complete subordination of individual will in the name of uniformity and efficiency. It followed, as Mexican War volunteer George C. Furber saw things, that a "regular soldier" of the army had "need for only so much brains as will enable him to stand erect, keep his clothing and tent clean and neat, and his arms bright; to enable him to go through the common evolutions, and to understand the common words of command, without explanation; to handle the musket, sword and pistol quickly; and just language enough to ask for his allowance of eatables and whatever else he may need to satisfy his appetite, and to be able, when out of hearing of his officers, to swear freely." Intelligence and independence beyond such basic levels were of "no value to him; for he never will be permitted to use them" as a professional soldier.[17]

Assertions like these were easily made, particularly when a central requirement of professional soldiering was the nearly complete surrender of one's individual rights. Officers, noncommissioned officers, and the daily routine of drill and other military functions seemingly reduced the individual regular's life to a harsh, mind-numbing, or dehumanizing routine. This picture, however, was too neat. It ignored two of the central features of life in the United States Army in this period: its voluntary, short-term enlistments and the relative freedom of action afforded to soldiers when off duty. Military life demanded more subordination and self-discipline than did civilian jobs, but the routines and difficulties associated with agricultural, craft, or factory work were every bit as mind-numbing as drill and just as subject to some form of regulation. Every form of work demanded some degree of self-abnegation by those who performed it. Soldiers voluntarily surrendered many, but not all, of their individual rights, and they did so voluntarily, and for only a short period of time.

If following orders was a burden for some American soldiers, the duties of leading these individualists was an equal or greater challenge. In 1813, Major General James Wilkinson ordered his officers to cease corresponding with the secretary of war, except in "cases of personal grievences, and then through the office of the Adjutant General." Wilkinson had to remind these officers that their "discordant opinions" caused him innumerable problems because of their tendency to "distract the public mind, break public confidence, and degrade the military character. The rights of a soldier," Wilkinson reminded them, are "few and those should be heedfully guarded." Soldiers were citizens, but "we must be careful not to confound republican freedom with military subordination, things as irreconcilable as opposite elements—the one being founded on equality the other resting on obedience."[18]

Commanders often called upon their men to exercise discretion so as not to bring disrepute upon themselves, the army, or their state. Men of the Old Line State marching to help suppress the Whiskey Rebellion were ordered to "remember you are Marylanders, remember the honours gained by your fellow citizens" in the Revolution, and "let no neglect of duty by us tarnish the military reputation of our state. We are now going into the deluded part of our country [western Pennsylvania]" and should "let our conduct be what I have observed on the march, that of good citizens." Bay State militiamen in 1814 had their attention called to the "disrepute" that had been "brought upon the [Massachusetts] *Militia* in the minds of some of the most worthy citizens by the boisterous revelry and Excess which has heretofore too often disgraced the *Muster*

Field." Cautions over conduct were not confined to any region. They were truly national.[19]

While campaigning against the Creek nation in 1813, Andrew Jackson called upon his soldiers as "fellow citizens" whose actions "must not disgrace the cause we are concerned in nor sully that reputation which we shall carry along with us." Victory in the Battle of Tullushatchee on 3 November "furnished another proof to the world that there is no soldier so valiant as the volunteer who takes up arms to defend the government of his choice." The regularity of commanders' appeals to their soldiers' ability to exercise self-discipline tacitly recognized their individualism and often succeeded. Frequently, however, soldiers chose to go their own way, ignoring the strictures of military discipline and causing countless problems for commanders and civilians alike. Augustus James Pleasonton was so frustrated by the indiscipline of the Philadelphia militia in 1838 that he cordially "wished all citisen soldiers most heartily at the devil." Perhaps, Pleasonton thought, Beelzebub could control his future charges.[20]

The conflict between soldiers' assertions of their personal independence and the demands of military discipline and order continually caused tensions. Soldiers were loathe to dispense with lifelong habits of personal independence and the "privileges and exemptions" they expected as their due. Men announced their personal independence by flouting seemingly minor points about the length or appearance of hair and the style of uniforms. One of the most celebrated incidents involved Colonel Thomas Butler, a veteran of the Revolution. Butler was court-martialed because he refused to cut his queue. In 1801, Brigadier General James Wilkinson had ordered all soldiers of the regular army to cut their hair. Styles had changed and Wilkinson consciously rejected the symbols so distinctive of the Continental army, including knee breeches, stockings, and shoe buckles. Although the Butler-Wilkinson row was at one level a personal affair and demonstrative of a still greater Federalist-Republican political conflict, it gives credence to the issue of individualism. Butler considered the order an infringement upon his personal liberties and retained his queue. The colonel was tried twice and received an official reprimand and a year's suspension of "command, pay, and allowances." Still wearing his queue, Butler died before the court enacted the suspension. Presumably, the colonel was interred with his hair intact.[21]

In another case, the First Massachusetts Volunteers staged a minor "mutiny" over the issue of uniforms following their landing at Vera Cruz, Mexico, in 1847. Militia companies had long had the right to design and select their uniforms according to their collective tastes. As it happened, the Massachusetts "mutineers" went to Mexico with a "gray uniform and the understanding that they were to buy their own clothes." Upon its arrival in Mexico, the regiment discovered that many of the "uniforms were worn out," and that "none of the same kind could be procured." Brigadier General Caleb Cushing thereupon ordered the Bay State volunteers to "wear the U.S. blue. One company refused, whereupon their Captain gave them a threatening speech and applied the epithet of scoundrel" to the men. When they continued to refuse the order, "Cushing gave them a dressing down and some more hard names and told them they were a disgrace to their country." Confinement and "hard work" at the fortress of San Juan de Ulloa followed this. The respite convinced forty-six out of forty-eight recalcitrant soldiers to don their "blue clothes . . . willy nilly." Although the Butler and Vera Cruz affairs seem ridiculously trivial, they point to the great esteem soldiers of all ranks had for their personal independence.[22]

The regular military hierarchy quickly subdued much of the spirit of independence among the soldiery but never fully quelled it in the volunteer ranks. Volunteers, with "varying degrees of emphasis, according to time and place," accepted the "notions that American warfare was unique and hardly required formal training." The popular image of the American citizen as a natural soldier convinced historian Don Higginbotham that for some Americans, the "militia ethos was almost as viable in the nineteenth century as in the republic's dawning days." A North Carolina volunteer colonel in Mexico, Robert Treat Paine, approvingly wrote that the "meanest soldier in our ranks considers that he does not meet his equal in battle, either in courage or character." Paine added that the "Mexican is destitute of every qualification which enobles man" and believed "cowardice and treachery are the two prominent traits of character belonging to the men of Mexico." Not surprisingly, the conduct of many United States volunteers in Mexico led many American soldiers and Mexican civilians to rue their contact with the citizen-soldier. When the individualism of soldiers was combined with their spirit of conquest, basic contempt for military order, virulent anti-Catholicism, and anti-Mexican racism, gross abuses against the conquered citizenry often resulted. Relations were highly problematic, to say the least. Letters from regulars and volunteers recorded a litany of volunteer abuses and indiscipline.[23]

Colonel Paine's attitude was not unique. It was a trait shared by many American soldiers in Mexico, volunteers and regulars. According to Brevet Major Lucien B. Webster of the First Artillery, Mexico was "not a civilized nation, and ought not to be treated as such." Webster thought, "Our indians are far superior to them as a race." In part, the attitude of Major Webster and other Americans toward Mexicans was premised upon a widely shared suspicion of Roman Catholicism's rituals and its strict hierarchy. Mexicans, according to Webster, had "mearly changed their form of idolatry, from their ancient mode of worship, to worshiping the cross and the images of the catholic church." Mexicans were clearly a docile and superstitious people who were unsuited for self-government. "I should be ashamed to acknowledge them as american citizens," wrote Webster. Incorporating Mexicans would be a "curse to us: and the sooner we vamos the better for us."[24]

Lieutenant George Gordon Meade, a graduate of the military academy and a not infrequent observer of volunteers, believed that the regular army understood it was waging "war against the Army and Government of Mexico and not against the people," who, he wrote, should be "left undisturbed in their peaceful avocations." Problems arose, however, because "always have the volunteers commenced to excite feelings and indignation and hatred in the bosom of the people by their outrages on them." With little exaggeration, Meade and others reported that "every day complaints are made of this man's cornfield being destroyed by the volunteer's horses . . . or another man's fence torn down by them for firewood or an outrage committed on some inoffensive person by some drunken volunteer." The excesses of volunteers were not confined to property damage, as they "killed" many "innocent people" or "committed outrages on the wife" of a Mexican citizen. Above all others, Meade considered the Texas "volunteers" as the "most outrageous" in their acts of violence and destruction. Texas's revolution and years of bitter border warfare created "fears and recollections of wrong done, which have been festering in them for 10 years." As Meade saw things, war between the United States and Mexico provided vengeful Texans the "guise of entering the U.S. service" so that they might "gratify personal revenge."[25]

Daniel Harvey Hill, a regular artillery officer, reserved his ire for another state's men. Hill concluded that "many of the Louisiana Volunteers" were a "lawless drunken rabble." Shortly after occupying a Mexican town, Hill discovered the Louisianans had "driven away the inhabitants taken possession of their houses and were emulating each other in making beasts of themselves." According to Hill, volunteer indiscipline caused 30 percent of the Matamoros population to evacuate the city. The young artillerist from North Carolina wrote that before the army captured the city on 1 August 1846, it "contained upwards of ten thousand inhabitants, [but] there are now in it not more than seven thousand. The rest, who were the wealthiest and most intelligent have fled in consequence of the wanton excesses of the Volunteers." Two days later, on 3 August 1846, Hill recorded, "We saw none of those drunken crowds [of volunteers] in Reynoso which [had] disgraced Matamoros." It was because the "Volunteers had not yet arrived." Unlike the population of Matamoros, the people of Camargo had not abandoned the city after its capture on 5 August 1846. With no little sense of satisfaction, Lieutenant Hill wrote that the people were now "living in a town held by the *licentious hirelings* of the Government; would that our noble citizen soldiers may behave so well when they come on" in their guise as soldiers.[26]

Regular officers were not the only ones who bemoaned the behavior of volunteers. North Carolina's Colonel Paine complained of many a volunteer officer in Mexico refusing "either to carry out in his own conduct or to enforce obedience among his men." Despondently, Paine wrote, "I sometimes sit down and curse them all, officers and men." As time passed, Colonel Paine became "more and more disgusted with the Volunteer service." It was "only by the strongest feeling of duty to the public" that Paine refrained from "retiring from the service." Elective office made Paine's attempts at enforcing discipline among volunteers all the more difficult. "I cannot discharge my duty as I think it should be discharged," wrote Paine, "without offending many." Prior to reembarkation for the United States, the North Carolinian wrote of "much dissatisfaction amongst the troops about going to sea again." He believed that about "forty men of the N[ew] Jersey battalion refused to take shipping and disbanded themselves" without authorization. As volunteer enlistments approached expiration, Paine noted that the "soldiers and officers began to act as if they were under no restraint." Company C of Paine's own regiment mutinied and ran the "commanding officer out of Camp." "Oh! The glories of a Volunteer Colonel!" lamented Paine. "How," he wondered, "could I have ever been so stupid and reckless ever to have permitted myself to be forced into such a situation?" How, indeed?[27]

Observers and participants alike recognized the inherent difficulty involved in disciplining independent men, especially those who served very limited enlistments. While campaigning in northern Mexico, topographical engineer George G. Meade knew it was "impossible for Genl [Zachary] Taylor to restrain these people," and that "Old Rough and Ready" had "neither the moral or physical force to do it." Lieutenant Meade feared that if "we advance with them into the interior," the volunteers might "exasperate the people against us, causing them to rise en masse" against the Americans. Meade, a perceptive officer, understood the great obstacles posed by the existence of elective office in a military organization. "The officers (many of whom are gentlemen and clever fellows)," wrote Meade, had "no command over their men." The twelve-month term of service and reliance upon electing commissioned and noncommissioned officers obviated any serious attempt to enforce discipline. Volunteer officers, following the expiration of their service, would "return to their homes" and the common soldiers would again be "their equals and their companions as they had been before." Consequently, volunteer officers exercised their authority very lightly. Major General Taylor tried to minimize volunteer misbehavior by keeping them as busy as possible, for "altho full of courage and zeal it is necessary to make use of them at once, and keep them constantly in motion, as they soon become tired and disgusted with the monotony of a camp life, and are impatient to be led against the enemy, or permitted to return home."[28]

The issue of volunteer independence and indiscipline continued within American armies through 1861. On 12 October of that year, George Meade, now a brigadier general commanding Pennsylvania volunteers, voiced his "private opinion of our force" to his wife, Margaret. Meade's experiences with citizen-soldiers in Mexico made him "certain" about one thing, and that was that "I am not confident of them" as a competent fighting force. However, despite grave reservations about his men, Meade was "not prepared to state positively they are not to be relied on" in battle. Toward the end of November, General Meade concluded the "men are good material, and with good officers might readily be molded into *soldiers*, but the officers, as a rule with but very few exceptions are *ignorant, inefficient, and worthless*." Volunteer officers' inability or unwillingness to exercise "control or command over the men" rekindled memories of 1846. Meade had little hope for his erstwhile civilians until the "vicious system of *electing*" officers ended. Toward the end of 1861, the future victor of Gettysburg wrote that "the volunteer system is and always has been a failure." Unlike Meade, however, the vast majority of volunteers celebrated their democratic traditions.[29]

Private Andrew Hero Jr. of New Orleans's Washington Artillery was "unable to state whether the right will be granted to us to elect our own officers or not." Hero wrote that his battalion found it "exceedingly mortifying" that their elective rights might be overridden by the Confederate government. The artillerymen preferred the "appointment of our own members to the officers over us" instead of having the "little squirts from the Virginia Military Institute and perfect strangers" commissioned as officers. Violating the traditional rights and privileges of citizen-soldiers sometimes caused open disobedience to orders. "There has been a fuss a brewing for a week and it has come to a crises" in the Sixth Massachusetts, wrote militiaman Lyman Van Buren Furber. Governor John Andrews had "appointed men; (I should say boys) over one or two companies as lieutenants." In Furber's opinion, the new lieutenants "dont know any thing about militia." On his first duty day, the "new lieutenant came out on drill" and became the "laughing stock of the whole regiment." Despite having been ordered to "parade rest," the company decided it was "bound not to obey" the new officer. Instead, the militiamen "terned their backs on him." Order was finally restored after the guard had been called out.[30]

In 1861, as in 1846, frustration with the volunteers' spirit of independence surfaced among the volunteers themselves. Although the men of the Fourth Alabama's Magnolia Cadets had elected Nathaniel Henry Rhodes Dawson their captain, Dawson thought that "our volunteer system must be disbanded, and a new one adopted. It is a failure." Dawson's privates thought they were "too good, generally, to endure the rules of discipline." He hoped for a force "made up of men who expect to obey, and to do their duties, or to be punished." Reflecting upon his officers and his fellow privates, Frank Liddell Richardson of the Second Louisiana had little good to say about Confederate citizens in uniform. He thought "those commissioned officers" were "just like the owners of slaves on plantations" who had "nothing to do but to strut about dress fine and enjoy themselves" as the common soldiers worked. Rather full of himself, Richardson looked down on his fellow enlisted men and thought they needed to be "treated as negros or they will not obey and besides they are a very low set of men being composed of these low Irish and the scum of creation."[31]

Not every observer in this period, however, saw or thought ill of the volunteers. A great many celebrated the volunteer's spirit of independence and the democratic nature of the volunteer company. "By the eighteenth century," wrote E. Wayne Carp, American militia and volunteer units had begun to "resemble a miniature commonwealth, clearly reflecting the community's inclusiveness, its stratified economic and social structure, and its hierarchical political world." The workings and character of the American republic were writ small in the volunteers. Republican practices were most evident in the democratic election of officers, the submission of petitions, and the common use of unit constitutions. Local men led by community leaders took it upon themselves to form their companies. These local initiatives are compelling proofs of the republican spirit in practice.[32]

Companies of militia began forming around York, Pennsylvania in 1774. The militia "infection," as John Adlum termed it, was "brought from Baltimore to York Town in Pennsa" by a German merchant, Bernard Eichelberger. Adlum and other local men believed that they had been pushed into action by the "British taxing and otherwise wishing to oppress us." Calling themselves the York Blues, the Pennsylvanians picked a veteran of the Royal American Regiment for their drillmaster. Working in concert with other local companies, the men decided to "form a Regiment and to choose a Colonel and other officers." Another group of militiamen, the "Associators of Militia of Captain Robert McCallen's Company of Lancaster County," Pennsylvania "Consentably Agree[d] to March to join the army of General Washington." Community, as it existed in the militia, was a powerful force that caused men to consider their actions in light of the expectations and the consequences of their decisions on fellow citizens. The selection of leaders was among the more important decisions made by soldiers. Communal concerns and rifts came to light in the course of elections and gave a glimpse of American political practices in action.[33]

Not surprisingly, volunteer and militia companies drafted and adopted constitutions to help govern their internal affairs. Constitutional governance made plain the nature and power of popular sovereignty at even this small level and the proper and allowable limits of government power. Members of constitutionally governed associations, whether sovereign states or militia companies, publicly declared their purposes for willingly joining together. Constitutions, therefore, were not simply collections of parliamentary rules and procedures but broad statements of meaningful purpose and declarations of the constituents' will. Citizen-soldiers' constitutions, albeit on a smaller scale, fulfilled much the same purpose as the United States Constitution.

A great deal of commonality existed within military constitutions. The democratic nature of constitution making was necessarily precluded in the regular army. Professional soldiering could tolerate some expressions of self-governance, but practical democracy was antithetical to good military order. It was important that soldiers state, at the outset, their purpose for joining together in arms. Their preambles were statements of intent that informed the reader and reminded the soldier of the purposes impelling military service. Early Revolutionary associations frequently (and sincerely) cast themselves as aggrieved citizens who had "taken up arms for the relief of our Brethren, and defence of their, as well as our just rights and privileges." Soldiers "solemnly and severally" swore to "Submit" themselves to "all the ordors and regulations of the army and faithfully to observe and obey all such ordors as we shall receive from time to time from our Superior officers." The associations of 1775 were simple and direct. Americans had voluntarily gathered together and armed themselves to preserve their traditional rights and liberties. Citizen-soldiers hoped their example would inspire other Americans to remain vigilant in defending liberty. As the nation matured, constitutions became more complex, but until 1861 ideas informing the constitutions and the fundamental purposes remained the same.[34]

Constitutions of the early national period continued to stress ideological motives for service, although their drafters more clearly delin-
eated the members' expectations of one another and rules and motives
governing their conduct. The constitution of the New Gloucester, Massachusetts (District of Maine) Association of the Friends of the Union
declared "'Every Government hath a right, especially in times actual or
impending Invasion, to command the PERSONAL SERVICES of ALL
its Members." The New Englanders placed government in a central role
and emphasized the positive power of law. In contrast, covenants and
constitutions had formerly been concerned solely with the individual
citizen and his responsibility to limit government's accretion and use of
power. But this association seems to have reversed the equation when it
declared "no member of the Body Politic can justly withdraw himself,
or decline to render, with promptitude and zeal, his utmost services in
behalf of the Government."[35]

New Gloucester's covenant recognized the responsibility of the self-
governing citizenry to defend its individual and communal interests as
a collective whole. Government was the organized representative power
of the political community and was, in the words of Earl J. Hess, the
"institutionalized" sum and substance of personal "liberty." By stressing
the power of government to call upon the services of the citizen-soldiery
and the citizenry's responsibility to heed that call, New Gloucester's
defenders acknowledged "institutionalized liberty" and their interest and responsibility to defend their right and ability to exercise self-
governance. Indeed, much as Robert Shalhope made plain about the
citizen-soldier, these constitutions embodied the "twin themes of personal right and communal responsibility." Bearing arms was the right
and responsibility of the virtuous citizen. The individual could not exist
outside of society.[36]

By the middle of the nineteenth century, the uniform quality of company constitutions was well established. Members continued to determine what provisions their companies adopted, but visiting companies
and technological advances in printing, transportation, and communication very likely contributed to the homogeneous character of the
documents. Preambles confirmed the members' beliefs that a "well organized and well disciplined Militia is a nation's bulwark and the sur-

est means of national defense." Members "individually, collectively and voluntarily agree[d]" among themselves to "raise" their companies and limit the membership to "any able bodied white male citizen" who had attained eighteen years of age.[37]

Among Confederate companies, citizenship provisions changed only slightly in 1861. Companies continued to require that each member demonstrate "good moral character" and "some means of visible support," but added the provision that he must be a "citizen of the Confederate States America." Except for this change of citizenship, Southern and Northern constitutions were virtually indistinguishable. Eligible men who fit the company's social, personal, and financial requirements were subject to a vote by the members of the company. Admission was not automatic. In general, constitutions stated, "No person shall be admitted to membership unless by vote of the Company by ballot; and if three votes are given against a candidate for admission, he shall be rejected." Citizen-soldiers trained for the "purpose of promoting and cultivating Military Science" and hoped that their upstanding character and behavior would stimulate the growth of "good moral character, and good standing in this community." While the volunteer companies were clearly exclusive social clubs, their members did take their military duties seriously. Mottoes like "WE DEFEND OUR RIGHTS" proclaimed their mission.[38]

The right to elect officers was one of the more hotly contested rights volunteers and militiamen so staunchly defended. William Whiting and Mark Hopkins reported the difficulty of recruiting troops from Hampshire County, Massachusetts, for an expedition to "Cannady" in 1776. On the one hand, experienced soldiers had an "Avertion" to "Inlisting before they know Who is to Command them and of Running the Risk of Such officers as may be Chosen by the Soldiers." For unexplained reasons, the "old Soldier[s]" did not trust that good officers would be elected by their peers. Whiting and Hopkins, "therefore thought [it] highly Propper that the Captains and Subaltern officers for the three Companies of this County should be Nominated Either by the Ginneral Assembly or by the field officers of the Regiment" in order to hasten recruiting. On the other hand, "Considerable Numbers of bravemen" refused to enlist out of fear that New York officers might receive commissions. Previous "Disputes" with the "N. York people Respecting the

Title" of "Lands" created a such a great "Avertion to the Yorkers that they [potential recruits] have the Greatest Reluctancy to Entering the Service." These men, thought Whiting and Hopkins, would "Chuse and insist on having their Company officers appointed [from] among themselves" before they would serve.[39]

Contests between competing politicians for national, state, or local offices sometimes carried over into the military sphere. In 1847, Musician Thomas Bailey of Company C, Fifth Indiana, noted a "mass meeting of soldiers" while on campaign in Mexico. Lieutenant Colonel Henry S. Lane had "asked of Democrats to repond to the nominations of Gen. [Lewis] Cass for President and Genl. W[illiam].O[rlando]. Butler for Vic. President" in the party's nominating process leading up to the 1848 election. More often than not, "many of the officers were candidates at home for the legislature, and other places of civil trust." It took little time for aspiring "officers" to begin "electioneering the men and doing the polite to those who are not aspiring to an office in the regiment." Political factions formed quickly and easily. "The different parties and friends are hard at work using every kind of artifice to insure success of their causes," wrote Lieutenant Charles Johnson of the Eleventh Louisiana to his wife, Lou. Johnson described in detail the process of electing field officers in his regiment. Each of the ten companies had four votes, and in order to be "elected" the candidate had to "receive twenty one votes, a majority of all to be cast." At the time of the election on 8 August 1861, "there were in camp but twenty eight votes," and in order to "elect therefore it was necessary that there should be no opposition." One faction was so well organized and ambitious that its electors went into "Caucus" and engineered a unanimous victory for the three leading candidates. Inevitably, losing factions complained of defeat by "political intrigues and dishonorable conduct." Whether honestly or through intrigue, the officers selected or put forward as candidates sometimes disappointed their constituencies.[40]

"We have chosen the wrong man for Colonel," declared William E. Mullin of the First Pennsylvania in 1847. Mullin was convinced that Colonel Francis M. Wynkoop would prevent the regiment from earning military glory and "an undying name" in the war with Mexico. A soldier of the Fifth New York, A. Davenport, thought an 1861 election in Company G split along class lines. Davenport reported a soldier named "Collins was our favorite" for company commander but that the "Officers" had "wanted some one of their Class, in education" and in other qualities. Collins graciously resigned and the winner, a Lieutenant Hamblin, invited Davenport's company to a "Social glass of Brandy and water."[41]

Unpopular appointments aroused far stronger emotions than electoral defeats. A number of Revolutionary volunteer "officers and men" in the southern theater "unanimously object[ed]" to Brigadier General Daniel Morgan's appointment as their commander in 1781. Colonel Otho Holland Williams of Maryland reported to Major General Nathanael Greene that "they actually decline[d] obeying him, and intimate[d] that they will not march under his orders." According to Williams, the volunteers wanted an officer of their own choosing: "They say they are Volunteers" and therefore they deserved to be "treated with distinction." Resignedly, Williams admitted it is "difficult to manage them." Appointments struck deeply at the very notion of self-governance in militia and volunteer units. These actions vitiated the democratic process in the selection of officers and caused men to wonder if they would lose even more rights. Following the appointment of "H.W." to the first lieutenancy of the Fifth New York's Company C in 1861, Private Davenport believed the post would be a "hot place for him, as they [the enlisted men] are determined not to do their duty under him, [for] he has few friends here among the Privates." Davenport wrote that although "Volunteer Corps have the right to elect Officers," that right was being taken away from the men. He feared that the soldiers of his regiment would soon have "no more rights that way than *Serfs*."[42]

Having actively participated in the governance of their units, volunteers and militiamen were understandably proud of their traditions. Some citizen-soldiers believed that their tradition of self-governance was the single most important quality of the volunteers and the militia. One volunteer turned regular proposed that the army reform itself by adopting the democratic practices of citizen-soldiers.[43]

Samuel Hamilton Walker of Maryland, a "native American, a lover of my country, and a true friend to the principles of freedom and justice," felt compelled to give his "fellow-citizens a few statements concerning the abuses of power and the tyrannical treatment of soldiers in the United States service." Walker's criticism of the army centered on its antidemocratic and authoritarian nature, the central ambiguity of the

American military experience in the nineteenth century. This veteran of the Seminole wars contended that "all republican armies should be conducted on purely republican and democratic principles, by giving them [soldiers] the privilege of electing all the officers." Furthermore, Walker thought the military justice system severely flawed. He called for "all persons in such service to have the right of trial by jury for any violation of the regulations of the army, and not to be thrown on the mercy of officers who receive their situations from those who are not immediately interested in the welfare of the private soldier." The introduction of democratic reforms would enhance the army's performance and its image, and, most importantly, make it an embodiment of republican values. One long-standing practice in the both civil and military spheres, however, would not require introduction—petitions.[44]

Soldiers' petitions were the primary means of giving voice to their concerns. Employed by soldiers of all ranks, the petition, unlike individual or group disobedience, often elicited respectful consideration from officers. The use of petitions, a well-known and respected act in American political culture, dated from the colonial era. Reasons for petitioning superiors included requests for the promotion or reinstatement of esteemed leaders, entreaties for the removal or court-martial of despised men, or pleas to change the conditions of service.

A petition from Captain Levi Spaulding's company of the Third New Hampshire to George Washington "'commend[ed] the conduct and undaunted courage of William Lee' at the Battle of Bunker Hill" in 1775. Spaulding's men held Lee in such great affection that they "desired" a commission for the esteemed "sergeant Lee." Major Samuel Eugene Hunter was clearly popular with the Fourth Louisiana's St. Helena Rifles in 1861. Following the notice of Hunter's transfer to another regiment, forty-nine "undersigned members" signed a petition to express their "extreme disappointment" over the transfer and to request Hunter's continued service in the company. In 1861, Colonel Maxcy Gregg apparently dismissed a Lieutenant Ryan from the First South Carolina's Irish Volunteers for drunkenness. In response, seventy-eight men "most respectfully" petitioned Colonel Gregg to "reinstate Lt. Ryan." Gregg's petitioners cited Ryan's skill in recruiting the company and added, "He is dear to each and everyone of us both as a Gentleman and a solder." Perhaps Ryan had been drunk, but "his faults if faults he had was in being an Irishman." Petitions that supported favored soldiers were not uncommon and attested to men's loyalties and their confidence that their voices would be heard and given due consideration by the military hierarchy. But the readiness with which soldiers submitted petitions on behalf on admired men was rivaled, if not surpassed by soldiers' calls to remove, chastise, or court-martial hated men.[45]

In February 1781, after nearly three years of voluntary retirement, Brigadier General George Weedon received the command of a brigade of Virginians. Weedon had initially resigned because his first brigade had been reduced in size and no commands equal to his rank and dignity as a brigadier general existed. Seriously displeased by Weedon's appointment, a Virginia "Board of Field Officers" protested to Major General Nathanael Greene. Two colonels, three lieutenant colonels, and four majors signed the petition out of great "confusion, disgust, and resignation." Weedon's unhappy officers considered the general's prolonged absence and easy restoration both "Irregular and unmilitary." Efforts to remove Weedon came to naught. He commanded his new brigade through the British surrender at Yorktown in 1781.[46]

Broken promises, unwise words, and offensive behavior precipitated a number of petitions calling for redress, court-martial, or resignation. Lieutenants of the Pennsylvania Line petitioned Congress in December 1780 for their promised "half Pay, and of the other Emoluments" voted for "Officers of our denomination." One month later, in January 1781, enlisted soldiers of the Pennsylvania Line mutinied and demanded that they be paid immediately and "without any fraud." The men wanted all "arrears of pay, depreciation of pay," and the "Cloathing" promised to them. Brigadier General Anthony Wayne of Pennsylvania sympathized with the mutineers and thought their "propositions are founded on principles of Justice and Honor, between the United States and the Soldiers, which is all that reasonable men can expect." The mutiny was really more of a protest by aggrieved citizens than an uprising by a disloyal soldiery. Pennsylvania's men simply wanted their promised due. It was, as Don Higginbotham has pointed out, an act that "could only have occurred in a country where many of the men were upstanding citizen-soldiers conscious of their rights . . . , liberties," and responsibilities.[47]

A number of regular officers serving in Texas and Mexico were clearly vexed by President James K. Polk's decision to officer the newly formed Regiment of Mounted Rifles with direct appointments from civil life. Their petition to Congress noted that "not a single officer of the Regular Army, who shared in the recent victories [at Palo Alto and Resaca de las Palmas in 1846] has been deemed worthy of promotion into this new Regiment but that an officer of Volunteers [Samuel Hamilton Walker] engaged in the same duty, present at the same battles, and who has been less than three months in service" had received a captaincy in the new regiment. Lieutenant Ulysses S. Grant thought that "Mr. Polk has done the Officers of the Army injustice" and believed "we have but little to expect from him." As far as the regular officers were concerned, Polk's actions constituted an "insult" to the honor of the army and to its officers.[48]

"The undersigned officers of the first and second Regiments of Illinois volunteers" were insulted by Colonel John J. Hardin's purported threat to send them "home in disgrace" following their arrests for indiscipline. Forty-nine officers, including the two regiments' colonels, resented Hardin's claim that they were "not worth a damn." Sucker State officers called on Hardin to retract these "insulting expressions respecting the officers," and told him his remarks were "unmerited, unbecoming a commanding officer, and would be degrading to us if we passed them by without notice." Hardin's officers acknowledged his "right to command" and promised to "obey all legal orders" despite the colonel's "bearing towards us." According to the offended men, they had no intention of "insubordination or mutiny" but thought it within their rights to remind Hardin that his "right to command us, does not include the right to insult us." Colonel Hardin's petitioners closed by "demand[ing] the unqualified retraction of the offensive expression respecting the officers of the Illinois Regiments." Hard feelings between Hardin and his command continued until his death at Buena Vista in 1847. Death redeemed the colonel's standing with his officers.[49]

Caleb Cushing's First Massachusetts suffered greatly from internal quarrels throughout much of its Mexican War service. Before departing from Boston for Vera Cruz, men from Company C, "believing ourselves agrieved, and believing that there are just causes of complaint," stated they could not serve in the "said regiment as an efficient company" until their "agrievances" had been "heard, and the cause of our complaint removed." The cause for complaint was "Theodore Ashley, first officer of said Company C." Thirty-four men charged that Captain Ashley's "Incompetency" and "Bad Moral character" contributed to his "Total want of capacity, to discharge the duties devolving upon him as first officer." In addition, the men noted that "his character and conduct is unbecoming an officer and we can place no confidence in him." Shortly after this contretemps the company requested that Cushing "withdraw all charges" against Ashley since "we *now* have the utmost confidence in" him. What had transpired to redeem the captain is a mystery. A similar incident in the Bay State regiment took place among the "subaltern Officers attached to Company H," who preferred court-martial charges against Captain Joseph Whiting for being "drunk at the Levee given by Mr. George Gibson in No 28 Pearl St.," for being "drunk at Quarters," for making a "habitual use of intoxicating liquors," and for "acting contrary to Army Regulations and against the advice of his officers" in freely giving his men passes which facilitated their desertion. While awaiting transportation to Mexico, Companies B, C, E, and F petitioned Cushing for furloughs to purchase personal articles in Boston. The men thought Cushing's restrictions on their freedom of movement "harsh and unjust treatment."[50]

Not every petition received a respectful hearing or reply. Officers of the Connecticut Light Horse reminded General George Washington of their state's laws, which made the unit "expressly exempt from Staying in Garrison, or doing Duty on Foot, apart from their Horses." A lack of forage did not allow the Light Horse to "Sustain their Horses" properly. Therefore, they asked for "Dismission" from the service. The petitioners' selfishness angered Washington and provoked him into replying to the officers that if "your men think themselves exempt from the Common duties of a Soldier" then "they can be no longer of Use" in the army. In closing, the Virginian curtly informed the cavalry officers that he did not "care how soon they are Dismiss'd."[51]

Self-governance touched upon all aspects of American life, and an appreciation of it is fundamental to any understanding of republican government and the American military character. As Charles Royster has pointed out, starting with the Revolutionary generation, many Americans "believed that God had chosen America to preserve and to exemplify self-government for the world." American character and government were self-reinforcing and so closely reliant upon one another that an "attack on American self-government meant an attack also on each American's psychological integrity—on each American's soul." United States military institutions, including the regular army, were "distinctive" exemplars of the "connections between a people and their army," especially in war. Government at all levels of the American political system was so small and poorly organized for military ventures that it could not defend the nation or wage war without voluntary popular support. Voluntary popular support in the military arena was, first and foremost, an act of republican self-governance.[52]

The American soldier's belief in his right to govern his life in some measure transcended chronological boundaries, and it affected in some way or another regular, volunteer, and militia order, discipline, and life. Republican soldiering relied in no small degree upon the willingness of the soldier to accept and shape its terms and conduct himself accordingly. Service was not a total surrender of the right of self-governance but was, instead, a voluntary, negotiated, and temporary abjuration of that right. By voluntarily placing himself under the demands, limitations, and expectations of military discipline, the American soldier signaled his responsibility as a citizen through his willingness to forgo the full exercise of his rights. For the American citizen as soldier, self-governance and military service were not mutually exclusive. They converged and reinforced one another, thus making plain the interdependence of republican citizenship and one of its most fundamental components, military service.

4

A Providentially Ordained Republic

God's Will and the National Mission

Americans' sense of divine election and their belief in themselves and in their mission as a chosen people to effect the spiritual or political regeneration of mankind has deep roots. Americans' belief in their "chosenness" was more than a simplistic or disingenuous rhetorical device to lend a veneer of legitimacy to smug self-righteousness and aggressive continental expansion. It was, instead, a means by which Americans and American soldiers understood their history, their present, and their future as a people and as a nation. Providential will, they believed, had caused early colonists to venture forth from Europe to the New World where they and their descendants established thriving and vibrant communities wrested from the wilderness and Indians. Throughout the course of their history Americans had benefited from God's munificence. His favor was plainly evident in the passage of time from colonial contact and conquest to the Revolution, the republic's demographic, economic, and continental expansion, and their political system.[1]

Chosenness, as Americans understood it, accounted for their exceptional fortune and informed them of their mission on earth. The foundations of the American sense of election, of exceptionalism, were both "Protestant and liberal" according to Anders Stephanson. American chosenness stressed "old biblical notions, recharged through the Reformation, of the predestined, redemptive role of God's chosen people in the Promised Land." Seventeenth-century Puritans, a "particularly fierce and uncompromising phalanx within the Reformation," had laid the foundation for the intellectual development of American choseness. Puritans, more than any other English emigrant group, embodied to an extreme degree the English belief in "destinarianism," the belief that they were "not only spatially but also spiritually separate" from the Old World and that they had a mission to establish a holy community that would stand as an example of what a godly people could and ought to do with their lives. In contradistinction to New England's theocratic elite, Virginians saw the Old Dominion as an *"extension* of God's chosen England, not as a qualitative break or an Exodus" from it. So although Virginians may not have brought with them the fervent separatist version of predestination, they did bring the conviction that they, like all Englishmen, were members of God's chosen people. The thought that emerged from these two regions, while formally dissimilar, was rooted in the English Reformation sense of national destiny and distinctiveness.[2]

New England and Virginian brands of destinarianism were not exclusive; rather, they represented polarities on an intellectual spectrum. Each reflected a different embodiment and degree of intensity of the same ethos; each was conjoined to the other through shared origins in Reformation thought and belief. To this spectrum must be added American republicanism and its emphasis on the supremacy of individual rights, liberties, and responsibilities within the limited strictures of a covenanted, constitutional, and rational society. The fusion of providential destinarianism and republican liberalism revealed itself in the aggressive, self-righteous, expansionist nature of American political culture, eventually known as Manifest Destiny, a convenient and descriptive phrase coined by journalist John L. O'Sullivan to denote the coalescence, presence, and active agency of destinarianism, republicanism, and expansionism throughout American history. God's will and the American sense of mission made continental and cultural expansion a "sacred-secular *project,* a mission of world-historical importance in a designated continental setting of no determinate limits."[3]

Americans' belief in God's will and in a national mission were powerful instruments in the shaping of "the idea of 'America'" and what it meant to be an American. Spreading American institutions over the length and breadth of the continent, achieving the republic's manifest destiny, was a "tradition that created a sense of national place and direction in a variety of historical settings, as a concept of anticipation and movement," and as such it was a part of the process of republican self-definition. The United States was not simply a nation but an ongoing force for regeneration and enlightenment that thrived under the aegis of divine guidance and revelation. The United States was, therefore, a "unique mission and project in time and space, a continuous *process*" for change. For proof of God's will and the "Blessing of Heaven," Americans had merely to reflect upon their dominion over the land and their success at arms against Indian and European foes. Because of God's favor, Americans had "Conquered their Enemys and turned the Wilderness into a Fruitfull Field" for future generations of godly people. The Americans who effected these accomplishments, soldiers among them, cast themselves as the agents of divine will, thereby reinforcing their belief in the profound relevance about being an American. The United States was the "Republican Israel," charged with fulfilling God's will on earth.[4]

Citizens from all walks of life hewed to the belief in national predestination and mission. Above all others, American soldiers believed themselves particularly suited to pushing forward the physical and cultural boundaries of the republic. Soldiers, the "agents of empire, who made possible the development of the American republic," were in the vanguard of American expansion and the creation of an empire that fostered and spread liberty. Republican men at arms secured the frontier and carried forward a "conscious and conscientious" acceptance and understanding of their role as the "agents of American empire and nationalism."[5]

Believing that God had predestined the republic for greatness, American soldiers had faith in their belief that he took a special interest in their lives. Soldiers took confidence from the knowledge that in performing their duties they were acting in his behalf as instruments for humanity's benefit. Revolutionary volunteers from New England announced *"To all Christian People believing in, and relying on, that God to whom our Enemies have at last forced us to appeal"* that their service followed "in the course of Divine Providence." These volunteers believed that God had selected them to hazard themselves in "defence of our Lives and Liberties," which were the "object of divine protection." Divine interest in America's "dear and Heavenborn Liberties" held out to men the promise of the "happiness of ages to come—of generations yet unborn." They went to war not simply for their own "Liberties" but for the "unalienable Rights of mankind" as well as the "priviledges which the God of nature hath bestowed upon them, and which they may not give up (unless unable to support them) without affronting that being who delights in the Liberty and prosperity of all his Creatures."[6]

Revolutionary soldiers were convinced that "God had chosen America to preserve and to exemplify self-government for the world." Their defense of self-government was a defense of God's plan for human governance that was calculated to inspire mankind and so lead humanity toward a godly way of life. So pervasive and vibrant was this thought that the "belief in God's design for the future of America and in his governance over the life of the individual influenced most American's understanding of their activities" and colored their dealings with the world beyond their borders.[7]

The belief that God had favored the United States and had picked the republic as his temporal deputy reaffirmed the inherent justness of American wars, much as others' belief that God had sanctioned so many other wars and had blessed so many other countries and peoples. Americans had made war, in part, to protect divinely sanctioned government, and to effect God's plan for mankind as well as his personal interest in the United States. Writing in 1836 while campaigning against the Creek Indians, Georgia quartermaster Iverson Lea Graves served as the "Christian souldier protecting the lives and property of my injured Countrymen." Graves believed the "Cause just, and my Conduct sanctioned by my God, who is greater than my own Conscience and Condemns me not." Graves, like other soldiers, believed that God's favor played a determinative role in their lives and in the life of the nation. This knowledge that soldiers were acting in accordance with the plans of the Almighty was a powerful reinforcing message to the army.[8]

Lewis Leonidas Allen, a Methodist Episcopal chaplain to Louisiana volunteers in Mexico, believed his flock to be "Men possessed of the loftiest feeling, and pure motives," whose minds were "actuated by the most sublime and holy principle which can possibly occupy the heart of man." According to Lewis, God had willed the war between the United States and Mexico as a means for "patriots and christians" to evangelize the "priest-ridden, ignorant and unhappy country . . . , for most assuredly this country will not only be revolutionized, but christianized" by Americans. It was destined that the United States would conquer and uplift Mexico and that the "go-ahead Anglo-Saxon" would not "rest until the stars and stripes wave, not only over the ruins of the halls of the Montezumas, but over every portion of North America." Lewis's vision of America's destiny was anything but uncommon. Robert Armstrong, an aide-de-camp to Major General Winfield Scott, "believed that Providence was interested directly in the affairs of nations," and he concluded that "his hand has been in this war" with Mexico. Divine interest in American affairs precluded Armstrong from questioning "the war we have waged, whether just or not in a political sense." Despite the Mexican string of defeats, Mexico had benefited most from the war. An American victory followed by a lengthy occupation would allow the United States to restore order to Mexico and to reform its politics. From Armstrong's perspective, the war "has thus far been a blessing to the people; and a vast majority of the intelligent population are anxious that our Army should remain in the country."[9]

Historian Robert Johannsen has written that "Patriotism and Providence were closely linked in the 19th-century mind by the belief that the United States was God's favored nation, its inhabitants God's favored people" and that their actions must, therefore, be indicative of God's will. It had to be so, "Because God had willed America's progress, its progress was foreordained," and to oppose the progress of the nation was take issue with the Almighty. The nation's political system, its republican culture, the "cause of liberty and democracy, the 'American idea,' was God's cause and, as so many Americans pointed out, it was the United States that was charged with bringing to fruition God's plan for all mankind." The plasticity and expansive boundaries of republican ideas, rhetoric, and culture allowed Americans to justify and make sense of their actions even as other Americans might questions those acts or deny their validity.[10]

Civil War soldiers drew strength from the same convictions that had informed previous generations of soldiers. They took courage from the knowledge that they, like their forebears, the men "who made the Revolution," were "firmly convinced that they were Heaven's favorites—that they were doing God's republican work in the world." To them America's political system had been ordained by Heaven, and to betray the republican system of government would be the equivalent of betraying God and working against his revealed word and will. Soldiers from both armies believed that they, and not their opponents, were the defenders of the true republican faith. Troops of the Civil War could not have served as they did without complete confidence in the justness of their respective causes. This sense of confidence, much of which was derived from their belief in God's will, drew men to service, sustained soldiers' will to fight, and enabled them to continue fighting fellow Americans in that first year of the war.[11]

Captain John Q. Winfield of the Seventh Virginia Cavalry wrote that the Confederacy was a *"New Jerusalem"* peopled by a citizenry with "high and noble instincts with the capacity for free government," who lived with the "blessing of God upon them." The Confederate States of America, which cemented slavery in its constitution, not the government of the corrupted Union, represented the "last hope of free government." Fellow Virginian William Nelson Pendleton linked his acceptance of an artillery command to the belief that a "defensive war cannot on gospel grounds . . . be condemned." Pendleton believed that the Confederate "government" existed for the "protection of rights," and that it had "God's emphatic sanction, indeed . . . His own ordinance." Because of God's interest in the Confederate government it was bound "to the extent of its ability" to "resist aggression."[12]

Morality, righteousness, and confidence in divine sanction were not solely the province of Southern soldiers. Within the ranks of the United States Army, according to Earl J. Hess, the "ideology of the Northern war effort was deeply concerned with morality and thus had a natural affinity with religion." Men's belief that God had sided with the Union before the post-1863 crusade to abolish slavery with fire and sword, sustained them in the field and in combat. God's support "ennobled the conflict, invested with a heady sense of righteousness" and gave greater meaning to the struggle. Illinois's William Harvey Lamb Wallace and Iowa's Caleb J. Allen fully believed that God took a special interest in the Northern war effort. Wallace expressed a commonly held belief that in "His hands are the destinies of nations, and He in His wisdom will in His own good time and for His own good purposes conduct and close this war." As Allen saw things, "Never had men nobler or more sacred cause for which to fight, and die" than that of maintaining the Union. According to Wallace, Union soldiers were the "humble instruments" of God's will who had but to "discharge the duties we have in hand, and leave the issue to him." Wallace's "fatalism" and that of so many other soldiers was "consistent with the general view of Providence held by most people in mid-nineteenth-century America." According to Hess, the "mass of ordinary Americans tended to associate Christianity with the gloom of Calvinism" and its strongly predestinarian tenets.[13]

Soldiering and fulfilling God's wishes were not incompatible. In fact, according to Chaplain Enos Hitchcock of the Continental army, godly men made for better soldiers. Hitchcock told the garrison at West Point that the soldier who "believed in the Deity and was actuated by a sense of moral obligation" was superior to all others. The devout soldier's "love to and reverence of his Maker animated him in the duties of his station" while keeping him from sinking into "vice and sensuality," or from surrendering to the "foulest blasphemies." Piety and faith, Hitchcock reminded the men of the garrison, would add "stability and lustre" to their "social and miletary virtues." By coming to understand and accept God's wishes and by living according to his dictates, the soldier could add to the "distinguished character of a patriot" the "more distinguished character of a virtuous, good, man" who, when he "quit this stage in the full blaze of honor," would then "receive a crown of glory" in Heaven.[14]

Captain Harvey Brown of the Fourth Artillery echoed the tone of Hitchcock's sermon while serving in Mexico. Brown felt "deeply the responsibility" of his duties as a company commander, and he hoped to make his men more than "good and efficient soldiers," but "better men." Captain Brown wrote, "I hope and trust that the obedience due my country is not inconsistent with that due to my Maker, and my God," for he believed the "better and more pious the man the more subordinate, faithful and efficient, the soldier." The artillerist noted that "piety and morality are not inconsistent with the character of a soldier" and that they ought to be encouraged among the men of the army. By making soldiers better Christians and thus men, chaplains and officers hoped to reveal God's plans for them and the nation as well as to assuage the concerns of men facing battle.[15]

The faith that Chaplain Hitchcock and Captain Brown spoke of was a source of comfort, assurance, and rationalizations for their actions. Soldiers consigned their lives to God in the hope that he would comfort and protect them, help them to behave honorably, or, if they did not survive, to die in a state of glory. Captain Richard Varick, Major General Philip Schuyler's secretary and a former New York lawyer, wanted nothing more than to be a good and brave soldier and to return home safely from the War for Independence. However, if it was "Divine Will," wrote Varick, that "I shall fall a Veteran" to the "Fury of my Enemies," he prayed that he might "fall with Honor to myself and Connections." Faith in God helped comfort Thomas Rodney when he parted from his family. It pained Rodney to take "leave of my loving wife pregnant with woe as well as child, one lovely boy five years old and as lovely a girl but two" when he left for the army on 15 December 1776. Rodney keenly missed his family, but, he wrote, "My dependence is in God that he will establish the just cause and disappoint the cruel ends of tyranny. Blessed be His name, amen."[16]

The thought of battle and the possibility of injury or death had the potential to unnerve soldiers if those fears went uncontrolled. A soldier's submission to Divine will helped to reconcile fears before an engagement. "Under all circumstances," wrote William Henry Tatum of Virginia's Richmond Howitzers in 1861, "we have but to do our duty and bow in humble submission to the will of God—nothing goes wrong with those who put their trust in Christ, although we may sometimes blindly think" that such is the case. Another Confederate soldier, Tristram Lowther Skinner of North Carolina, approached the war with a stoicism derived from his religious faith. Speculating about one's fate was an exercise in futility. It was better, Skinner thought, to "await with patience and resignation Gods holy will as will be shown in the result." Mason Gordon of the Second Virginia Cavalry's Albemarle Light Horse reminded his niece Lucy that not even a "sparrow falls unless it be the will of the all merciful and omniscient author of our being." Gordon was proud that he could serve God as a soldier in "defence of their country and the rights of Mankind" and he considered it his "duty to submit to his [God's] decree without complaint." Death was a possibility, but under the circumstance, there could be "no death more honourable and more glorious."[17]

The American sense of predestination manifested itself directly in the national mission to effect a general uplifting of humanity or, at the very least, of the southern reaches of the continent after British Canada had rebuffed American advances in the War for Independence and the War of 1812. Revolutionary soldiers understood that "Heaven hath decreed that Tottering Empire Britain to irretreivable ruin; and thanks to God, since Providence hath so determined, America must Raise an Empire of

Permanent Duration, supported upon the grand Pillars of Truth, Freedom and Religion, encouraged by the smiles of Justice and defended by her own Patriotic sons" whose proofs of virtue and duty would inspire other nations to follow in their stead. This sense of mission would later help soldiers explain and understand western expansion, Indian removal, war with Mexico, and civil war. Man's redemption via the agency of America was a moral, social, and political mission that would bring formerly benighted or corrupt peoples into a way of life and system of governance that more perfectly accorded with God's wishes for mankind. God's plan for man was, of course, one of republican virtue and individual liberty.[18]

Beginning with the first generation of American soldiers, the "widely shared vision of America's future" accorded the revolt a "central role in the redemption of the world. Americans could be God's instruments to smash tyranny and to cast out the vices on which tyranny had long battened." Word of the American example and triumph over British "tyranny" would "spread" far and wide "to other countries by people who would emulate American resistance" and cause their own "liberation." Continentals, militiamen, and volunteers "saw themselves as righteous men fighting for a righteous cause." Philadelphia lawyer and militiaman James Allen wrote "it is a great and glorious cause" upon which the American people had embarked. "The Eyes of Europe are upon us," Allen believed, and if "we fall, Liberty no longer continues on inhabitants of this Globe: for England is running fast to Slavery." James McHenry, a Marylander and future secretary of war, enlisted in 1775 to "defend the liberties of Americans and mankind against the enemies of both." Victory was not simply a matter of colonial independence but a mission to save mankind through the example set by a virtuous people and its soldiery.[19]

It mattered dearly to the Continentals and their compatriots that they proved by their example their worthiness to lead the world. American victories would "produce a Conviction to the World that the Sons of America can and dare face, fight, or Defeat, not only the Troops of Britain but of all her adherents." Success by the "Sword" would "Determine whether we shall be freemen or Slaves."[20]

Battlefield successes were not the sole means by which victory would be attained. Keeping the army together in the face of British pressure would not only help preserve the revolutionary spirit and provide a means of resistance, it would also demonstrate American earnestness in the fight for liberty and hearten liberty-seeking people throughout the world. Pennsylvania's Brigadier General Anthony Wayne boasted that "our Growing Country can meet with considerable losses" which might, for a while "embarrass us," but the British would soon discover that "they can't Subjugate the free Sons of America who very shortly will produce a Conviction to the World that they diserve to be free."[21]

The conduct by which Americans hoped to ignite the fires of liberty among other nations was more than a matter of valorous action on the battlefield. It extended to the everyday conduct of individual soldiers. Thus soldiers' behavior in garrison and when off duty mattered as much as physical and moral bravery. Their "aid" was thought to be "essential to the preservation of the Rights of Human Nature and the Liberty of America." Colonel John Patton of the Pennsylvania Line found the attempts by some of his officers "seeking by dirty and base Means the promotion of their own dishonest gain" to be a "matter of extraordinary consequence and concern." Dishonorable actions on behalf of private interest would not do "when the united Efforts of America are exerted in defence of the common rights and liberties of Mankind." This was especially so in an officer corps of an "Army constituted for so noble a purpose." When Major General Alexander McDougall approved the court-martial conviction of Lieutenant Isaac Barber for "beating and kicking a Lieutenant Freeman's servant, Edward Hand, and rendering him unfit for Duty," he found it "painfull" that any "Officer in the American Army, raised for the express purpose of defending the Rights of and Liberty of Humanity, should forget" those purposes and treat a man so brutally. This understanding that American conduct would regenerate the world continued well past the Revolution. However, leadership by moral example alone was not enough. Republican empire, the extension of American borders and culture meant that the forceful incorporation of new lands and peoples were part of the nation's divinely ordained mission.[22]

The American mission to teach humanity how to govern itself by example alone was not enough. The aggressive spirit and "pungent rhetoric of Manifest Destiny" and its companion belief in Anglo-Saxon racial superiority, always present if only as an undercurrent in eighteenth-century American thought, asserted itself in the nineteenth century. Manifest Destiny's "central assumption" about the redemptive nature of the United States, that the "American nation and empire was divinely ordained" and that America had a mission to enlighten humanity, intensified following the War for Independence. Edward Larkin has suggested that a trajectory existed from the colonial era, in which the colonies came to resemble the mother country in its imperial aspirations, to the creation of the republic as empire. The Revolution had temporarily slowed the growth of American empire even as it laid the foundations for the continental expansion of a republican empire.[23]

Equating the American republic with imperialism is not contradictory. Indeed, as Richard H. Immerman has written, when "Perceived through the lens of America's ideology, empire and liberty are mutually reinforcing." Empire, as Americans from the Revolution through the Civil War understood it, was not a pejorative term. At its worst, empire was "ambiguous" to American sensibilities. Most, however, thought the "word *empire* benign." For the founding generation, empire did not carry the emotionally charged meanings of later generations. Simply put, an empire was "a polity" with dominion over a great geographic expanse over whose constituent parts ruled a metropolitan center. The population "included many peoples of diverse 'races' (as broadly defined at that time) and nationalities." Empire, as with the American republic, accepted individual social and political "inequality, limited citizenship and possibilities for assimilation" and understood that "rule was not necessarily consensual." Empire meant state, but an expansive, growing state in terms of population, territory, production, riches, and power. These interchangeable meanings continued into the nineteenth century, into the period of the Civil War, and only began changing during the Civil War and Reconstruction as Southern whites and others challenged the right of the federal government to exercise rule over them.[24]

Thus, instead of leading mankind solely by force of example, America would also lead mankind by force of national will and by force of the nation's arms. The United States would achieve its manifest destiny by annexation and assume direct responsibility for regenerating mankind by incorporating members of it, albeit often reluctantly, into the American empire. The new inhabitants acquired by territorial expansion would require education and uplifting, removal, or, if they refused the benefits of American civilization, war until their better senses prevailed and they recognized the inevitability of American political and cultural rule. There could be no other way for a superior people. God had destined American empire, and in the early nineteenth century science and nationalism had sanctioned it.

As the United States entered the first decades of the nineteenth century it entered a changing definitional landscape of race and the conflation of race with destiny. In the eighteenth century, Americans and Europeans had used race, ethnicity, and nationality interchangeably. Europeans understood one another as members of different races and had discerned and assigned various behavioral traits to one another. In the 1820s, however, race was coming to be understood in a pseudoscientific manner that argued for qualitative ranking of peoples based on physical and cultural attributes, and emphasized things like "racial destiny" and the inherent superiority and inferiority of races. This is not to say that Americans had not thought of themselves as superior to others. Indeed, as Ann M. Little noted about warfare in colonial New England, "Portraying one's enemies as utterly strange and different—as savage, irrational, weak, or foolish (as opposed to oneself: civilized, rational, strong, and wise)—undoubtedly served the psychological needs and political agendas on all sides" of a conflict. Moreover, English reasons for waging war in America in the seventeenth and eighteenth centuries, for the conquest, displacement, or extermination of Indians or the simple conquest and displacement of Catholic French and Spanish colonists, dovetailed with the expansion of the colonial plantation complex and the rising need for the slave labor that fueled it. Thus the ground was well prepared for influences from Europe.[25]

In the early nineteenth century, following the French victories over Austria in 1805 and Prussia in 1806, and the subsequent dissolution of the Holy Roman Empire that year, nationalist German thinkers who sought to inspire a sense of unity among the quarrelsome states of Germany appealed to what they saw as the elements of German identity as they stressed shared traits over those that divided them. Intellectuals like "[Johann Gottlieb] Fichte, [Friedrich Ernst Daniel] Schleiermacher, and eventually [Georg Wilhelm Friedrich] Hegel exalted the state, the language, and the German people" so that Germans might transcend their differences and unite on a basis of their common traits. For Fichte,

Schleiermacher, Hegel, and company, the primary engine of German unification was the institution of the state.[26]

These nationalist philosophers purposefully exalted the "state as an instrument of divine purpose" that existed to "stimulate the growth of a German nation." They interpreted history as a divinely ordered story of progress in which a particular people occupied the center stage of world events for a finite period of time. Ultimately, history was the story of mankind's steady procession toward an age of liberty. In order for Germans to seize their world-historical moment, they had to be led by the divinely ordained state. It alone could harness the energies of a politically divided but linguistically and culturally related people and lead them as a unitary nation-state. Elements of German thought profoundly influenced American intellectuals like George Bancroft, whose ten-volume *History of the United States of America, from the Discovery of the American Continent* stressed in romantic nationalist thought and prose the righteousness of American republicanism and the country's inevitable rise to glory. Bancroft captured the triumphalist tone in American political culture and melded neatly with long-standing American beliefs of predestination and chosenness.[27]

Changes in the tone of the rhetoric but not in the underlying assumptions about the United States' mission to expand, enlighten, and uplift others were so widely accepted that by "1850 American expansion was viewed in the United States less as a victory for the principles of free democratic republicanism than as evidence of the innate superiority of the American Anglo-Saxon branch of the Caucasian race." Conquest and expansion at the expense of Indians and Mexicans provided "abundant empirical proof of God's choice" of the United States for continental hegemony.[28]

American expansion took place under the loosely organized auspices of the state, but the state, in this case, represented the collective will of citizens who wished to push forward the physical, political, and cultural boundaries of the United States. The regular army was chief among the institutions advancing the growth of American civilization. Francis Paul Prucha credited the regular army officer corps for its role as "able representatives of the nationalistic spirit of the age" and considered them an "outstanding expression of the romantic impulse which marked so much of early nineteenth-century America." Considered in the aggregate, however, soldiers' attitudes toward blacks, Indians, Mexicans, people of mixed race, and other less fortunate peoples were generally disparaging. Expressions of smug superiority were abundant, as were resignation to the will of God, regret for having to make war upon inferior peoples, joy for the opportunity to lend a hand in the civilizing mission, and hopefulness for the future.[29]

While reflecting upon *"the Gallant Conduct of the Nine Graduates of the Military Academy, and other Officers of the United States Army"* who had died in 1835 and 1836 against the Seminoles in Florida, Lieutenant Benjamin Alvord declared that "it was never intended by the God of Nature that this beautiful and magnificent continent should sleep on in benighted barbarism under perpetual vassalage to hordes of ignorant savages." Leaving to nature productive land that otherwise might be put to use by God's chosen people would be to "arrest and blot out all that has been done to advance civilization, christianity, political and religious freedom on this western continent," and might also "annihilate many of the brightest glories in the history of our race." Because the Indians had not settled and cultivated the land in accordance with white American norms, they had obviously wasted God's gift and were undeserving of further dominion. Alvord had no intention of "extenuat[ing] in the slightest degree, any of the numerous wrongs which have been committed against the red man" but decided, upon reflection, that "warfare appears to have been an inseparable concomitant of the advance of whites into this country. Perhaps Heaven, in its wise Providence, willed that" that should be the case.[30]

America's aggressive and racially tinged spirit of national mission went forward with its soldiers into Mexico, the preeminent example of American expansionism. Soldiers expressed sentiments of racism, paternalism, contempt, pity, and the desire to aid Mexico by refashioning it in the image of the United States. Continuing in the pattern established by their ancestors, "Many of the soldiers were convinced that they were instruments of an overruling Providence" and that they were "pioneers, carrying the tenets of republican government and extending the bounds of American civilization" to the benighted reaches of the world. Soldiers' letters conveyed the belief that, if ever a country needed American civilization, surely it had to be Mexico. Colonel Henry Smith Lane of the First Indiana Volunteers thought the Mexicans were "lazy, ignorant and perfidious with no patriotism, no public spirit, no enterprise" and that they were "bigotted Roman Catholics" who had no ability to govern themselves. The altogether liberal and enlightened Lane believed that Mexico could not defy the all "grasping and all conquering genius of genuine Americanism" and thought it "would be a great mercy to them to take their country and give them a settled form of free government and Americanize their Republic."[31]

Race loomed large for the men of the invading army. Weaned on "Revolutionary republicanism" and influenced by nationalist thinking that equated the level of a society's accomplishments with its race, Americans had come to associate their form of government, their societal norms, and their material progress with the inherent superiority of the Anglo-Saxon race, particularly its American branch. The concept of race was evolving, but it was not clearly defined or uniformly accepted in the nineteenth-century United States. Some Americans understood it as a designation of "inherent biological characteristics." However, most Americans, according to Robert Johannsen, accepted race as a "community of individuals united by a distinctive cultural configuration, implying descent from a common stock but also suggesting a peculiar amalgam of varied influences both inherited and acquired." Nonetheless, in both cases it was understood that every people embodied a "particular spirit or genius, an identifying characteristic that set it apart from other peoples. This was good romantic doctrine" that infused the existing sense of chosenness with an even greater "sense of uniqueness."[32]

Captain Joseph H. Lamotte of the First Infantry certainly agreed that race determined the fate of nations. He credited Major General Zachary Taylor's 1846 victory at Monterey to the inherent superiority of the "bold and hardy Anglo-Saxon race." Grandiloquently, Lamotte characterized the Anglo-Saxons as a "race that has plucked from Glorys wreath laurels, equally amid the frozen barriers of the North as under the eternal sunshine of the South; a race (if ever there was one) whose whole history would to be prove invincible."[33]

Compared to the people of the United States, Captain James Willoughby Anderson found the "Mexicans . . . a strange people" who stubbornly refused to accept the inevitability of their defeat by the colossus of the North. Perhaps, Anderson thought, "God, for his own wise purposes, hardens their heart, in order that the whole country shall not only be conquered but populated by our race." Anderson, a veteran of the Seminole War, saw the problem as an issue of race, particularly the miscegenation that had taken place in Mexico since the Spanish conquest. Drawing upon his experiences with the Seminoles, he could not help but "think that the Almighty has cursed the Indian race and that he has hardened the hearts of the Mexicans against peace measures in order that they may be swept from the face of the earth as a nation." Writing to his wife, Ellen, Anderson gloomily predicted that the "Indian is doomed and there is too much of the Indian blood here for Mexico to escape" the eventual demise of its people. "There is a curse upon the country that is being fulfilled," wrote Anderson, and the "day is not far distant when Mexico will contain more yankees than Mestizzoes."[34]

Most observers were not as gloomy as Captain Anderson. The prevailing consensus was that Mexicans were an inferior race whose mixed parentage of Roman Catholic Spaniards and savage Indians had consigned them to a perpetual state of inferiority. But many Americans believed, nonetheless, that Mexicans did manifest a degree of educability and docility and that their country promised Americans an outlet for their redemptive and commercial zeal. Rather than misfortune, involvement in Mexico offered the United States the prospect of channeling its energies into the wholesale reform of a people while at the same time earning a profitable return. Economic considerations were ancillary to regeneration. Profit was a by-product of accomplishing the national mission, not its driving force. Once the people of Mexico had "witnessed the blessings of liberty imported to their shores by the free born sons of a land scarce out of sight of their own," wrote Captain Lamotte, they would welcome and assist in the transformation of their country.[35]

To enable Mexico's transformation into a proper republic, three tasks had to be undertaken. First, racially purer and superior Protestant Americans had to break the power, prestige, and religious monopoly of the Roman Catholic Church. Second, the system of education had to be improved by establishing a publicly supported one free of Catholic influence. Third, the United States would have to establish cultural, economic, and political suzerainty over Mexico to safeguard the country from regression or interlopers. As a result, Mexico would benefit from the United States and the United States would benefit from Mexico's challenge to the American spirit and from the country's resources. All of these acts would help introduce liberalized thought into Mexican life and allow for missionary Americans to proselytize for Protestantism, republicanism, and commercial enterprise. Writing to his brother Frederick, Pennsylvania volunteer J. Jacob Oswandel believed that Mexico's regeneration would be impossible "until the United States government takes hold of its [Mexico] dominion, under whose government every man, woman and child can worship God according to their own belief." Lieutenant James Wall Schureman of the Second Infantry held that the church's "monopoly of Religion," like "all monopolies," was inherently "adverse to republicanism and tend in the end to enslave the masses."[36]

Oswandel's and Schureman's opinions reveal a generalized belief that Roman Catholicism's hierarchical and centralized nature was antithetical to the self-governing nature of American religious and political life. Temporal or spiritual allegiance to any authority outside of the Protestant and republican tradition of the United States divided the citizen's loyalty and threatened the nation's tradition of individualism and self-governance by introducing elements of foreign or papist influence into the body politic. A religiously plural community, preferably without Roman Catholics, complemented a society whose fundamental political organization relied upon individual self-governance and free association. Based upon this assumption, Roman Catholicism's stranglehold on the soul and mind of Mexico had to be broken in order for the United States to lead Mexico onto the path of reform. In addition to the issue of religious pluralism, reform-minded soldiers addressed the pressing need for a system of free public education to liberate and inform the minds of Mexico's future generations.

Regular army officers occupying Mexico City in 1848 proposed to "establish free schools for the education of the poor Mexican children." Lieutenant Schureman thought that the idea was the finest "yet hit upon for making this people prosperous and happy and if fully carried out will make the future generations bless the invaders of the North." The task of properly educating Mexico's children would probably require the United States to "stay here for years to show the people the great benefits to be derived from such institutions for should our Army leave before fruit could be gathered from the tree that they planted, the Military despots and vile clergy would use all their endeavours to destroy it root and branch for in it they would see the instrument of downfall of their power, the people." Schureman placed great stock in the self-governing potential of an educated Mexican people. He believed that the "people with their eyes open and their reasoning powers brought into play; would at once behold the cause of their former misery [military dictators and priests]; and direct their efforts aright to remove it." Once educated and free from religious monopoly and the thrall of the army, Mexico might begin an extended period of American-dominated tutelage or even annexation. In either case, Mexico would learn from its northern neighbor how to conduct itself in a proper republican manner.[37]

There was no doubt that Mexico and the United States would benefit from the extension of American dominion. American rule would be a blessing for this "poor . . . miserable race" of people who had suffered from a combination of bad "luck an[d] the effects of bad Government." Brigadier General John A. Quitman of Mississippi was quite "satisfied that we are but the instruments of a benevolent providence to improve this country and its condition" and that "our invasion will result in the establishment in some good government and in conferring blessings upon the people." Samuel Hamilton Walker, a captain of mounted rifles and former Texas Ranger, fought with the "hope of producing results that will be beneficial to my country and mankind generally; I believe," writing that the "extension of the Area of freedom over this benighted Land . . . will do more to extend the great principles of freedom than anything else that has transpired since the Revolution." For this to happen, the United States would be compelled to take "military possession of the country." The United States' possession would "result in the Annexation of Mexico and open a new and extensive field for the display of American Genius and enterprise" in the country and in territories beyond.[38]

Soldiers who surveyed the prospect of Mexican annexation also believed that the newly acquired territories would result in direct and tangible commercial benefits for the United States. Writing to Senator Henry S. Foote of Mississippi, General Quitman demanded that the United States turn its occupation into formal annexation. Quitman, in contrast to more hopeful officers, had no faith in Mexico's ability to establish a competent or honest government. Quitman, nicknamed "Old Chapultepec" for his "services at the Halls of Montezuma," imagined that if the Mexicans were left to their own devices the country would sink into anarchy and civil war, which would ultimately result in a British seizure of the country. "Hold on to this country," counseled Old Chapultepec, "It is destiny, it is ours. We are compelled to this policy—We cannot avoid it." Commercial and geopolitical responsibilities and self-interest demanded that the United States rule Mexico and exploit it for its commercial value. "Let the road be opened," he stated, and "let foreign goods be brought to this capitol under our low system of duties, and we should sustain a moral conquest over this country which would soon bring peace." Small wonder that filibusters and other expansionists looked with approval upon Old Chapultepec.[39]

Former Texas Ranger Samuel Hamilton Walker had visions of American commercial success premised upon the establishment of a "Government" that was amenable to American wishes. Friendly relations between the United States and its Mexican puppet would "eventually Result in good to ourselves and the conquered people" who would then "witness . . . the completion of the [transisthmian] Canal or Railroad communication" from the Gulf of Mexico to the "Pacific Ocean." An American-ruled Mexico would allow the full exploitation of Mexico's "resources and open the doors to emigration for millions of enterprising inhabitants." Walker's dreams of a southern American empire were motivated by more than crass economic interest. He believed the results of the war would be "beneficial to my country and mankind generally." American expansion meant an "extension of the Area of freedom over this benighted Land and the completion of the great internal improvement to which I have alluded." The combined power of American-inspired political and economic advancement would do "more to extend the great principles of freedom than anything else that has transpired since the Revolution." Walker, like many other visionaries and agents of Manifest Destiny, understood the war as a stage in the "commencement of a new Era in the history of our great nation" and the world.[40]

Walker's thoughts were not unique to the "Army of Manifest Destiny" or among the American population at large. There existed a widespread "belief that the Mexican War constituted a stage in world progress" and that the United States was fulfilling its divinely ordained national mission to overspread the continent or even the world. The rhetoric of Manifest Destiny was not a cynical exercise in wordplay to mask land grabbing. The sentiments and words trumpeting territorial expansion were sincere, if self-righteous, simplistic, and strident. No matter how naïve the words sounded, "the belief that it was America's duty to redeem the Mexican people was simply too widespread, too pervasive, to be dismissed as nothing more than an attempt to mask ulterior desires for power and gain." Thus Walker and those like him believed an Americanized Mexico would "arouse Emperors and Kings throughout the World to a proper sense of their position and teach them that they were but men and they alone were not made to Govern the world." The United States had arrived on the stage of world history. The nation's expansion would, or so Walker thought, "soon bring us into close proximity to China the most gigantic nation in the world and the influence of our institutions with their continual improvements would soon be felt by China as well as Mexico."[41]

War with Mexico had been a resounding success for American arms. The republic's expanded dominion confirmed to many soldiers the "superiority of their race and governmental institutions" and caused some men to call for further expansion through filibustering expeditions in Latin America. Filibusters cited the victory over Mexico as the most recent proof of the nation's "moral right" to expand its borders through conquest. Besides demonstrating the righteous nature of expansion, the war had given men the chance to rise in social and political prominence through their feats of arms. Illegal expansion promised both the fulfillment of the nation's mission and an opportunity for personal reward.[42]

While the regular army and the states' militias did not participate in the filibusters' extraterritorial adventures, many of their veterans were attracted by the prospects that filibustering promised. According to Robert E. May, the battlefield successes of West Point graduates created a "Mexican War legend" that "helped mold West Point into a breeding ground for Manifest Destiny apostles." The attraction was so strong that some regulars deserted in order to accompany men like William Walker of Tennessee on their adventures.[43]

Dreams of a global American empire for liberty caused Private Edward Ashley Bowen Phelps of the Regiment of Mounted Rifles to wax rhapsodic about his military service and the role the army would play as the vanguard of American expansion. Phelps was excited by the prospect of participating in this important stage of world history. Writing from Mexico to his brother Samuel, Phelps reported that he was "more

in love than ever with the *Service*—except the *Killing* part." Phelps ab-
horred the possibility that he might be forced to "wound or inflict the
smallest pain or injury upon a fellow creature," and he confessed that "I
would rather die a thousand deaths than" harm someone. Speaking to
his brother Samuel as a "citizen of the world," Edward admitted his pride
and sense of "usefulness" as a member of the army, "The forerunner of
civilization." He dreamed of "soldier emigrants" who would "overrun"
the land from the "west and south from the isthmus of Darien to Ber-
ring Straits." Phelps celebrated "*The American Army*" for its central role
in America's impending growth. He could not conceive that there was a
"spot of the earth it is not destined to visit and aid" in the providentially
ordained "cause of Truth and Justice, as *we* understand it, not as defined
by the usurpers and tyrants of the age."[44]

Given to some measure of introspection, Phelps wondered what
power "brought us here" to Mexico City? It had not been American
military talent, he mused. Indeed, "Had our fortunes depended upon
'*skill in the art of war*' we would never have passed Cerro Gordo." This
was odd stuff coming from the soldier of a victorious army. Dismissing
the army's skill at war, Phelps posited that the Americans had advanced
so deeply into a hostile nation because of the innate superiority of the
"institutions of the north, the anglo saxon spirit of endurance, [and]
the *individuality* of the men who compose the american army." These
were men whose spirit "would take them to the Capital of Prussia with
scarcely a murmur" of complaint.[45]

If Phelps lauded the accomplishments and superiority of Anglo-
Saxons and the might of American soldiers, he did not do so for the
parochial purposes of national aggrandizement. "My sympathies though
none the less" for brother Samuel and the United States were for "all
mankind. *I Know*," wrote Phelps, that the "spread of our Citizens over
the continent is a blessing" for all the peoples of North America who
longed for liberty and a better way of life. Not caring "whether they
[Americans] go as soldiers, farmers or mechanics," Phelps's "only hope
[was] that our conquests may extend *the world* over." He easily envi-
sioned "Entering England, France and Spain from the East." Conquering
Mexico was the first stage in an imminently triumphal American march
to the establishment of global liberty. God had destined "our National
Flag to wave above the walls of every capital of the old world, so called,

leaving South America and Africa the last." With a profound sense of anticipation, Phelps penned that the "uproar of freedom has scarcely begun."[46]

American expansion alone would satisfy the "universal and rushing demand for liberty and light," but it would also probably entail serious opposition from would-be tyrants. "Will the aristocrats, monarchists," and other opponents of the United States' Manifest Destiny "go suffer the yankees to 'come in' without a few fights[?]" asked Phelps. He thought not. The "horrors of war," despite Phelps's aversion to killing, were unavoidable. Looking to the future, Phelps conceded that "*The Rifle* is bound to have its share in carrying forward and promoting" the "liberties and advantages" of American republicanism and civilization "to its freed millions."[47]

Private Phelps's celebration of Manifest Destiny was highly charged, but it was not beyond the general ken of American expansionism. As a proponent of Manifest Destiny, however, he stands out for his liberal opinions on Mexicans. Phelps believed in the superiority of the American line of Anglo-Saxon racial development, but thought that intermarriage between Americans and Mexicans would produce a superior people who could conquer the world. The result of joining "the swarthy suple soft, pliant race of beings" in Mexico with "our sterner natures of the North" would be a "glorious combination." To Phelps, this issue was so important that it was a necessary precursor to successful expansion. "We ought to mingle races" before moving to the next stage of conquest, he wrote. "Our qualities are just such as should be mingled to make a happy union" and a superior race. "Before our conquests extend across, *westward*," circumnavigating the globe before returning to the "Atlantic shore" it was imperative that "we should join to our sterner world the loving south."[48]

Phelps's advocacy of sexual union was part and parcel of the "all-Mexico movement," a grouping of expansionists who called for the United States to annex all of Mexico. Phelps and his kindred spirits believed that "that Mexicans were socially, politically, and, especially, racially inferior to Americans." These subscribers to Anglo-Saxon, especially American, racial superiority "could express [with] utter confidence that in the end the characteristics of the superior race would win out." According to these men, "sexual union" with Mexican women was the answer. Their progeny, sired by vigorous, martial Anglo-Saxons would absorb the conquered people into the republican empire. What, however, of the effeminate Mexican men? Were they to be denied sexual unions in order to allow the race to die out in a kinder and gentler form of genocide, or did these people envision another servile caste in the United States' racial hierarchy?[49]

Expansionists' sexual fantasies aside, they illuminate both the complexities of Manifest Destiny and the simplistic, almost childlike faith of Americans in their choseness and in the national mission. Not a monolithic ideology, Manifest Destiny was at once both complex and naïve. Within its complexity there was self-contradiction. Most of the military adherents hoped to uplift and Americanize people for whom they had a basic contempt. They wished to introduce an American style of republicanism that emphasized the rights and responsibilities of self-governance to people who, if understood solely by some American views, were incapable of exercising any degree of self-governance. The naïveté of Manifest Destiny was in the assumption, and not for the first time, that Americans could make war upon their neighbors and then expect to be welcomed as liberators. Manifest Destiny embodied, expressed, and aroused American aggressiveness, self-righteousness, racism, hope, and contempt. Its spirit had motivated the nation into expanding westward and undertaking a foreign war that nearly doubled the size of the United States. The debate that followed the Mexican War over how best to integrate the territories of the Mexican Cession contributed to the sectional crisis and the outbreak of civil war.

The American soldier's belief in the United States' divine election and in its national mission provided him with another means to understand and define himself as a soldier, but, more importantly, as a republican citizen. God's revealed will and his divine election of the nation as his temporal agents for human regeneration made the American experiment in republican government a holy undertaking and imbued the people of the nation with a belief in the profound importance of American citizenship. Because God had called upon Americans to teach humanity a better way, citizenship had implications that reached beyond the nation's boundaries.

The means to effect the national mission were mixed, but the basic impetus, the spread of American republicanism, remained constant. Soldiers of the revolutionary generation understood the means to be one of universal example and inspiration, a break from their recent imperial past. Their revolution in the cause of liberty would inspire other peoples to establish like republics. They had a hopeful faith in the self-perfecting and regenerative capacity of mankind. By the 1820s, however, America's faith in inspiration from afar had reverted to its older patterns, albeit with an overt racial tone. Inspired by theories of Anglo-Saxon racial superiority and by a belief in nationally dominated world-historical stages leading to an age of universal liberty, Americans pushed the nation's borders westward. Americans' short-lived faith in humanity's ability to learn from the American example had waned. Thereafter, it was through conquest and annexation that American enlightenment was to spread throughout the benighted territories.

Faith in God's will and in the national mission contributed powerfully to the American sense of identity. Believing themselves to be a chosen people, Americans confidently proceeded from the assumption that their form of government, indeed, their society, was a model worthy of global emulation and that the republic's duty to God and to humanity was to propagate that model.

5

Questing for Personal Distinction

Glory, Honor, and Fame

All of the elements underpinning American soldiers' understanding of service and citizenship joined together in the adherence to and pursuit of glory, honor, and fame. Concern for these abstractions of proper behavior and for their very real rewards and recognition was not peculiarly American. Many, if not most, soldiers in the Western tradition held in high regard proper deportment, manhood, bravery, reputations, and the commensurate accolades derived from gallantry in battle. Exemplary service and performance, and, especially, bravery in combat were among the keys to success in a military life. But for U.S. soldiers, very few of whom were long-service professionals, glory, honor, and fame went beyond the boundaries of the military world. These highly militarized values spoke not merely to a valorous soldierly mien but to the soldier's core, to his character and standing as a man, as a soldier, and as an American citizen. Glory, honor, and fame functioned as the guides and goals of reputable conduct.

Glory, honor, and fame took on added importance because of the rather austere nature of American republicanism, the political nation having consciously rejected hereditary monarchical and aristocratic privileges, transmissible titles, and their affiliated distinctions and trappings. Most conspicuously, the regulars and militia had rejected formal military decorations, unlike the groaning abundance available in the United States Army in the late twentieth and early twenty-first centuries. Embracing plainness and simplicity in address and uniforms spoke to the symbolic but very real need of Americans for national and personal identity and distinctiveness.[1]

The absence of an official system of publicly recognized distinctions did not, however, mean that U.S. soldiers did not want to earn popular or soldierly acclaim. Indeed, the dearth of titles and decorations made soldiers even more anxious to earn public approbation. Without titles of distinction, medals, or other tangible forms of recognition, glory, honor, and fame were the rarefied social coin of the republic. By earning glory, honor, or fame, men were raised in the public's esteem and as a result acquired particularly distinctive badges of social status. Men who had earned this form of public recognition were evidence of the nation's natural aristocracy coming to the fore and indicated a growing trend toward meritocracy. Soldiers accrued glory, honor, and fame through acts of bravery and virtue. These attributes were at the core of a soldier's identity and reputation; they reflected on his manhood and virtue. In this way, glory, honor, and fame were at one and the same time the guides, results, and public images of virtuous republican military service.[2]

When soldiers wrote of glory, honor, or fame they assumed that their correspondents were familiar with these concepts. The three elements were very closely related and were often used interchangeably by soldiers, creating therein some confusion. Douglass Adair's study of "*fame* and its cognates *glory* and *honor*" in the lives of the Founding Fathers forms a solid foundation from which to proceed to a greater understanding of the American soldier's relationship with these values. According to Adair, glory, honor, and fame share similar attributes but proceed from discrete sources which thereby endow the individual concepts and their possessors with unique characteristics. One's adherence to and acceptance of these concepts served a useful purpose, not only because the virtuous or duty-bound soldier admired and pursued these laurels, but because glory, honor, and fame helped channel otherwise selfish energies into activities that benefited society at large. Thus, ambitious men with a regard for public and private opinion willingly submitted themselves to a pervasive form of social control and self-discipline.[3]

Glory, honor, and fame revealed much about a soldier's character and spirit. Virtuous soldiers performed their duties despite the hardships of military service; they were prepared to sacrifice their emotional and material comforts and, if necessary, their lives on behalf of a greater cause or for their comrades. Thomas C. Linn, in his examination of military ethics and warfare, suggested that a high degree of altruism is necessary in soldiers because of the "magnitudes of power and responsibility that have been entrusted to them." In Linn's view, the ideal soldier is primarily an "individual who derives satisfaction from giving of himself" in the "general interests of society." Linn's account, however, is only one dimension of a complex idea. Virtue alone cannot account for the pursuit of glory, honor, and fame. Soldiers consciously sought recognition and acclamation deriving from acts of military gallantry. Hence, the self-interested pursuit of glory, honor, and fame was a vital spark to motivate soldiers to perform their duties.[4]

Through their pursuit of glory, honor, and fame soldiers satisfied their self-interest, which quite often coincided with the needs of the republic. Soldiers used their military service to attain distinction and thereby transform their "egotism and self-aggrandizing impulses into public service; public service nobly (and selfishly) performed was the surest way to build 'lasting monuments' and earn the perpetual remembrance of posterity."[5]

E. Wayne Carp's study of the Continental army's administration and its connection with republican ideology and governance showed that "patriotism, esprit de corps, and most of all honor and reputation— provide the key to understanding staff officers' willingness to undergo the hardship and strain of public service." Carp found that in the "staff officers' hierarchy of values, the army shared place of honor with serving one's country." For these men the "link was logical: American independence rested on the army," and service with the army would clearly "add luster to their individual reputations," thereby enhancing their military standing, but also their place within society. Edward M. Coffman noted similar connections in his examination of the peacetime army from 1784 to 1898. For many commissioned officers, military life was an "unending competition" that they waged with fellow officers for "better positions and more awards."[6]

The pursuit and high valuation of glory, honor, and fame were at their most pronounced within the officer corps. Although many enlisted soldiers also set great store by these distinctions, until the Civil War references to these distinctions did not appear in their writings as frequently as in the correspondence of officers. Officers' educations and aspirations likely account for the greater esteem accorded and occurrence of these ideas in the records. Men who were more widely read, men who sought social, political, or military leadership and preeminence valued such things more highly. Moreover, the attributes and ideals of glory, honor, and fame, which were "derived in part from an inherited aristocratic tradition and in part from America's deferential society" of the seventeenth and eighteenth centuries, likely informed officers. In the broader social and intellectual milieu of American society these propositions were "associated with wealth, family, education, and social connections." A man's "reputation denoted character, integrity, honesty, and dependability," and was a manifestation of his and his peers' "desire for the respect and approval of their fellow citizens."[7]

Serving the public interest through military service held out the opportunity for individual distinction while acting for the good of society. In this way, selfishness united with the needs of the common weal. The best way to insure the immortality of name and repute was to pursue and accumulate glory, honor, or fame. The quest for a reputation based upon these achievements was a "spur and a goad" that impelled some men toward military service. By chasing after these distinctions, soldiers transformed their "egotism and self-aggrandizing impulses into public service." Beginning with the Revolution, military service in the cause of independence made "self-interest identical with public good. By erecting a republican government and ensuring the preservation of liberty and justice," soldiers of that generation "planned on paying themselves off in the only coin they coveted: fame, the everlasting applause of contemporaries, and the undying gratitude of generations unborn." Similar sentiments continually appeared in soldiers' correspondence through the end of 1861. The example and ethos of 1775 resonated for the men of 1861. Union and Confederate soldiers, like their eighteenth-century forbears, believed that noble behavior would receive immediate reward and would also perpetuate the man's name and bequeath to his kin no small measure of regard in the eyes of fellow republicans. Because of the mutually reinforcing nature of citizenship and soldiering in the idealized American republic, glory, honor, and fame spoke not simply to the soldier, or to the citizenship of the soldier, but to the republic itself.[8]

Republican men-at-arms were not simply anxious for their present reputations but were, as Douglass Adair noted, "fantastically concerned with posterity's judgment of their behavior." Not long after accepting his commission as commander of the Continental army, George Washington prayed for the Almighty to "grant" that his "acceptance of it may be attended with some good to the common cause and without Injury (from want of knowledge) to my own reputation." Washington understood that a soldier's "reputation derives its principal support from success" and that his own good name was dependent upon American victory. Washington exhorted his officers "most earnestly" to "shew an Example" of valorous behavior in the cause of American independence. He reminded them that as "brave and good Officers," they "shall be honor'd with every mark of distinction and regard." So highly did Washington esteem "Reputation" that he believed it "ought ever to be dearer than Life" to a soldier.[9]

As Adair suggested, "*Glory*, in its core meaning, is an attribute of God and, strictly speaking, of God alone." Understood thus, the soldier who served for glory's sake sought to make known to himself and to the public his membership in a very select group—men who had been selected by God or had earned God's approbation and blessing. By hewing to the "concept of *glory*," soldiers presumed that God unceasingly kept an eye on his children "and that those men who, conscious that God's eye is continually on them, behave with such piety and goodness in rendering homage to Him, will shine with reflections of His glory." Glory, therefore, was more of a premodern construct, wherein God's involvement in man's life was regular and not unexpected. The longevity of glory in the ethos and lives of American soldiers attests to its force and vitality.[10]

Earning or demonstrating God's favor was no small feat. According to Colonel Joseph Ward of the Continental army, the "Soldier, who in Freedom's Cause has borne all the ills misery had in store and braved death in every form," had accomplished "deeds of glory" for his country and for posterity. The "joys" of glory proceeded from a "source beyond the reach of fortune or the smile of mortals, from conscious Virtue," which had its source in the favor of the Almighty. The soldier who had "true glory" as his "aim" would experience "tranquil joy in constant streams," which would "raise the genuine transport of the Soul; for conscious worth outweighs the wealth of worlds." Ward's words make clear that military glory was only attainable through great feats of courage. In 1777, Brigadier General Anthony Wayne said as much when he counseled President Thomas Wharton of Pennsylvania that the "few troops you have are second to none in the field—they have stepped the first for glory" in the struggle against Britain. Revolutionary soldiers knew that combat would afford them an opportunity to earn glory. Corporal

Thomas Fanning of Colonel Samuel Blatchley Webb's Additional Continental Regiment heard the "Drum beat with the impulse that Warms / the Soldiers Brave heart" in his "War Song." Fanning believed that "war is the Scene where true Glory is won" and that combat was a "Lofty Conception [to] Enrapture the Soul." In 1783, Lieutenant Benjamin Gilbert of the Third Massachusetts Continentals complimented recently discharged soldiers, those "brave men," for their services on the "field of Glory." To Gilbert, the field of battle was the province of glory, and as the degree of danger increased, so too did the commensurate glory.[11]

When Alexander Scammell, colonel of the First New Hampshire Continentals, wrote to congratulate the First Maryland's Colonel Otho Holland Williams on the successes of the Southern Army in 1781, he believed that to "baffle an army of veterans superior in Numbers and well formed with a few ragged, half famished, pennyless, clever fellows, reflects a double radiency of military glory." For Williams, the success was particularly sweet. The British Army had nearly destroyed the entire Maryland Line, including Williams' own Sixth Maryland, at the Battle of Camden, South Carolina, on 18 August 1780. Williams now commanded the reconstituted First Maryland, a composite regiment comprised of the remnants of Maryland Line.[12]

Twenty-two years later, in the Old Northwest, Colonel James Mills reminded his Ohio militiamen that in their 1813 campaign for the "preservation of the lives of helpless thousands, [they] honor[ed] . . . the American Country in arms." No motivation beyond an "opportunity to share the glory of defeating the enemy," according to Mills, was necessary to inspire the men from Ohio. On the western frontier the following year, Captain James Callaway of Missouri's St. Charles County Mounted Rangers did not think that a "man embarking in his Country's Cause" was necessarily "honourable." It was, instead, his "Duty," when it was "invaded by a cruel and savage foe" like Britain's Indian allies. Surely, Callaway's sentiments about invading savages were not ironic. If Callaway died while performing his duty his death would be an "honourable" act, one he "trust[ed] no man may have it in his power to add a cowardly one." Following the repulse of British forces at the Battle of Baltimore in 1814, Major George Armistead, commander of Fort McHenry, reflected upon the recognition he had received for his spirited and successful defense of the post. Armistead reported to his wife, Louisa, that along with a promotion to colonel, he had received a "very handsome compliment" from President James Madison. "So you see my Dear Wife," Armistead wrote, "all is well, at least your husband has got a name and standing that nothing but divine providence could have given him." President Madison's congratulations and proffered promotion were public recognition for Armistead's divinely inspired success against the heretofore victorious British.[13]

Battle was the favored arena in which to earn God's favor. Risking life, limb, and reputation in the service of the republic made one an exemplar of manly readiness to sacrifice all for a greater good while earning a greater name. Surely, imagined soldiers, God would look favorably upon men who ran the risks of war in their nation's name. Self-interested in the quest for repute was the handmaiden of military glory. As Lieutenant Isaac Bowen and the First Artillery prepared to "march upon Monterey [Mexico]" in 1846, he did so hoping to "cover myself with that bubble 'Glory' which I am *so anxious* to attain." Bowen understood the necessity of combat as a test which he and other soldiers had to master so that God's grace might devolve upon them. Soldiers like Bowen desired glory so much that they feared there might not be a battle in which they could test and prove their mettle. Anxious for a fight, Bowen wrote that it was "generally believed that there will be no opposition to our entering Monterey. I almost hope they will [fight] for I, as well as every one else, will feel disposed to fight somebody after going so far for that purpose."[14]

A singularity of purpose motivated Colonel Elmer E. Ellsworth, commander of the Eleventh New York, the "First Fire Zouaves." Ellsworth was a prewar volunteer-militia enthusiast and former law clerk for Abraham Lincoln. While attempting to remove an offending Confederate flag from atop an Alexandria, Virginia, hotel in May 1861, he was shot by the hotel's proprietor. Ellsworth's death became the focus of popular adoration for many Northerners. The young colonel had shed his blood in defense of the Union. J. Henry Mason of the Bay State Artillery mourned the "brave Ellsworth" but believed himself unable to fully "express in writing" the powerful emotions wrought by his "feelings" over Ellsworth's death. Despite Mason's perceived inadequacy at letters, the sincerity of his emotions came through clearly. "We know and feel," wrote the young man, that "we have lost a brother, that one has left us, whom we all loved and respected, and who we had placed our implicit confidence." Ellsworth had "won for himself unsought, a name that shall be as lasting as the mountains stand, and may it serve as a watchword for us, and if it be in accordance with the wishes of the Divine Providence, may we have sweet revenge for his dear life." Ellsworth's death and the images it conjured touched Mason and his comrades deeply.[15]

Death was a distinct possibility for soldiers, whether at peace or at war. A "Good Death," however, elevated a soldier's sacrifice into something blessed and morally admirable because he had sacrificed himself for others and on behalf of a glorious cause. War was therefore the arena for good deaths. Ellsworth's death certainly illustrates this point. Comrades of slain men "derived moral exaltation from bloodshed in a virtuous cause" and were thus inspired to greater heights of accomplishment and sacrifice. Whether some divine entity truly had selected some men for glory is unimportant. It is important that soldiers believed that it was so.[16]

Honor, like glory, was both the "goal of character formation and an instrument of social control" that caused the individual to demand from himself a "pattern of behavior calculated to win praise from his contemporaries who are his social equals or superiors." Equally important, the man of honor expected reciprocity of behavior from his peers. Honor, unlike glory and its dependence upon divine favor, was attainable, indeed fashionable, by acts of individual will or conduct. As a form of social regulation, but also as guide to individual behavior, a soldier's honor proceeded from his "sense of due self-esteem, of proper pride, of dignity appropriate to his station." Honor acted like "conscience for a practicing Christian," and it was "capable of inspiring" within its possessor "systematized and regularized conduct that is noble, magnanimous, and admirable." Honor, Adair wrote, is "elitist, for small male in-groups" and serves "primarily a private ethic that links a person's identity with social stratification or occupational specialization. It is an ethic of competition, of combat, of struggle for eminence and distinction; and therefore is traditionally antithetical to the Christian demands for humility, abnegation, altruism." It was a code admirably fitted to the military culture of republic and its people.[17]

As a newly arrived people, Americans were highly conscious of their standing in the world as a republic and as a people who had created and preserved their national existence and legitimacy through revolution and war. Because the young republic lacked a long and reassuring history and because its purpose-built concepts of nationhood and citizenship were new and untested, Americans could be prone to braggadocio in order to project conviction and an image of sureness and national mission. The American sense of honor and self-image was sensitive, prickly, combative, often bombastic, and not prone to respect the rank of one who insulted it.[18]

The overtly combative and competitive nature of honor suited many American soldiers, but it also created many problems. In February 1779, Colonel Otho Holland Williams, commanding the Sixth Maryland Continentals before their destruction at Camden, recounted some of the turmoil within the Maryland Division that arose over slighted honor and personal conflicts. Colonel Mordecai Gist's promotion to brigadier general on 9 January 1779 caused Colonel Thomas Price, commander of the Second Maryland Continentals, "to quit our line." Gist had previously commanded the Third Maryland. Another Line State colonel, Josias Carvel Hall of the Fourth Maryland, refused to serve under the command of Brigadier General William Smallwood, who commanded the "division of Maryland troops." Williams, meanwhile, was temporarily commanding the second Maryland Brigade while its normal commander, Colonel William Richardson, was "absent." Williams thought the "Duty by no means agreeable in Quarters where there's more fateague than Danger and consequently more business than Honor." For Williams, honor could neither be served nor obtained without the risks of combat. For some of Williams' fellow regimental commanders, honor was a deeply personal affair.[19]

Captain George W. Melvin of the First Artillery reacted vigorously to an alleged slur against his personal honor in February 1814. Melvin informed his fellow regular, Major Asa B. Sizer of the Twenty-ninth Infantry, that he had heard that Sizer had "circulated a report injurious to my reputation (ie.) that I carried women of loose character out of town to a dinner and returned with them to Albany, and while in their company was guilty of disorderly conduct." Melvin was clearly incensed, and he called on the major for an "immediate answer that I may govern myself accordingly." Sizer may well have been a gossip who delighted in impugning the character and honor of fellow officers, because lieutenants John McCarty of the Twenty-third Infantry and David Foot of the

Ninth Infantry also wrote to Major Sizer that same February regarding "Reports" that were "Derogatory to our character" and charged him to answer their inquiry. Officers were not alone in their concern over matters of personal honor. Writing to Lieutenant Christopher Quarles Tompkins while incarcerated, Corporal S. Johnson of the Third Artillery believed he had been imprisoned unjustly and requested a transfer to Tompkins's command and a new court-martial to clear his name. Pleading that "I set no higher value on my life than a soldier should," Johnson forthrightly stated, "My honour is as dear to me an enlisted soldier as if I held a commission, and although my life in the strict sense of the word belongs to my country and at the disposal of any superiors, yet my honour remains my own"[20]

For the republic's soldiery, "Honor not only required a man to uphold his rank, keep his word, and demand the same of others; it also required that he resent any insult" and readily respond to it. A certain quickness of temper and readiness to resort to violence kept a "gentleman's self-esteem inviolable" and helped to sustain his independence of thought, action, and existence among his peers and society in general. That quickness of temper was readily demonstrated by Colonel John J. Hardin of the First Illinois Volunteers in November 1846. Hardin's First Illinois was one of several volunteer regiments assigned to Brigadier General John E. Wool's division in northern Mexico. Wool, a regular, tried, with mixed results, to train and discipline his volunteers. While en route to Monclova, Mexico, Wool had a "major contretemps with Colonel Hardin, during which he castigated the entire volunteer officer corps." According to Hardin's account, "Wool told him to 'go tell my men that he had confidence in them and a damned sight more than he had in me or any of my officers.'"[21]

Later, while at Monclova, Wool doubled down on the state of Illinois when he allegedly told the officers of both the First and the Second Illinois that they were "not worth a damn" and threatened them with discharges for the continued indiscipline of their regiments. Honor forced Hardin to respond to Wool's "insulting expressions respecting the officers," for to ignore them "would be degrading." The Illinoisians presented to Wool their "claim to have been gentlemen when we joined the army as volunteers, and we intend to be treated as such while we are in the service." Although the volunteers recognized Wool's "right to command us," they rejected his "right to insult us" and issued a "demand" for the "unqualified retraction of the offensive expression respecting the officers of the Illinois Regiments." The affair was not settled. Shortly after the exchange of insults and demands, Hardin was killed at Buena Vista. Hardin's conflict with Wool and his readiness to respond boldly illustrates the serious nature of military honor to all forms of soldiers. The tone of his letter was combative, but respectful. The Sucker State colonel reacted in the only way open to a republican man of honor.[22]

In his work on American democracy in the age of Andrew Jackson, Alexis de Tocqueville observed that in "democratic armies all the soldiers may become officers, and that fact makes desire for promotion general and opens almost infinite doors to military ambition." Although Tocqueville oversimplified the nature of American military promotions, it bore more than a grain of truth. An officer's "standing in society," observed the aristocrat, "almost always depends on his rank in the army." Rank supported an officer's dignity and fortune and often constituted his sole "claim to distinction" through the "military honors" he had garnered in service. The condition of "equality" and the availability of individual opportunity and self-improvement enhanced the value of "military honors" and made those military distinctions all the more valuable to the republican soldiery.[23]

In practical terms, honor advertised a man's reputation to society. To safeguard honor was to safeguard repute. In the War for Independence, some militia organizations, like the "New England companies" at Princeton and the "Philadelphia militia" were fellow townsmen. These soldiers "knew one another; they had something to prove to one another; they had their 'honor' to protect" in the army and at home. Honor stressed the bonds of loyalty and mutual respect among soldiers. It called upon men of honor to adhere voluntarily to the precepts of the code and to assume personal responsibility for their actions. It demanded of those who followed it that they keep their word in distressing circumstances and avoid quibbling and base legalisms to escape onerous responsibilities. Ultimately, honor helped bind together men from different backgrounds through an accepted and understood consanguinity of culture and ideology.[24]

Captain Joseph Bloomfield regarded the soldiers in his company of the Third New Jersey Continentals as his military "Family." He felt an "affectionate Regard" for them. Bloomfield's men were "dear" to him because they had entrusted their lives to him, and in return the captain hoped to "behave with Tenderness and humanity to them" so that he might "gain the Love and Esteem" of his company and bring "Credit" to himself and his "family" name. For these men, highly sensitive to their honor, the "challenge to behave like men was not an empty one. Courage, honor, gallantry in the service of liberty . . . defined manhood" for many Continentals and for their descendants. George Washington, after advertising to the Continental Congress his availability for command of the Continental army and then receiving an offer to do so, found it "utterly out of my power to refuse this appointment without exposing my Character to such censures as would have reflected dishonour upon myself."[25]

Seemingly echoing Washington's sentiments, Private Philip Gooch Ferguson, a Missouri volunteer serving in Mexico, sounded familiar sentiments about reputation and honor that were wholly consonant with those of the previous century. Upon enlisting with the "Rough and Ready" Company from Washington County, Ferguson "resolved" in his journal that "should I live to read over these pages in future years, there shall here be found recorded no act of mine which might bring shame on the soldier or the man." Lieutenant Carnot Posey of the Mississippi Rifles, a famed regiment in the Mexican War, believed there was "scarcely a man in our company, who would not rather sacrafice himself a victim to temerity, than to have the *slightest* imputation cast upon his *name* or character, while *waring* for the honor of their Country." Cadet Charles R. Adams, a Mississippian enrolled at West Point, hoped to "avoid the *disgrace* of being found deficient" in mathematics and so wrote to "Pa [Simeon Roe Adams] for permission to resign" from the academy. Cadet Adams was clearly pained by his decision but opted for a course of action that would allow him to preserve his honor. Dismissal was a distinct possibility for Adams, but by taking the initiative and assuming responsibility for his own removal from West Point, Adams maintained the appearance of exercising his free will, thus preserving his reputation and his honor.[26]

Writing from the arsenal at Harpers Ferry in 1861, Lieutenant Roger Jones, an officer in the Regiment of Mounted Rifles, reflected upon the secession crisis, his duty, and his honor. Jones found it a "most painful idea to have to fight against one's countrymen" and "would not willingly do it, but situated" as he was, a regular officer, Jones found that he could not "avoid it with honor." Resignedly, Jones wrote that he and his men were "determined to do our duty" and were "prepared for whatever may come."[27]

Jones was not the only regular in 1861 whose sense of honor steeled his conduct. Sergeant John S. R. Miller, a North Carolinian in the Tenth Infantry, supported the Southern states' secession and recognized the threat of civil war and the possibility of his having to suppress the rebellion as regular. As a loyal soldier and as a Southerner, Miller considered himself in a "peculiar position" but vowed that he would "not swerve from the path of duty." As Miller considered his position, he believed that if his home state of North Carolina seceded he could "claim a discharge (which I certainly will do) and then I can act without a stain upon my honor." Although service against North Carolina would be "painful," it was more important that he "stick to the path of duty and honor, and not bring shame upon my name and family."[28]

As soon as Brigadier General Albert Sidney Johnston "learned the course adopted" by Texas, he submitted his "*resignation* to the President." Until Johnston received notification of the acceptance of his resignation, however, he determined to serve "faithfully" as an officer of the regular army until he had been "properly relieved." Johnston saw "no dishonor" in his resignation, but were he to remain in regular service "without the proper animus" there would be "dishonor." Pennsylvania's George Gordon Meade remained with the regular army out of a "sense of duty because I could not with honor stay away." Meade, like his fellow regulars, found the prospect of civil war painful but found the other option, abjuring his honor by avoiding his duties and responsibilities, even more distasteful.[29]

Volunteers and militiamen were as concerned with their honor as were the regulars. Avoiding active service by joining "that home guard," advised Richard Ackerman, was disgraceful. Ackerman, a soldier in the Fifth New York, thought that the home guard was filled with the "meanest that can be kicked out" of the active regiments and by volunteering to serve in it, it "looks like saying 'You do my fighting and I'll back you' or 'I'd like to but daresn't.'" As for himself, Ackerman was not at all "bloodthirsty," but he certainly did not want to return to home as a "member of the glorious fifth which shirked duty or rather fighting." Patriotic volunteers found the idea of avoiding combat "till the war is over . . . perfectly horrible." While more than one volunteer found military service "disgusting . . . , repulsive" or "intolerable," these men gritted their way through army life because the "condition of affairs makes the presence of Every man a test of his honour and patriotism." It was more important to preserve one's honor through the hardship than to satisfy the longing for comfort.[30]

The volunteers of 1861 confronted the dilemma of reconciling their wishes for limited tenures of enlistment with the armies' manpower needs. Northern and Southern forces desperately needed great numbers of men and called upon their experienced troops to reenlist for longer terms. Thomas Corwin Honnell, a private in the Fifteenth Ohio Infantry, was troubled upon hearing the rumor that his colonel had volunteered the regiment for three years' service. Honnell did "not know what to do." He had no desire to extend his service and clearly preferred to return home, but he worried that his reputation would suffer upon his arrival at home and that it might be said of him that he was a "coward and afraid to meet the enemy." Unhappy with military life, William Augustin M. Larue of the Sixth Virginia Cavalry badly wanted to go home and marry his fiancée, Eliza Cornelia Grantham. Rather than run off to marry his sweetheart, Larue decided to "remain in state servise until our specified tim expires." To do otherwise would have been a "disonerable act." It was better to "act honorable and stand to My post iff death be the penalty" rather than to dishonor himself.[31]

Soldiers were motivated to enhance and preserve honor and pass on the reputation and its reciprocal obligations of behavior and duty to succeeding generations. They expected their descendants to follow this generalized pattern of conduct so that additional luster would attach itself to the family name. Brigadier General Anthony Wayne insisted to his wife, Mary, that his "Son must be made the first of Scholars," because this would "put him above the frowns of Fortune and enable him to make figure in the World." Scholarly endeavors and personal success alone, however, were only a small part of Wayne's expectations of his son. Wayne was anything but mad when he added that "when ever his Country may Demand his Service either in Council or the Field, I trust that he will not turn aside from Honor, Altho' the path should be marked with his fathers Blood." Calls for descendants to adhere to honorable conduct were more than personal or familial vanity to be preserved beyond the grave; they were reminders of individual obligations to enhance the intangible but ever so important reputation and standing of the family. Through this, individual actions, interests, and wants were channeled toward actions that would benefit the greatest number of people who shared a common interest and continue the improvement of family name so as to advance the interests of future generations.[32]

Bequeathing honor and enhancing personal and familial stature continued as a guiding motive for soldiers as the United States made its way through the nineteenth century. From Mexico, Tennessee's Brigadier General Gideon J. Pillow tried to explain to his son why his "Pa cannot come home . . . now as you wish without being *disgraced* and bringing *dishonour* upon his name and family." Pillow tried to convey the complexities of personal honor and repute to his son Gideon Jr. by emphasizing the significance of keeping his word. "Pa," wrote the elder Pillow, had "entered the Army to *fight* for his *country* and is the General Commanding 5000 men and if he were to come home every body would *laugh* at him, and he would be disgraced in the opinion of the world." Despite Pillow's longing to return to his "dear sweet, good" wife and "all his dear little children," he had to wait until the end of the war. Young Gideon learned from his father that the senior Pillow had "fought the Mexicans hard because it was his duty to his country to do so, and [so] that he might have *honour* and reputation with his country, and reflect credit upon his Dear wife and children." To return home would be "wrong and dishonourable."[33]

Would-be soldiers respectful of their parents' wishes or still subject to their parents' authority asked for permission to enlist "as soon as possible" so that they might go to war with comrades of their own choosing and to avoid soldiering with "dregs of the parish" militia. To serve alongside such men or to have been drafted, thought Andrew McCollam Jr. of Louisiana, would have been "very mortifying not only to me, but to the whole family." Young McCollam promptly joined St. Mary's Cannoniers, an artillery battery. Fathers like Captain James Trooper Armstrong of the Ninth Arkansas, Captain William Anderson of the Fourth South Carolina, and Lieutenant Colonel William Preston Johnston of the First Kentucky, Confederates all, "could not bear the idea of not being in this war" for fear that their "children would be ashamed" of them when in "aftertimes this war is spoken" of and they "should not have figured in it." Present and future family "honour" demanded the presence of these men in the army. Armstrong, Anderson, Johnston, and others believed that their service would be a "greater source of happiness for our posterity to say my Father did his duty in the great struggle," than to have "it said your Father only half accomplished the duties required of him." Johnston best expressed this view of honor as a familial inheritance to his wife, Rosa Duncan Johnston. This Kentucky colonel believed that his honor, his military reputation, his "name," would be a "birthright to my children."[34]

To Major General Anthony Wayne, commander of the Legion of the United States, the honor of the republic and of its army was at stake in 1793. In 1790 and 1791, the Miami Indians under Little Turtle had soundly defeated ill-trained United States forces; Wayne was determined to prepare his troops thoroughly and reassert United States authority in the Ohio country. For Wayne, the success of his mission, the "safety of the western frontiers, the reputation of the Legion, the dignity and interest of the nation all forbid a retrograde manoeuvre" by his forces "until the enemy are compelled to sue for peace." Wayne's efforts went well, and in 1794 he and the Legion triumphed over an Indian force at Fallen Timbers, Indiana. Prior to battle, Wayne conveyed his conviction to Secretary of War Henry Knox that "America will no longer be insulted with impunity," and he committed his "gallant Army" and his self to an "all-powerful and just God." Importuning troops as the armed and disciplined representatives of the nation's honor was an integral component of American military life.[35]

Toward the end of the Second Seminole War (1835–1843), both Colonel Stephen Watts Kearny of the First Dragoons and Major Ethan Allen Hitchcock of the Eighth Infantry agreed that the "interest of the Country requires that Peace be restored to Florida." The war had been an exasperating, ruinous, and "embarrassing affair" for the army and for the United States. Despite Kearny's wishes for peace, however, it was clear that the "honor of the Army is not concerned in obtaining that Peace by the purchase of the Indians." Honor, in Kearny's mind, could be served only by successfully removing the Seminole from Florida. A negotiated settlement with the Indians would vitiate the sacrifices and "tact and courage" demonstrated by the "officers and men" who had "proven themselves worthy of their Countrys notice." Honor notwithstanding, Kearny's notions were atypical of his brother officers' views on the war. Most of them hoped for a negotiated end to the conflict.[36]

National and professional honor were not the sole preserve of highly placed officers. Had not most enlisted men and junior officers sub-scribed to the rubric of honor, all calls to adhere to those precepts would have been for naught. Writing from Mexico in 1848, the Third Artillery's Captain William Austine wished "most devoutly" that the United States would "never again have occasion to invade a foreign land." Despite Austine's hope, he believed that this "war with Mexico" was "inevitable" because of Mexican insults to "our flag and citizens within their limits" and Mexico having "libel[ed] us with foreign powers." Austine saw no other choice but war. To continue to acquiesce passively to such conduct would diminish "our reputation, and as a consequent, our commerce, would have suffered vastly the world over." National honor could be re-claimed by war alone.[37]

Many regular officers bound and even conflated their own sense of personal honor, and that "reputation which is dearer to the sol-dier than his life," with that of the regular army. Americans' enduring popular fear of a standing army as a potential source of corruption or tyranny continued unabated into the nineteenth century. When Ameri-cans extolled militiamen and volunteers it was usually at the expense of the regular soldier. Regular officers were understandably sensitive to any real or perceived slights and looked for opportunities to re-deem themselves in the public eye or, at the very least, to shame the amateur soldiers. Best of all, if redemption could be accomplished to the detriment of the "Cowardly, lying and villainous Volunteers" and militia who "defame and misrepresent us," so much the better. Lieu-tenant Daniel Harvey Hill of the Fourth Artillery eagerly awaited any opportunity to knock down the volunteers and militia in the eyes of the public and in the minds of the "false-hearted Knaves in Congress." Hill's friend, Lieutenant Isaac Bowen of the First Artillery, considered the war with Mexico a chance to show Congress that the officers were not "'epauletted loafers'" or "'idle vagabonds' draining the public trea-sury," or popinjays who strutted about or lounged as their "'hireling'" soldiers, "the 'scum of society,'" toiled and drank. After the early (and unassisted) regular army victories over Mexican forces in 1846, Bowen thought that "certainly the Army must rise in public estimation after the important services it has rendered" to the country in the early days of the Mexican War.[38]

On 8 and 9 May 1846 Major General Zachary Taylor's Army of Occupation won a pair of stunning victories over General of Division Mariano Arista's Army of the North. Captain William Chetwood De Hart congratulated his friend and fellow officer of the Second Artillery, Captain Charles Ferguson Smith, on the "glorious and spirit stirring news of the victory" by Taylor's "'gallant little army.'" De Hart was clearly pleased by the "thankfulness which was expressed over and over again" by the regular army's newfound "friends (which are *now* numerous)" and by their utterances of "'Thank God! There was no *Militia* there to help them; they fought it out most nobly by themselves alone, and to them alone belong the honor and credit of the achievement'!" Moreover, De Hart was convinced that the nature of the victories had taken place under the "most fortunate circumstance." It was well, De Hart noted, that the regulars "should have beaten the enemy before the arrival of the Volunteers—Had this latter force been present, whatever might have been the facts—they would have arrogated to themselves all the credit, and then have destroyed the army."[39]

In addition to serving as a goal for character formation, honor also augmented the maintenance of military order and discipline. Acting as an adjunct to the formal rules of discipline, honor appealed to soldiers' personal and communal pride. Soldiers were confronted with the specter of public humiliation and shame for acts that might impugn their honor or that of the army or of the republic. Commanders, instead of cowing soldiers with promises of punishment, sometimes called upon their soldiers to "Pay the Strictest attention to their Duty and Exert them Selves to Learn that Discipline so Necessary to their own Honour and Safety; that they will behave with Decency to their Fellow Citizens Whose Persons and Property they were ordained to Protect and Defend; and that they will not by any unworthy Conduct Disgrace the Honourable Profession of a Soldier." Officers purposefully couched appeals to professional pride or to the "Honor of the Regiment" in terms that reminded soldiers to avoid shameful conduct and to "gain the Esteem of the Inhabitants, where ever it may be their lot to be on duty."[40]

Despite the many entreaties to honor, there were always deviants and those supreme individualists who did not submit to military order on behalf of honor, or for any other reason. Whether through acts of omission, commission, or by happenstance, the army and militia had their fair share of such soldiers. According to Colonel Andrew Hynes of the Tennessee Militia in 1814, it was in the "power of a few men, by their refractory conduct, to bring disgrace on the whole army." Sensitive to such conduct and to its ramifications, commanders went to great lengths to prevent and punish indiscipline.[41]

As he prepared to invade Canada in 1813, Major General James Wilkinson stressed to his men that the army's "character, its honor, and that of the American people are entrusted, deeply entrusted" to the care of the soldiery, and that any deviation would stain the country's repute. Wilkinson added an additional caveat to ensure compliance by men who might not be inclined to uphold national honor. Severe punishment, including "death," for "rapine and plunder" or for "marauding" was promised to all offenders. Wilkinson's admonitions about honor are not without more than a little irony. Strange stuff indeed: an appeal to honor from a traitor to his country, Spanish Agent 13.[42]

Even in the aftermath of a successful battle, soldiers' behavior was capable of devolving. Charges and countercharges by Louisiana and Kentucky volunteers against one another quickly followed the 1815 Battle of New Orleans. Men from the contending states charged one another with the "unmanly defence of their line" against British assaults. Major General Andrew Jackson's chief engineer, Major Howell O. Tatum, offered his own assessment of the row in his journal. Tatum was of the "opinion that neither of the contending parties acted with that manly bravery and fortitude their country expected of them, or that their own reputation required." Less than commendable conduct was not the sole province of volunteers, militiamen, or even enlisted men, however. Cadets at the military academy were fully capable of giving offense.[43]

On the evening of 27 July 1852, Professor Dennis Hart Mahan's "attention was arrested by a group of Cadets" at the military academy, "one or two of whom had in their mouths cigars, and from the midst of whom proceeded swearing and such blasphemous language as I should blush to repeat here even in writing." Mahan, a graduate of the academy and formerly a lieutenant of engineers, was highly vexed by the conduct of the offending cadets. Writing to a senior cadet and future major general of volunteers, James Birdseye McPherson, Mahan reported that he had "no interests apart from the Corps." The young men had dishonored themselves and the Corps of Cadets, and "as their reputation so must be mine." Mahan's sense of probity was anything but rare.[44]

At the close of 1861, Lieutenant Henry C. McCook, chaplain of the Forty-first Illinois, resigned his commission over honor and fugitive slaves. Chaplain McCook noted that particular "Officers, Lieutenants, brought into our Camp fugitive slaves who had placed themselves under their protection at the Pickets, and afterwards delivered them over to their masters receiving therefore sums ranging from Fifty to Twenty Dollars each." McCook considered the act a "gross prostitution of the honor of the Officers and of the good name of the Regiment." Turning to his commanding officer, Colonel Isaac C. Pugh, for an acceptable resolution, McCook found that his commander had no desire to act upon the matter. Refusing to "submit to share this disgrace" and believing that he could not "comfortably associate with, as officers, and feel bound to treat as gentlemen those who I believe to have forfeited every claim to consideration as either Officers or gentlemen," the chaplain forwarded his resignation, stating emphatically that he did "not desire to be one of a Regiment where *slave-trading* Officers" went unpunished. Morality and simple human justice, even if not explicitly stated, informed McCook's sense of honor. Captain John C. Kelton, assistant adjutant general for the Department of the West, noted that McCook's resignation was accepted with "much regret."[45]

Honor was as much a guide as it was a goal for soldiers. Hence it was as much a cultural imperative as it was a form of agency. Acting honorably or earning honor might very well point to individual glory, that divinely inspired element in soldiering. However, if glory was restricted to God's elect, fame was open to a much broader population of the soldiery. It required no special gift of grace or depth of learning, and its devotees were not a circumscribed group. Instead, fame's "audience" was the present and future generations of "humanity." Fame's sole demand was the individual thirst for "renown and immortality." Indeed, above all, noted Douglass Adair, "fame is a pure spur to action." The would-be possessor of fame believed that future generations would remember his "name and his actions," and that the memories of him would not soon fade and pass. Fame was immortality secularized. For the generations of American soldiers between 1775 and 1861, fame was a "dynamic element in the historical process" which called upon each man to make a "strenuous effort to *become*" a shaper, a force, and a figure of history. Desirous of history's approbation, soldiers channeled their "ambition and self-interest" toward the benefit of society.[46]

Fame is distinguished from glory because of human agency's determinative role in its attainment and enjoyment. Fame, as cultural historian Leo Braudy has noted, is "inseparable from the ideal of personal freedom" in the Western world, and as such it reinforces individual distinctiveness in society. In a phrase, fame represented a person's "liberation from powerless anonymity." According to Braudy, "America had been founded in fame." The United States' "dynamic present," as Braudy deemed the age of the American Revolution, "superseded the past of all those who made it up, and national self-consciousness was the support or crutch for the individual inspiration of each of its inhabitants." Moreover, the Continental army and the states' militias were part and parcel of an age in which "citizen-armies . . . defend a nation rather than the privileges of a particular group." Fame thus was a response of self-awareness and determinism. Man, not God as was the case of glory, became the measure and agency of his own destiny.[47]

Brigadier General Nathanael Greene, no small disciple of fame, related the 14 July 1775 arrival of "His Excellency General Washington" in camp. The Virginian, noted Greene, was "universally admired" by the men, and "Joy was visable in every countenance and, it seemed as if the Spirit of conquest breathed the Whole Army." Greene hoped that the fledgling army would model itself after Washington. He believed that "they that assume this Character and possess a happy Genius, accompanied with a prudent conduct, and fortune smiles on their endeavours, have an opportunity of traveling the shortest Road to the greatest heights of Ambition; and may the deserving obtain what their merit enables them to" do. As Greene saw things, ambition channeled and pursued properly was the key to American independence and personal fame. Major General Marie Jean Paul Joseph Roch Yves Gilbert du Motier, better known as the Marquis de Lafayette, echoed the Rhode Islander's sentiments. Above all else, the younger man wanted to do "some thing by myself, and justify that love of glory which I left be known in the world." Lafayette, an "ardent lover of laurels," freely admitted that his service represented the joining of the "pure ambition of glory" with his "other ambitions of advancement, rank, and fortune." Self-interest directed for the good of the community would reward both the soldier and society.[48]

Soldiers wrote unabashedly of their ambitions to gain fame and renown. They understood that combat was the only arena in which they could garner these public laurels. Neither warmongers nor callous brutes, these men were the products of an age that took a "romanticized view of history." Americans of the eighteenth and nineteenth centuries believed that "soldiering was an adventure; death in battle was a glorious sacrifice for country and a good cause." One soldier of the Revolution, Corporal Thomas Fanning of Colonel Samuel Blachley Webb's Additional Regiment, wrote or copied "A War Song" extolling the opportunities that a war for independence presented to the fame-seeking soldier:

> The Lightnings that Play and the thunders that roll
> With Lofty Conception Enrapture the Soul
> the Cause which we fight for let no man Disown
> for we fight for a Caus that will cloth with renown
>
> The ages to Come Shall convey his fame Down
> And the World Shall Surround with Eternal Renown
> Then Let us to arms and Encounter the foe
> Tis to bright beaming glory and Conquest we go
>
> We shall drive them from hill and from vale and from Plain
> to measure the Ocean and Sail back again
> the General who commands is the brave Washington
> With him we shall vanquish and rise to renown[49]

Ultimately, war was a chance to win fame and immortality of name. After a period of recruiting duty, Captain Benjamin Smead of the Eleventh Infantry was "glad for the opportunity to return" to his regiment and active duty. Smead's regiment had fought successfully at the 1814 battles of the Chippewa and Lundy's Lane and was sharing vicariously in the glow of the victories. He hoped for the chance to "share exploits with" those "worthy" soldiers of his regiment so that he might earn the "never fading wreaths with which their brow are already entwined."[50]

Writing half a dozen years later, Quartermaster General Thomas Sidney Jesup, an ambitious and capable regular officer, "abandoned forever the idea of a political life and of a residence in the West" in 1820 and "resolved to continue in the Army." Jesup, a thirty-two year-old brigadier general and self-confessed "votary at the shrine of ambition," was coldly honest about the passions that drove him. He could with "truth disclose" to his friend Colonel Joseph Swift Gardner of the Corps of Enginers that he was not "animated" by the "petty aspirations of the office which govern grovelling souls," or by a "thirst for power merely for its pomp, which is satisfied with a glittering exterior." Jesup knew that he possessed that "pride of character which covets applause for the good produced which aspires only to the promoting of the welfare of society and of the country."[51]

Philip St. George Cooke, colonel of the Second Dragoons, thought his life and "rank and power" were "unenviable." Although Cooke commanded one of the finest regiments in the army, he saw no opportunity for "Fame" while policing the frontier and becoming a "conqueror of Indians!" Cooke's dragoons were scattered about the western frontier in small detachments, pacifying Indians who refused to fight pitched battles. This was not the kind of warfare that led to fame. Cooke longed for a "*fair field* of battle" in a war against a "civilized foe." When Cooke got his wish, his son-in-law, Confederate brigadier general J. E. B. Stuart, humiliated him in a circuitous chase around the Union army in 1862. Stuart had won the fame that Cooke had so eagerly sought.[52]

Like Cooke, not every soldier questing after fame attained it. "There is war it seems among our western Indians," and "I am ingloriously safe," lamented the First Infantry's Captain Ethan Allen Hitchcock in 1827. Citing his company's superior arms and preparation in 1846, Captain Robert Anderson requested that his company of the Third Artillery be sent to the seat of war in Mexico. The future hero of Fort Sumter feared that the war against Mexico might be the "only chance of distinction, which may be afforded us in our life time." Lieutenant Ulysses S. Grant, regimental quartermaster of the Fourth Infantry, wrote a "protest" to Lieutenant Colonel John Garland of the same regiment while in Mexico and asked to return to his "place in the line" so that he might share in the "dangers and honors of service with my company at the front." Another young officer serving in the same war, engineer Lieutenant George Brinton McClellan, was vexed when he "found that every confounded Voluntario" serving in Mexico "ranked" him. McClellan damned the average volunteer officer as a "soldier of yesterday, a miserable thing with buttons on it, that knows nothing whatever," and decided to "resign" if he was unable to advance his *rank in this war.*" Eager for promotion, McClellan went to Mexico with "high hopes, with pleasing anticipations of distinction, of being in hard fought battles and acquiring a name and reputation as a stepping stone to a still greater eminence in some future and greater war." Frustrated in Mexico, McClellan earned a name of sorts in the Civil War.[53]

The "confounded Voluntario[s]" who so angered Lieutenant McClellan shared his hopes for fame, as well as his frustrations with the circumstances that prevented them from gaining it. William E. Mullin, a private in the First Pennsylvania Volunteers, feared that the newly elected colonel, Francis M. Wynkoop, was the "wrong man" to command the regiment and that he would prevent the Pennsylvanians from earning an "undying name." A spirit of melancholia seemed to have gripped Lieutenant Colonel Henry Clay Jr. in 1847. Writing to his father, Clay was "without the hope of any distinction" and was, therefore, "only endeavoring to avoid disgrace." Nearly despondent, Clay feared that if the Second Kentucky was "disgraced," he would "go with it" to shame, and that "Should it win distinction the fame" would devolve "upon another." Young Clay was mistaken in his fears. He won fame; however it was through his death in battle at Buena Vista in 1847.[54]

American success on the battlefield punctuated the United States' war with Mexico at every turn. Small armies competently led and made up of well-trained regulars and spirited volunteers had defeated superior Mexican forces in every engagement. Brevet promotions and public accolade had followed every battle. The fame and excitement that derived from the war were intoxicating for many men. War promised fame, adventure, and territorial expansion and it exercised a great "appeal and meaning to America's young males," especially to those who dreamed of extending slavery's dominion through filibustering. It was not solely an appeal to former volunteers or to men who had missed the war, but to the men of the army itself. Indeed, as historian Robert E. May has pointed out, it "would be wrong to exempt United States soldiers from filibustering's spell. The army held up a cultural mirror to its nation" and reflected the nation's spirit, although, as May noted, most regular army officers "disparaged" the filibusters as they upheld the "nation's honor."[55]

The pursuit of fame was not only a means to satisfy ambition, but, like glory and honor, was a guide for the actions of those who would have it. While the pursuit was an exercise in ambition and self-interest, it largely channeled those desires toward the public good, but not always. Brigadier General Thomas Sumter of the South Carolina Militia lamented the uncontrolled self-interest and avarice of his fellow Carolinians in a 1781 letter to Nathanael Greene. The Gamecock apologized to Greene for his having "discovered" what he termed an "injudicious thirst for enterprise, private Gain, or personal Glory." Sumter feared that his own "endeavour, together with the Good people of South Carolina, have not tended in the least Degree to promote the publick Good." It was not self-interest that Sumter decried, but the form that it took. As he saw things, "private Gain is the primary Object with many, and as much lament that the desire of Fame is not more sought after" by the people. Before any other consideration, self-interest had to answer first to the needs of the "publick Good"[56]

Ambition and self-interest directed toward the attainment of fame handsomely complimented the spirit of republican self-governance. "What," in the words of Brevet Major General John A. Quitman, but "motives, similar to those that prompted the soldier of republican Greece or Rome, to rally round his country's standard, and perform prodigies of valor, could have stimulated such men to subject themselves voluntarily to the deprivations, discomforts and toils of war, and to the perils and dangers of the battle field!" Quitman, a volunteer who had accorded himself well in the war with Mexico, discerned that "whatever may have been the motives, whether a patriotic desire to serve their country, the love of glory, or the ambition of personal distinction, they indicate an elementary material, from which invincible armies are constituted." American success and the fame that followed were due to personal ambition and patriotic self-interest.[57]

Achieving immortality of name and reputation seriously concerned many soldiers. Their desire for immortality seems, upon first consideration, to have been one of vanity, but this was only a part of their motivation. It was more than simple conceit that caused men to risk themselves in battle. Immortality through fame confirmed the worth of the soldier's services, reassuring him and his family that his actions had meaning and were worthy of emulation and respect by future generations. Immortality comforted the soldier's mind and quelled any doubts about his undertaking in war.

Colonel Otho Holland Williams was very much concerned about how future generations would remember American soldiers when he pondered the 1781 Battle of Eutaw Springs, South Carolina. American forces under the command of Nathanael Greene had taken part in what Williams termed "obstinate fair field fighting." Williams thought it "worthy of remark that it happened on the same spot of ground where according to the tradition of this Country, a very bloody, desperate Battle was fought, about a century ago, between the *Savage* Natives and the *barbarous* Europeans who came to disposses them of their possessions." All that remained of the then century-old battle was a "monument or mound of Earth, said to have been erected over the bodies of the brave Indians who fell in defence of their Country. Will any such honorable testimony be erected to the memory of our departed heroes?" wondered Williams.[58]

Soldiers under the command of Colonel Samuel Blachley Webb in November 1782 voiced similar concerns. Webb's men had selected him to represent their interests to Congress. Congressional and state parsimony, poor planning, and indifference had resulted in an underpaid and poorly clothed and fed army. Soldiers simply wanted redress for their legitimate grievances. They believed that the "patriotic firmness and Virtue of the Army will bear them on the most Brilliant pages of the Book of Fame with veneration and applause" to their "posterity." Webb's soldiers, the "Citizens of America in the Field," prayed that their "Conduct on this Occasion may not be marked with an Intemperate Zeal," and that they would continue to display to the "World the most Astonishing Spectacle of *persevering Patriotism* and *Virtue in distress*." Above all, they did not want to "cast a shade upon that fame, which we hold equally dear with our Lives." The Continentals, according to John Gooch, an assistant deputy quartermaster general, would indeed be remembered for their services. Gooch remarked that "their firmness and Virtue will ever make me revere them" for their service and conduct.[59]

Troops of the Continental army won the immortality that so many of them desired. Their example set a standard by which the succeeding generations of American soldiers would be judged and would judge themselves. Likewise, the soldiers who followed the Revolutionary generation hoped to set their own examples to attain immortality. William Atherton, a Kentucky private in the War of 1812 thought it "proper that the rising generation should know what their fathers suffered, and how they acted in the hour of danger; that they sustained the double character of '*Americans* and *Kentuckians*.'" Charleston, South Carolina's Washington Light Infantry, in the words of William E. Mikell, a planter, lawyer, and later private in the Third South Carolina Cavalry, served to "obtain the approbation of mankind, stamped upon the truthful tablets of history."[60]

American soldiers readily adopted glory, honor, and fame into the military ethos of republicanism. They defined themselves to their society and to posterity according to the standards of conduct conducive to attaining and maintaining these goals. Glory, honor, and fame were more than goals; they were standards of conduct that governed soldiers' behavior. The self-regulatory nature of glorious, honorable, or famous conduct had a special resonance with the character of the republic. Americans were engaged in a process of defining their role in the world and the nature of their society. They were determining the republic's place in the world according to the standards by which they chose to govern themselves. Soldiers of the republic could do no less for their own sense of self and place in the army and in society.

Epilogue

Disunion, Civil War, and Shared Ideals

South Carolina, Mississippi, Florida, Alabama, Georgia, Louisiana, and Texas, the roll call of secession as one slaveholding state after another declared its independence from the United States and overthrew the federal government within in its borders during the Secession Winter of 1860–1861. In February 1861, this "harvest of disunion" joined in a provisional confederation. The following month, the new Confederate States Congress authorized a 100,000-man army. Abraham Lincoln had yet to be inaugurated as president of the United States, and the federal government had not taken any action against the rebellious states. On 12 April 1861, South Carolina troops fired on the United States Army garrison at Fort Sumter, in Charleston Harbor. Major Robert Anderson, a Kentuckian and former slaveholder, commanded the post. Running short of supplies, unable to return effective fire, and with little hope of relief, Anderson surrendered after two days of bombardment. The following day, President Lincoln called 75,000 militiamen to the colors. In the wake of Lincoln's call to arms, Virginia, Arkansas, North Carolina, and Tennessee joined the roll call of rebellion.[1]

Northerners and Southerners rushed forward to volunteer by the hundreds of thousands. Ultimately, more than a million Americans served in the Civil War. They looked to their past, real and imagined, for inspiration. These men expressed their motives for service with a fierce intensity that spoke to the deep and abiding emotions and beliefs that they held about their republics, about being American citizens, and about being soldiers. The thoughts and beliefs of those who volunteered to fight against their fellow Americans resonated in their shared civic-martial culture, the military ethos of republicanism, one that drew inspirational, ideological, and moral sanction from the revolutionary generation's example.[2]

"Although I am a most ultra Secessionist, I am still proud of the American Flag," wrote Cadet John Pelham of Alabama. Enrolled at the United States Military Academy, Pelham resigned from it before his graduation in 1861 and offered his services to the Confederacy. Pelham quickly gained fame as a commander of horse artillery in Brigadier General J. E. B. Stuart's cavalry division in the Army of Northern Virginia. The flag, wrote Pelham, "does not belong to the North any more than to us, and has never had anything to do with our wrongs. I think that both sides ought in justice to the illustrious dead, lay it aside as a memento of our past greatness and of our Revolutionary renown." Pelham saw no contradiction or even the slightest sense of irony in simultaneously proclaiming his pride in the symbolic power of the United States' flag, the country's shared revolutionary heritage, or in being "a most ultra Secessionist." It was time for a Southern republic, thought Pelham. The United States' past seemed to provide a firm foundation for a new country and a new future. More than a few Northerners, however, disagreed with the young Alabamian's assessment even as they declared sentiments that also drew from their shared past and ideals.[3]

"Liberty or Death! Tomorrow I start" for the army, wrote George Smith Avery to his fiancée, Elizabeth Little, as he set off to enlist as a private in the Twelfth Illinois Volunteers, a three-month regiment. A mere six days after Lincoln's call for volunteers, Avery vowed "never to return until this terrible contest between freedom and anarchy shall have been brought to an end." Telling his fiancée that "I regard the rights of an American citizen dearer than life itself," Avery "for one have resolved to die rather than have one of those rights taken away." Fatalistically, the young soldier reflected that "it appears that we have hoped & prayed in vain [for a peaceful resolution]—there is no alternative left us but war." Throughout 1861, Avery's letters to Little resounded with sincere patriotic sentiments. "Can you sit unconcerned," asked Avery rhetorically, "when our liberties are invaded?" Secession threatened to devolve the country into an anarchic state of nature in which no rights were secure and individual freedom was threatened. Querying his fiancée, Avery asked Little, "Can you look in silence upon the public robery? Can you see the noble Flag of our country hurled from its proud position— trampled in the dust, & spit upon without exciting your indignation?" The answer, of course, was no. Avery's manhood, his standing as a citizen, and his own self-respect would not tolerate passivity in a time of crisis. As a result, neither Avery nor Pelham nor, indeed, hundreds of thousands of others could have done otherwise. To have stood by idly would have been to have ignored their obligations to the republic, their communities, their families, and themselves.[4]

In going to war against one another over the ideas and ideals made manifest in their culture, Americans drew on powerful symbols and language from their collective past, reminders that resonated as strongly in 1861 as they did in 1775. The Civil War generation and those preceding it judged themselves and their conduct according to norms set by the founding generation in 1775. The military ethos of republicanism was broad enough in its spectrum and flexible enough in its structure to accommodate a wide array of variations on shared themes. The culture's elasticity, its ability to hold so many distinctive voices and views, was a reminder of its vibrancy and vitality. Its expansive breadth allowed seemingly discordant thoughts to exist alongside one another without fracturing the continuity of the ethos or shortening its longevity. Indeed, the ethos's breadth and elasticity accommodated often refractive thoughts but were among the signal elements in its long life and continuity.

The durability and continuity of the military ethos of republicanism attest to its vigor and to the centrality of republicanism in American life. The historical and intellectual themes embodied in the United States' civic-military culture, which were so central to American soldiers' identity, remained constant from 1775 to 1861. Throughout these years, soldiers made sense of their place within the republic and the republic's place in the world through the agency of their military service. Beginning in 1775 and continuing through 1861, the ethos doubled as a guide and a goal that helped soldiers understand and shape the meaning and significance of their service and citizenship. Soldiers referred to and drew upon a culture that citizens and soldiers had shaped and shared for nearly a century. The military ethos of republicanism, far from producing soldiers of complacency and little reflection, reminded officers and men of their national past and future, and of the standards they had to maintain and uphold if they were to keep faith with the military element of republican citizenship.

Soldiers' shared military and civic identities, much like their shared history as Americans, were inseparable; indeed, they were inextricably bound to one another. When these soldiers contemplated their place in the republic and the meaning of their service and their citizenship in 1861, they framed their expectations and actions according to commonly held beliefs that had been firmly rooted in American society and culture since 1775. American soldiers' understanding of their military service and their citizenship informed the intellectual unity that they derived from the history and culture of the United States. Immigrants and African Americans who hoped to establish their own legitimacy as loyal citizens readily assimilated the larger patterns of this ethos, even if the broader society rejected them. There were individual, regional, and sectional variances in opinion, yet all fell within boundaries fully consistent with this civic-martial culture. By 1861, as Charles Royster has pointed out, the "Revolution's sanction of ideological war had become clear to both sections [of the country], even as they disputed the interpretation of [common] ideals." Even with the creation of the Confederacy and the dissolution of the Union by an illegitimate rebellion against the results of a constitutional election, Americans "could agree on one thing: they must shed blood. The mystic music of remembered battles might encourage rather than discourage violence in those who heard it. In nothing were both sides more American than in killing for the sake of ideals," ideals that formed the basis for a shared identity and also for disunion. Union and Confederate soldiers went to war out of a desire to preserve or to restore the union of states as they understood it.[5]

Much like the generation that went to war in 1775 with the Mother Country in order to sustain its traditional rights and privileges within the empire, most of the men who volunteered in 1861 did so out of a profound sense of conservatism, not out of a revolutionary conviction. In both wars, as well as during the intervening years and conflicts, many soldiers' views changed, but they still remained within the broader contours of the military ethos of republicanism. American citizens and soldiers idealized their beliefs over the connection between bearing arms and holding citizenship. Soldiers defined themselves as republicans through their service. From 1775 to 1861, American military values were part of the larger ideological and philosophical constructs of American society. Understanding the military ethos of American republicanism sheds light on the broader landscape of American political, social, and intellectual life then and now.

American citizens have expressed pride in the performance of their armed forces over the past several years. Small regular forces, bolstered by the reserves and the National Guard and joined by small contingents of allied military forces, have waged long, grinding wars involving regime change, occupation, irregular warfare, counterinsurgency, and nation building in Iraq and Afghanistan. They have waged numerous smaller, often obscure actions across the face of the globe. In the wake of the United States' change of mission in Iraq and Afghanistan it is worth reflecting upon the civic-martial tradition that informed American military service from the country's founding in war through the opening year of the Civil War. In light of the wars in Iraq and Afghanistan, it is an appropriate time to consider the United States' civic-military tradition and how it shaped American soldiers' identities in the country's formative decades.[6]

NOTES

OHS Ohio Historical Society, Columbus

SHC Southern Historical Collection, Manuscripts Department, Wilson Library, University of North Carolina, Chapel Hill

SCHS South Carolina Historical Society, Charleston

SCL South Caroliniana Library, University of South Carolina, Columbia

SHSW State Historical Society of Wisconsin, Madison

TNSL Tennessee State Library and Archives, Nashville

TULANE Howard-Tilton Memorial Library, Tulane University, New Orleans

TXSL Texas State Library and Archives, Austin

USAMHI United States Army Military History Institute, Carlisle Barracks, Pennsylvania

USMA Special Collections and Archives, Cadet Library, United States Military Academy, West Point

UTA Special Collections, University of Texas at Arlington Library

UVA Special Collections, University of Virginia Library, Charlottesville

VHS Virginia Historical Society, Richmond

WLCL William L. Clements Library, University of Michigan, Ann Arbor

WMC Special Collections, Earl Gregg Swem Library, College of William and Mary Library, Williamsburg

WRC Williams Research Center of the Historic New Orleans Collection, New Orleans

PREFACE

1 James Wright, *Those Who Have Borne the Battle: A History of America's Wars and Those Who Fought Them* (New York: Public Affairs, 2012), 13–14, 19, 23.

2 See Paul Taylor, ed., *The Military-Civilian Gap: War and Sacrifice in the Post 9/11 Era* (Washington, DC: Pew Research Center, 2011). On United States civil-military relations and military views of American society, see Samuel P. Huntington, *The Soldier and the State: The Theory and the State of Civil-Military Relations* (Cambridge, MA: Belknap Press of Harvard University, 1957); Morris Janowitz, *The Professional Soldier: A Social and Political Portrait* (New York: Free Press, 1971); Richard H. Kohn, ed., *The United States Military under the Constitution of the United States, 1789–1989* (New York: New York University Press, 1991); Eliot A. Cohen, *Supreme Command: Soldiers, Statesmen, and Leadership in Wartime* (New York: Anchor Books, 2003); Thomas S. Langston, *Uneasy Balance: Civil-Military Relations in Peacetime America since 1783* (Baltimore: Johns Hopkins University Press, 2003); Andrew J. Bacevich, *The New American Militarism: How Americans Are Seduced by War* (New York: Oxford University Press, 2005); Suzanne C. Neilson and Don M. Snider, eds., *American Civil-Military Relations: The Soldier*

and the State in a New Era (Baltimore: Johns Hopkins University Press, 2009); and Mackubin Thomas Edwards, *US Civil-Military Relations After 9/11: Renegotiating the Civil-Military Bargain* (New York: Continuum, 2011).

3 Earl J. Hess, in *The Union Soldier in Battle: Enduring the Ordeal of Combat* (Lawrence: University Press of Kansas, 1997), convincingly argued for the strength, breadth, and depth of the shared belief system of Union soldiers. It was so pervasive and accepted that few soldiers needed to enunciate fully all of its principles.

4 Jack C. Lane, "Ideology and the American Military Experience: A Reexamination of Early American Attitudes toward the Military," in *Soldiers and Civilians: The U. S. Army and the American People: The U. S. Army and the American People*, ed. Garry D. Ryan and Timothy K. Nenninger (Washington, DC: National Archives and Records Administration, 1987), 17; Sarah J. Purcell, *Sealed with Blood: War, Sacrifice, and Memory in Revolutionary America* (Philadelphia: University of Pennsylvania Press, 2002), 3.

INTRODUCTION

1 On a practical level, the expenses associated with regular armies and the nation's physical separation from Europe demanded and allowed the maintenance of a small professional establishment. However, these considerations should not be construed as the primary motives for the size and organization of the United States' military establishment.

2 Officer resignation averaged less than 4 percent per annum between 1823 and 1859. William B. Skelton, *An American Profession of Arms* (Lawrence: University Press of Kansas, 1992), 216. On the eve of the Civil War, there were only 1,108 officers in the Regular Army, 313 of whom resigned. Something over 15,000 enlisted men comprised the rank and file. Russell F. Weigley, *History of the United States Army* (New York: Macmillan, 1967), 199; Marcus Cunliffe, *Soldiers and Civilians: The Martial Spirit in America, 1775–1865* (Boston: Little, Brown, 1968; reprint, New York: Free Press, 1973), 26, 17, xii. Although regulars often did most of the fighting or outnumbered volunteers and militiamen in certain theaters or campaigns, their overall numbers paled when "nine out of ten infantrymen in the War of 1812 were militiamen. Only one out of ten foot soldiers was a militiaman in the Mexican War; three were Regulars, and six were war volunteers." John K. Mahon and Roman Danysh, *Infantry*, pt. 1, *Regular Army* (Washington, DC: Office of the Chief of Military History, 1972), 23.

3 See Bernard Bailyn, *The Ideological Origins of the American Revolution*, enl. ed. (Cambridge, MA: Belknap Press of Harvard University, 1992); Gordon S. Wood, *The Creation of the American Republic, 1776–1787* (Chapel Hill: University of North Carolina Press, 1969; reprint, New York: W. W. Norton for the Institute of Early American History and Culture, 1972); Gordon S. Wood, *The Radicalism of the American Revolution* (New York: Alfred A. Knopf, 1992); and Michal Jan Rozbicki, *Culture and Liberty in the Age of the American Revolution* (Charlottesville: University of Virginia Press, 2011). There is a lacuna in studies

examining American identity and American styles of warfare. John Grenier, *The First Way of War: American War Making on the Frontier* (New York: Cambridge University Press, 2005), 222.

4   Cunliffe, *Soldiers and Civilians*, 65, 68.

5   Jeremy Black, *War and the Cultural Turn* (Malden, MA: Polity, 2012), 10, 15.

6   See Edmund S. Morgan, *Inventing the People: The Rise of Popular Sovereignty in England and America* (New York: W. W. Norton, 1988) on the place, role, utility, and value of fictions; Rozbicki, *Culture and Liberty*, 117, 118, 115; Charles Royster, "Founding a Nation in Blood: Military Conflict and American Nationality," in *Arms and Independence: The Military Character of the American Revolution*, ed. Ronald Hoffman and Peter J. Albert (Charlottesville: University Press of Virginia, 1984), 25, 30. For a review and incisive consideration on the use, misuse, and nature of the recent cultural bent in military history, see Jeremy Black, *War and the Cultural Turn* (Malden, MA: Polity, 2012). Edward Tabor Linenthal, *Sacred Ground: Americans and Their Battlefields, Lexington and Concord, The Alamo, Gettysburg, The Little Bighorn, Pearl Harbor* (Champaign: University of Illinois Press, 1991) is a thoughtful reflection on war and American identity. Jon Butler, *Becoming America: The Revolution before 1776* (Cambridge, MA: Harvard University Press, 2000) contended that a modern American identity had emerged before the Revolution. See David Hackett Fischer, *Albion's Seed: Four British Folkways in America* (New York: Oxford University Press, 1989) for a thoroughgoing examination of Britishness in North America.

7   Americans' creation of memory as a bond and means of instilling a national identity following the War for Independence is the focus of Sarah J. Purcell, *Sealed with Blood: War, Sacrifice, and Memory in Revolutionary America* (Philadelphia: University of Pennsylvania Press, 2002).

8   Joyce Appleby, "Republicanism in Old and New Contexts," *William and Mary Quarterly*, 3rd ser., 43, no. 1 (January 1986): 21–23; Daniel T. Rodgers, "Republicanism: The Career of a Concept," *Journal of American History* 79, no. 1 (June 1992): 38; Black, *War and the Cultural Turn*, 42, describes it as "Culture: Malleable, Nebulous, but Useful," in a particularly apt section heading. For the breadth and depth of Americans' views see Joyce Appleby, ed., "Republicanism in the History and Historiography of the United States," *American Quarterly* 37, no. 4 (Autumn 1985); Andy Doolen, "Early American Civics: Rehistoricizing the Power of Republicanism," *American Literary History* 19, no. 1 (Spring 2007): 120–140. Michael Kammen, *People of Paradox: An Inquiry Concerning the Origins of American Civilization* (1972; reprint, Ithaca, NY: Cornell University Press, 1990) considers the often contradictory nature of American culture and civilization.

9   Joyce Appleby, "Republicanism and Ideology," *American Quarterly* 37, no. 4 (Autumn 1985): 461; Robert Shalhope, "Republicanism and Early American Historiography," *William and Mary Quarterly*, 3rd ser., 39, no. 2 (April 1982): 356; Jean Baker, "From Belief into Culture: Republicanism in the Antebellum North,"

American Quarterly 37, no. 4 (Autumn 1985): 536, 542, 549. See Rodgers, "Republicanism: The Career of a Concept," 11–38, for an analysis of the arc of republicanism. The history of republicanism is far too extensive to list in any definitive sense or treat fully in an endnote. That notwithstanding, there are a number of salient works in the field: Bailyn, *Ideological Origins of the American Revolution*; Isaac Kramnick, *Bolingbroke and His Circle: The Politics of Nostalgia in the Age of Walpole* (Cambridge, MA: Harvard University Press, 1968); Wood, *Creation of the American Republic*; Robert Shalhope, "Toward a Republican Synthesis: The Emergence of an Understanding of Republicanism in American Historiography," *William and Mary Quarterly*, 3rd ser., 29 (January 1972): 49–80; J. G. A. Pocock, *The Machiavellian Moment: Florentine Political Thought and the Atlantic Republican Tradition* (Princeton, NJ: Princeton University Press, 1975); Lance Banning, *The Jeffersonian Persuasion: Evolution of a Party Ideology* (Ithaca, NY: Cornell University Press, 1978); Drew R. McCoy, *The Elusive Republic: Political Economy in Jeffersonian America* (Chapel Hill: University of North Carolina Press, 1980); James T. Kloppenberg, "The Virtues of Liberalism: Christianity, Republicanism, and Ethics in American Political Discourse," *Journal of American History* 74, no. 1 (June 1987): 9–33; J.G.A. Pocock, "Between Gog and Magog: The Republican Thesis and the *Ideologia Americana*," *Journal of the History of Ideas* 48, no. 2 (April–June 1987): 325–346; Major L. Wilson, "Republicanism and the Idea of Party in the Jacksonian Period," *Journal of the Early Republic* 8 (1988): 419–432; Isaac Kramnick, *Republicanism and Bourgeois Radicalism: Political Ideology in Late-Eighteenth Century England and America* (Ithaca, NY: Cornell University Press, 1990); Wood, *Radicalism of the American Revolution*; Joyce Appleby, *Liberalism and Republicanism in the Historical Imagination* (Cambridge, MA: Harvard University Press, 1992); Paul A. Rahe, *Republics Ancient and Modern: Classical Republicanism and the American Revolution* (Chapel Hill: University of North Carolina Press, 1992); Marc W. Kruman, "The Second American Party System and the Transformation of Revolutionary Republicanism," *Journal of the Early Republic* 12 (1992): 509–537; Major L. Wilson, "The 'Country' versus the 'Court': A Republican Consensus and Party Debate in the Bank War," *Journal of the Early Republic* 15 (1995): 619–647.

10 Baker, "From Belief into Culture," 535, 538–39, 549–50; James Oakes, "From Republicanism to Liberalism: Ideological Change and the Crisis of the Old South," *American Quarterly* 37, no. 4 (Autumn 1985): 551–571; John Hope Franklin, *The Militant South, 1800–1861* (Cambridge, MA: Harvard University Press, 1956); David F. Ericson, "The Nullification Crisis, American Republicanism, and the Force Bill Debate," *Journal of Southern History* 61, no. 2 (May 1995): 249–270; Thomas E. Rodgers, "Billy Yank and G. I. Joe: An Exploratory Essay on the Sociopolitical Dimensions of Soldier Motivation," *Journal of Military History* 69, no. 1 (January 2005): 93–121.

11 Richard H. Kohn, "The American Soldier: Myths in Need of History," in *Soldiers and Civilians: The U. S. Army and the American People*, ed. Garry D. Ryan and

Timothy K. Nenninger (Washington, DC: National Archives and Records Administration, 1987), 53, 54.

12 Ibid; Richard H. Kohn, "The Social History of the American Soldier: A Review and Prospectus for Research," *American Historical Review* 86 (June 1981): 556; Andrew J. Goodpaster, "West Point, the Army, and Society: American Institutions in Constellation," in Ryan and Nenninger, *Soldiers and Civilians: The U. S. Army and the American People*, 4–6.

13 17 June 1775, 20 June 1775, *Journals of the Continental Congress*, vol. 2, *10 May–20 September 1775*, ed. Worthington Chauncey Ford (Washington, DC: Government Printing Office, 1905), 96, 100–101.

14 14 June 1775, 30 June 1775, *Journals of the Continental Congress*, 2:90, 111–112; Robert K. Wright, *The Continental Army* (Washington, DC: U.S. Army Center of Military History, 1983), 25; Goodpaster, "West Point, the Army, and Society," 4–6; Kohn, "The American Soldier: Myths in Need of History," 53, 54.

15 Wayne E. Lee, "Mind and Matter—Cultural Analysis in American Military History: A Look at the State of the Field," *Journal of American History* 93, no. 4 (March 2007): 1116–1142; Rozbicki, *Culture and Liberty*, 7; Edward M. Coffman, *The Old Army: A Portrait of the American Army in Peacetime, 1784–1898* (New York: Oxford University Press, 1986), vii–viii; Skelton, *An American Profession of Arms*; Richard H. Kohn, "The Social History of the American Soldier: A Review and Prospectus for Research," *American Historical Review* 86, no. 3 (June 1981): 553–567; Kohn, "The American Soldier: Myths in Need of History," 53, 54; Don Higginbotham, "The Early American Way of War: Reconnaissance and Appraisal," *William and Mary Quarterly*, 3rd ser., 44, no. 2 (April 1987): 230–273; Maurice Matloff, "The Nature and Scope of Military History," in *New Dimensions in Military History: An Anthology*, ed. Russell F. Weigley (San Rafael, CA: Presidio, 1975), 388, 389–390. Examples of these broadened approaches include, but are not limited to, Gerald F. Linderman, *Embattled Courage: The Experience of Combat in the American Civil War* (New York: Free Press, 1987); John Shy, "The Cultural Approach to the History of War," *Journal of Military History* 57, no. 5 (October 1993): 13–26; Reid Mitchell, *The Vacant Chair: The Northern Soldier Leaves Home* (New York: Oxford University Press, 1993); Rita Roberts, "Patriotism and Political Criticism: The Evolution of Political Consciousness in the Mind of a Black Revolutionary Soldier," in "African-American Culture in the Eighteenth-Century," ed. Rose Zimbardo and Benilde Montgomery, special issue, *Eighteenth-Century Studies* 27, no. 4, (Summer 1994): 569–588; Samuel J. Watson, "Religion and Combat Motivation in the Confederate Armies," *Journal of Military History* 58, no. 1 (January 1994): 29–55; Holly A. Mayer, *Belonging to the Army: Camp Followers and Community during the American Revolution* (Columbia: University of South Carolina Press, 1996); Joseph Allan Frank, *With Ballot and Bayonet: The Political Socialization of American Civil War Soldiers* (Athens: University of Georgia Press, 1998); Kurt Daniel Kortenhof, "Republican Ideology and Wartime Reality: Thomas Mifflin's Struggle as the First Quartermaster General of the Continental

Army, 1775–1778," *Pennsylvania Magazine of History and Biography* 122, no. 3 (July 1998): 179–210; Michael A. McDonnell, "Popular Mobilization and Political Culture in Revolutionary Virginia: The Failure of the Minutemen and the Revolution from Below," *Journal of American History* 85, no. 3 (December 1998): 946–981; Mark A. Weitz, "Drill, Training, and the Combat Performance of the Civil War Soldier: Dispelling the Myth of the Poor Soldier, Great Fighter," *Journal of Military History* 62, no. 2 (April 1998): 263–289; John Resch, *Suffering Soldiers: Revolutionary War Veterans, Moral Sentiment, and Political Culture in the Early Republic* (Amherst: University of Massachusetts Press, 1999); R. Claire Snyder, *Citizen-Soldiers and Manly Warriors: Military Service and Gender in the Civic Republican Tradition* (Lanham, MD: Rowman and Littlefield, 1999); Joseph Allan Frank and Barbara Duteau, "Measuring the Political Articulateness of United States Civil War Soldiers: The Wisconsin Militia," *Journal of Military History* 64, no. 1 (January 2000): 53–77; Edward M. Coffman, "The Duality of the American Military Tradition: A Commentary," *Journal of Military History* 64, no. 4 (October 2000): 967–980; J. C. A. Stagg, "Soldiers in Peace and War: Comparative Perspectives on the Recruitment of the United States Army, 1802–1815," *William and Mary Quarterly*, 3rd ser., 57, no. 1 (January 2000): 79–120; Charles E. Brooks, "The Social and Cultural Dynamics of Soldiering in Hood's Texas Brigade," *Journal of Southern History* 67, no. 3 (August 2001): 535–572; Richard F. Miller, "Brahmin Janissaries: John A. Andrew Mobilizes Massachusetts' Upper Class for the Civil War," *New England Quarterly* 75, no. 2 (June 2002): 204–234; Purcell, *Sealed with Blood: War*; Gregory T. Knouff, *The Soldiers' Revolution: Pennsylvanians in Arms and the Forging of American Identity* (University Park: Pennsylvania State University Press, 2003); Mary Ellen Rowe, *Bulwark of the Republic: The American Militia in [the] Antebellum West* (Westport, CT: Praeger, 2003); Christopher P. Magra, "'Soldiers . . . Bred to the Sea': Maritime Marblehead, Massachusetts, and the Origins and Progress of the American Revolution," *New England Quarterly* 77, no. 4 (December 2004): 531–562; Amy S. Greenberg, *Manifest Manhood and the Antebellum American Empire* (New York: Cambridge University Press, 2005); Harry S. Laver, *Citizens More Than Soldiers: The Kentucky Militia and Society in the Early Republic* (Lincoln: University of Nebraska Press, 2007); Ann M. Little, *Abraham in Arms: War and Gender in Colonial New England* (Philadelphia: University of Pennsylvania Press, 2007); Marc Milner, "In Search of the American Way of War: The Need for a Wider National and International Context," *Journal of American History* 93, no. 4 (March 2007): 1151–1153; John Resch and Walter Sargent, eds., *War and Society in the American Revolution* (DeKalb: Northern Illinois University Press, 2007); Mark S. Schantz, *Awaiting the Heavenly Country: The Civil War and America's Culture of Death* (Ithaca, NY: Cornell University Press, 2008); Lorien Foote, *Gentlemen and the Roughs: Violence, Honor, and Manhood in the Union Army* (New York: New York University Press, 2010); George C. Rable, *God's Almost Chosen Peoples: A Religious History of the American Civil War* (Chapel Hill: University of North Carolina

Press, 2010); Lee, *Barbarians and Brothers: Anglo-American Warfare, 1500–1865* (New York: Oxford University Press, 2011); Joshua M. Smith, "The Yankee Soldier's Might: The District of Maine and the Reputation of the Massachusetts Militia, 1800–1812," *New England Quarterly* 84, no. 2 (June 2011): 234–264; Nicole Eustace, *1812: War and the Passions of Patriotism* (Philadelphia: University of Philadelphia Press, 2012).

16 Rozbicki, *Culture and Liberty*, 7, 86.

17 Nate Probasco, "The Role of Commoners and Print in Elizabethan England's Acceptance of Firearms," *Journal of Military History* 76, no. 2 (April 2012): 357; Keith Roberts, *Cromwell's War Machine: The New Model Army, 1646–1660* (Barnsley, UK: Pen and Sword, 2005), 42–47; Steven C. Eames, *Rustic Warriors: Warfare and the Provincial Soldier on the New England Frontier, 1689–1748* (New York: New York University Press, 2011), 21–47.

18 Lindsay Boynton, *The Elizabethan Militia, 1588–1638* (London: Routledge and Kegan Paul, 1967), 37–38, 91–92, 96–106, 110, 175–176, 291–293; J. R. Western, *The English Militia in the Eighteenth Century: The Story of a Political Issue, 1660–1802* (London: Routledge and Kegan Paul, 1967); Marie L. Ahearn, *The Rhetoric of War: Training Day, the Militia, and the Military Sermon* (New York: Greenwood, 1989), 17–18; Douglas Edward Leach, *Arms for Empire: A Military History of the British Colonies in North America, 1607–1763* (New York: Macmillan, 1973), 7–38; Kyle F. Zelner, *A Rabble in Arms: Massachusetts Towns and Militiamen in King Philip's War* (New York: New York University Press, 2009), 15–39.

19 Zelner, *A Rabble in Arms*, 8–10; John E. Ferling, *A Wilderness of Miseries: War and Warriors in Early America* (Westport, CT: Greenwood, 1980), 78–79.

20 Ferling, *A Wilderness of Miseries*, 82, 91, 170, 201.

21 Fred Anderson, *A People's Army: Massachusetts Soldiers and Society in the Seven Years' War* (Chapel Hill: University of North Carolina Press for the Institute of Early American History and Culture, 1984), 39, 195; Little, *Abraham in Arms*, 2, 3, 14, 24–25, 166, 167.

22 Anderson, *A People's Army*, viii. See also James Titus, *The Old Dominion at War: Society, Politics, and Warfare in Late Colonial Virginia* (Columbia: University of South Carolina Press, 1991), for a study of provincial Virginia soldiers in the Seven Years' War; John Shy, *Toward Lexington: The Role of the British Army in the Coming of the American Revolution* (Princeton, NJ: Princeton University Press, 1965); Leach, *Arms for Empire*; Douglas Edward Leach, *Roots of Conflict: British Armed Forces and Colonial Americans, 1677–1783* (Chapel Hill: University of North Carolina Press, 1986); and Sylvia R. Frey, *The British Soldier in America: A Social History of Military Life in the Revolutionary Period* (Austin: University of Texas Press, 1981), for an understanding of the British Army in North America.

23 Anderson, *A People's Army*, 168.

24 S. E. Finer, *The Man on Horseback: The Role of the Military in Politics*, 2nd ed., rev., enl., and updated (Boulder, CO: Westview, 1962), 7, 29.

25 Don Higginbotham, *The War for American Independence: Military Attitudes, Policies, and Practice, 1763–1789* (New York: Macmillan, 1971), 93, 404, 413.

26 Charles Royster, *A Revolutionary People at War: The Continental Army and American Character, 1775–1783* (Chapel Hill: University of North Carolina Press, 1979; reprint, New York: W. W. Norton for the Institute of Early American History and Culture, 1981), vii, 3, 373–378; Edward C. Papenfuse and Gregory A. Stiverson, "General Smallwood's Recruits: The Peacetime Career of the Revolutionary War Private," *William and Mary Quarterly*, 3rd ser., 30 (1973): 117–132; James Kirby Martin and Mark Edward Lender, *A Respectable Army: The Military Origins of the Republic, 1763–1789*, 2nd ed. (Arlington Heights, IL: Harlan Davidson, 2006).

27 Don Higginbotham, *War and Society in Revolutionary America: The Wider Dimensions of Conflict* (Columbia: University of South Carolina Press, 1988), 97, 99; Caroline Cox, *A Proper Sense of Honor: Service and Sacrifice in George Washington's Army* (Chapel Hill: University of North Carolina Press, 2004), 73–117.

28 Richard H. Kohn, *Eagle and Sword: The Federalists and the Creation of the Military Establishment in America, 1783–1802* (New York: Free Press, 1975), 284. For institutional histories of the states' militias see John K. Mahon, *History of the Militia and the National Guard* (New York: Macmillan, 1983); Jerry Cooper, *The Rise of the National Guard: The Evolution of the American Militia, 1865–1920* (Lincoln: University of Nebraska Press, 1997); and Michael D. Doubler, *Civilian in Peace, Soldier in War: The Army National Guard, 1636–2000* (Lawrence: University Press of Kansas, 2003).

29 Lawrence Delbert Cress, *Citizens in Arms: The Army and the Militia in American Society to the War of 1812* (Chapel Hill: University of North Carolina Press, 1982), xi. See also John Todd White, "Standing Armies in Time of War: Republican Theory and Military Practice during the American Revolution" (PhD diss., George Washington University, 1978). William H. Gaines surveyed the organization and recruiting efforts for the new armies in "The Forgotten Army: Recruiting for a National Emergency (1799–1800)," *Virginia Magazine of History and Biography* 56 (1948): 267–279.

30 See Robert Gough, "Officering the American Army, 1798," *William and Mary Quarterly*, 3rd ser., 43, no. 3 (July 1986): 460–71, for a quantitative examination of the men thought suitable for appointment as the army's senior generals. For a discussion of West Point and treasonous alumni see James Tyrus Seidule, "'Treason is Treason': Civil War Memory at West Point, 1861–1902," *Journal of Military History* 76, no. 2 (April 2012): 427–452; Theodore J. Crackel, "The Founding of West Point: Thomas Jefferson and the Politics of Security," *Armed Forces and Society* 12, no. 4 (Summer 1981): 529–543; Theodore J. Crackel, "Jefferson, Politics, and the Army: An Examination of the Military Peace Establishment Act of 1802," *Journal of the Early Republic* 2 (1982): 21–38; Theodore J. Crackel, *Mr. Jefferson's Army: Political and Social Reform of the Military Establishment, 1801–1809* (New York: New York University Press, 1987). See also

Samuel J. Watson, "Developing 'Republican Machines': West Point and the Struggle to Render the Officer Corps Safe for America" in *Thomas Jefferson's Military Academy: Founding West Point*, ed. Robert M. S. McDonald (Charlottesville: University of Virginia Press, 2004), 154–181, which suggests limits to the Academy's early success; Samuel J. Watson, *Jackson's Sword: The Army Officer Corps on the American Frontier, 1810–1821* (Lawrence: University Press of Kansas, 2012); Samuel J. Watson, *Peacekeepers and Conquerors: The Army Officer Corps on the American Frontier, 1821–1846* (Lawrence: University Press of Kansas, 2013).

31 For incisive examinations of the war see Donald R. Hickey, *The War of 1812: A Forgotten Conflict* (Urbana: University of Illinois Press, 1989); Alan Taylor, *The Civil War of 1812: American Citizens, British Subjects, Irish Rebels, & Indian Allies* (New York: Alfred A. Knopf, 2010); Stagg, *The War of 1812: Conflict for a Continent* (New York: Cambridge University Press, 2012); Troy Bickham, *The Weight of Vengeance: The United States, the British Empire, and the War of 1812* (New York: Oxford University Press, 2012); Cress, *Citizens in Arms*; Stagg, "Soldiers in Peace and War," 79–120; Reginald C. Stuart, *Civil-Military Relations during the War of 1812* (Santa Barbara, CA: ABC-Clio, 2009); Robert P. Wettemann, Jr., *Privilege vs. Equality: Civil-Military Relations in the Jacksonian Era, 1815–1845* (Santa Barbara, CA: ABC-Clio, 2009).

32 Kenneth Otis McCreedy, "Palladium of Liberty: The American Militia System, 1815–1861" (PhD diss., University of California, Berkeley, 1991) and Mark Pitcavage, "An Equitable Burden: The Decline of the State Militias, 1783–1858" (PhD diss., Ohio State University, 1995) examine widespread militia service and its decline against the backdrop of politics, continental expansion, citizenship, and individual military responsibility. Don Higginbotham, *George Washington and the American Military Tradition* (Athens: University of Georgia Press, 1985), 12.

33 Dean Paul Baker, "The Partridge Connection: Alden Partridge and Southern Military Education" (PhD diss., University of North Carolina, Chapel Hill, 1986); *The Eclaireur, a military journal* . . . . 3 vols., ed. John Watts De Peyster and Augustus T. Cowman (Hyde Park, NY: Platt and Schram, 1853–1856); *New York Military Magazine; Devoted to the Interests of the Militia Throughout the Union*, vol. 1, ed. William W. Tompkins (New York: Labree and Stockton, 1841).

34 Robert W. Johannsen, *To the Halls of the Montezumas: The Mexican War in the American Imagination* (New York: Oxford University Press, 1985), 30, 40.

35 Johannsen, *To the Halls of the Montezumas*, 49, 51, 112, 170, 281; Paul Foos, *A Short, Offhand, Killing Affair: Soldiers and Social Conflict in the Mexican-American War* (Chapel Hill: University of North Carolina Press, 2002), 33.

36 James M. McCaffrey, *Army of Manifest Destiny: The American Soldier in the Mexican War, 1846–1848* (New York: New York University Press, 1992), 31, 68, 79, 210. The underside of American imperialism is highlighted in Robert E. May, *Manifest Destiny's Underworld: Filibustering in Antebellum America* (Chapel Hill: University of North Carolina Press, 2002).

37 Richard Bruce Winders, *Mr. Polk's Army: The American Military Experience in the Mexican War* (College Station: Texas A&M University Press, 1997), 65, 78, 64, 14. See also John C. Pinheiro, *Manifest Ambition: James K. Polk and Civil-Military Relations during the Mexican War* (Santa Barbara, CA: ABC-Clio, 2007).

38 Anonymous reviewer to author, e-mailed manuscript review, 14 April 2014; William B. Skelton, "The Army in the Age of the Common Man, 1815–1845," in *Against All Enemies: Interpretations of American Military History from Colonial Times to the Present* (New York: Greenwood, 1986), 106. See also Coffman, *The Old Army*, 1–211, on the army's isolation. Francis Paul Prucha, *Broadax and Bayonet: The Role of the United States Army in the Development of the Northwest, 1815–1860* (Madison: State Historical Society of Wisconsin, 1953); Francis Paul Prucha, *The Sword of the Republic: The United States Army on the Frontier, 1783–1846* (New York: Macmillan, 1969), xvi; Robert M. Utley, *Frontiersmen in Blue: The United States Army and the Indian, 1848–1865* (New York: Macmillan, 1967). See also Norman W. Caldwell, "The Frontier Army Officer, 1794–1814," *Mid-America: An Historical Review* 37 (April 1955): 101–128; Robert P. Wettemann Jr. "A Part or Apart: The Alleged Isolation of Antebellum U.S. Army Officers," *American Nineteenth Century History* 7, no. 2 (June 2006): 193–217.

39 Watson, *Jackson's Sword*; Watson, *Peacekeepers and Conquerors*; William H. Goetzmann, *Army Exploration in the American West, 1803–1863* (New Haven, CT: Yale University Press, 1959); Marilyn Anne Kindred, "The Army Officer Corps and the Arts: Artistic Patronage and Practice in America, 1820–85" (PhD diss., University of Kansas, 1981).

40 Reviewer to author, 14 April 2014; Michael L. Tate, "The Multi-Purpose Army on the Frontier: A Call for Further Research," in *The American West: Essays in Honor of W. Eugene Hollon*, ed. Ronald Lora (Toledo, OH: University of Toledo Press, 1980), 171–208; Michael L. Tate, *The Frontier Army in the Settlement of the West* (Norman: University of Oklahoma Press, 1999); Durwood Ball, *Army Regulars on the Frontier, 1848–1861* (Norman: University of Oklahoma Press, 2001); Robert Wooster, *The American Military Frontiers: The United States Army in the West, 1783–1900* (Albuquerque: University of New Mexico Press, 2009).

41 Gerald F. Linderman, *Embattled Courage: The Experience of Combat in the American Civil War* (New York: Macmillan, Free Press, 1987), 2; Earl J. Hess, *The Union Soldier in Battle: Enduring the Ordeal of Combat* (Lawrence: University Press of Kansas, 1997); Earl J. Hess, *Liberty, Virtue, and Progress: Northerners and Their War for the Union* (New York: New York University Press, 1988), 1, 2, 13.

42 Ricardo A. Herrera, "Self-Governance and the American Citizen as Soldier, 1775–1861," *Journal of Military History* 65, no. 1 (January 2001): 21–52; Skelton, *American Profession of Arms*, xv; Daniel T. Rodgers, "Republicanism: The Career of a Concept," *Journal of American History* 79 (June 1992): 11–38; Rozbicki, *Culture and Liberty*, 8; Purcell, *Sealed with Blood*, 16. Franklin, in *The Militant South*, saw a distinctive antebellum Southern character, which developed in

response to social, political, and economic changes. He did not, however, satisfactorily address the shared ideological bedrock upon which American intellectuals and others based their beliefs and conduct. Cunliffe's *Soldiers and Civilians* disputed Franklin's arguments for a distinctively militant Southern character. See Mark Wahlgren Summers, in "'Freedom and Law Must Die Ere They Sever': The North," in *Why the Civil War Came*, ed. Gabor Boritt (New York, 1996), 177–200.

CHAPTER 1. SERVICE, SACRIFICE, AND DUTY

1 John A. Logan, *The Volunteer Soldier of America, with Memoir of the Author and Military Reminiscences from General Logan's Private Journal* (Chicago: R. S. Peale, 1887), 90, 88, 380; John Polley, 1775, Orderly Book, Orderly Book Collection, WLCL. On the gendered equation of soldiering, republicanism, and masculinity in the American tradition see R. Claire Snyder, *Citizen-Soldiers and Manly Warriors: Military Service and Gender in the Civic Republic Tradition* (Lanham, MD: Rowman and Littlefield, 1999), 1–2, 81, 85–87.

2 Robert E. Shalhope, "Douglass Adair and the Historiography of Republicanism," in *Fame and the Founding Fathers: Essays by Douglass Adair*, ed. Trevor Colbourn (New York: W. W. Norton for the Institute of Early American History and Culture, 1974), xxv; Washington Light Infantry, 18 December 1858, Minutes of the Washington Light Infantry, 330, SCL.

3 Allan R. Millett, "The Constitution and the Citizen-Soldier," in *The United States Military Under the Constitution, 1789–1989*, ed. Richard H. Kohn (New York: New York University Press, 1991), 97; Henry S. Lane, "Sketch of the Remarks of Lt. Col. H.S. Lane, made on the 22d of Feb 1847, at a dinner given by Capt. S. Lasselle to his Company in Matamoros, Mexico," Lasselle Family Papers, INSL.

4 Joseph Ward to Samuel Adams, 3 March 1777, Joseph Ward Papers, NYHS (microfilm, CHS); Enos Hitchcock, "A Devout Soldier: A Sermon Preached at West Point, June 23, 1782; At Providence, February 2, 1783," in "Diary of Enos Hitchcock, D. D., A Chaplain in the Revolutionary Army. With a Memoir," ed. William B. Weeden, *Publications of the Rhode Island Historical Society*, n.s., 7, no. 2 (July 1899): 100–106.

5 Maarten Ultee, "Adapting to Conditions," in *Adapting to Conditions: War and Society in the Eighteenth Century*, ed. Maarten Ultee (University: University of Alabama Press, 1986), 5–6.

6 E. Wayne Carp, "The Problem of National Defense in the Early American Republic," in *The American Revolution: Its Character and Limits*, ed. Jack P. Greene (New York: New York University Press, 1987), 21; Lawrence Delbert Cress, *Citizens in Arms: The Army and the Militia in American Society to the War of 1812* (Chapel Hill: University of North Carolina Press, 1982), xi, 8, 23–24, 28–33, 55, 72; Charles Royster, *Light-Horse Harry Lee and the Legacy of the American Revolution* (New York: Alfred A. Knopf, 1981; reprint, Baton Rouge: Louisiana State University Press, 1994), 16–17.

7 Late Captain of Infantry, *Hints Bearing on the United States Army, with an Aim at the Adaptation, Availability, Efficiency and Economy Thereof* (Philadelphia: Henry B. Ashmead, 1858), 27.

8 William B. Skelton, *An American Profession of Arms: The Army Officer Corps, 1784–1861* (Lawrence: University Press of Kansas, 1992), 59–61, 212–17.

9 Thomas C. Linn, "Ethics Versus Self-Interest in How We Fight," in *Moral Obligation and the Military: Collected Essays* (Washington, DC: National Defense University Press, 1988), 220, 222; Lane, "Sketch of the Remarks of Lt. Col. H. S. Lane," Lasselle Family Papers; Lane, "Mexican War Journal," 417; Benjamin Alvord, *Address before the Dialectic Society of the Corps of Cadets . . .* (New York: Wiley and Putnam, 1839), 6.

10 Charles Royster, "A Society and Its War," in *Adapting to Conditions: War and Society in the Eighteenth Century*, ed. Maarten Ultee (University: University of Alabama Press, 1986), 180; Mason Gordon to Elizabeth L. Gordon, 4 August 1861, Gordon Family Papers, UVA; Thomas J. Goree to Robert Daniel Goree, 20 December 1861, in *Longstreet's Aide: The Civil War Letters of Major Thomas J. Goree*, ed. Thomas W. Cutrer (Charlottesville: University Press of Virginia, 1995), 64.

11 Marcus Cunliffe, *Soldiers and Civilians: The Martial Spirit in America, 1775–1865*, 2nd ed. (Boston: Little, Brown, 1968; reprint, New York: Free Press, 1973), 215–216, 219; Thomas R Vardell, "Address, on the Presentation of a Pair of Silver Pitchers by the Moultrie Guards, a Uniform Corps attached to the 16th Regt of Infantry to their Commander Capt Edward McCrady by Tho R. Vardell Orderly Sergt and Chairman of the Committee, on Monday the 26th July 1844," Edward McCrady Sr. Collections SCHS.

12 Cunliffe, *Soldiers and Civilians*, 241, 242, 230; Elmer Ephraim Ellsworth, Enlisting Orders, U. S. Zouave Cadets, Governor's Guards of Illinois, Company Orders No. 22 [ca. 1859], Elmer Ephraim Ellsworth Collection, CHS.

13 *Constitution and By-Laws of the Marion Corps of Baltimore* (Baltimore: Sands and Neilson, 1831), 3; Caleb J. Allen to Nellie Allen, 5 November 1861, Samuel T. Allen Papers, CAH.

14 James M. McPherson, *For Cause and Comrades: Why Men Fought in the Civil War* (New York: Oxford University Press, 1997), 23; Charles Royster, *A Revolutionary People at War: The Continental Army and American Character, 1775–1783* (Chapel Hill: University of North Carolina Press, 1979; reprint, New York: W. W. Norton for the Institute of Early American History and Culture, 1981), 22–23; Robert E. Shalhope, "The Armed Citizen in the Early Republic," *Law and Contemporary Politics* 49, no. 1 (Winter 1986): 125–141.

15 George Smith Avery to Elizabeth Little, 23 September 1861, George Smith Avery Letters, Civil War Letters Collection, CHS.

16 George Washington, Address to Massachusetts Provincial Congress, ca.4 July 1775, *The Papers of George Washington*, ed. W. W. Abbot et al., Revolutionary War Series, *June-September 1775*, vol. 1, ed. Philander D. Chase (Charlottesville: University of Virginia Press, 1985), 59–60.

17 Thomas Cushman, 12 May 1775, Diary, MAHS; John Whitcomb to Massachusetts
    Provincial Congress, 21 March 1775, United States Revolution Collection, AAS;
    Nathanael Greene to Samuel Ward, 14 July 1775, Nathanael Greene Papers, WLCL;
    Enos Hitchock to John Low, 2 October 1778, "Diary," *Publications of the Rhode
    Island Historical Society*, 90.

18 Joseph Bloomfield, *Citizen-Soldier: The Revolutionary War Journal of Joseph
    Bloomfield*, ed. Mark E. Lender and James Kirby Martin (Newark: New Jersey
    Historical Society, 1982), 37; Isaac Foster Jr. to Isaac Foster Sr., 7 July 1776, Isaac
    Foster Family Papers, LC; James Clinton to Philip Schuyler, James and George
    Clinton Papers, 7 August 1777, LC.

19 Inhabitants of New Gloucester, Maine, "An Association of the Friends of the
    Union," War of 1812 Collection, WLCL; Fairfield, Connecticut Volunteers,
    "Proposed Rules for a Company of Musquetry (Volunteers)," War of 1812
    Collection, WLCL.

20 Jacob Jennings Brown to the Cadets of the United States Military Academy, 4
    December 1815, Jacob Jennings Brown Papers, WLCL; Iverson Lea Graves to
    Sarah Dutton Graves, 3 June 1836, Graves Family Papers, SHC.

21 *New York Military Magazine; Devoted to the Interests of the Militia Throughout the
    Union* 1, no. 5, (10 July 1841): 78; Kimball Hale Dimmick to George Holcomb, E. B.
    Dimmick, and others, 28 July 1846, Kimball Hale Dimmick Correspondence and
    Papers, Bancroft; Henry Smith Lane to Samuel Stone, 5 November 1846, Henry
    Smith Lane Papers, Filson; Frederick W. Hopkins, *Discourses at Norwich, Vermont,
    during the Obsequies of Truman B. Ransom, Colonel of the New England Regiment,
    February Twenty-second, 1848* (Hanover, NH: Dartmouth and Journal, 1848), 22, 23.

22 Caleb J. Allen to Matilda T. Allen, 4 September 1861, Samuel T. Allen Papers.

23 Dexter F. Parker to Alonzo Hill, 21 April 1861, Letters to Rev. Alonzo Hill, AAS; Peter
    Warden to Mrs. Henry Vreeland, 22 September 1861, Warden Family Papers, CHS.

24 Lewis Leonidas Allen to Elenor Jay, Mary Kingsbury, Mary A. Johnson, Martha
    Haygood, Julia Garrison, and Sarah Kellogg, 1, 27 June 1846; Allen to the editor of
    the *Saint Louis American*, 11 August 1846.

25 John Bramblett Beall, *In Barrack and Field: Poems and Sketches of Army Life*
    (Nashville, TN: Smith and Lamar, 1906), 292; Benjamin F. Peterson to William P.
    Corthell, 12 June 1861, Letters to William P. Corthell, AAS; Charles B. Fox, 10
    November 1861, Journal, MAHS; Thomas Wentworth Higginson, *Massachusetts
    in the Army and the Navy during the War of 1861–1865*, vol. 2 (Boston: Wright and
    Potter, 1895), 394; William O. Crutcher to Emily Shannon Crutcher, 23 November
    1861, Crutcher-Shannon Family Papers, CAH.

26 Robert Treat Paine to Lavinia Paine, 22 May, 25 July 1847, Robert Treat Paine
    Papers, SHC; Lane, "Mexican War Journal," 390, 406.

27 John Bratton to Elizabeth Porcher DuBose Bratton, 11, 14 June 1861, John Bratton
    Letters, SCHS.

28 Ibid; Ezra J. Warner, *Generals in Gray: Lives of the Confederate Commanders*
    (Baton Rouge: Louisiana State University Press, 1959), 33–34.

29 David Gregg McIntosh, *Reminiscences of Early Life in South Carolina*, ed. Horace Fraser Rudisill (Florence, SC: St. David's Society, 1985), 97.

30 John S. R. Miller to Elisha P. Miller, 16 December 1858, John S. R. Miller Papers, SHC, John S. R. Miller to Mrs. Elisha P. Miller, 6 May 1860, John S. R. Miller Papers; John S. R. Miller to Elisha P. Miller, 5 February 1861, John S. R. Miller Papers.

31 Albert Sidney Johnston to Dr. Johnston, 14 April 1861, Frederick M. Dearborn Collection, Confederate Generals, Houghton.

32 Ulysses S. Grant to Jesse Root Grant, 21 April 1861, *The Papers of Ulysses S. Grant: April–September 1861*, vol. 2, ed. John Y. Simon (Carbondale: Southern Illinois University Press, 1969), 6; John E. Anderson, "Reminiscences of John E. Anderson," n.d., 6, Civil War Collection, AAS.

33 James B. Walton to Emma Louisa Walton, 25 July 1861, Walton-Glenny Family Papers, WRC; George Mitchell to Parents, 28 April 186l, George Mitchell Letters, NYHS; Thomas Corwin Honnell to Benjamin Epler, 21 May 1861, Thomas Corwin Honnell Papers, OHS; Oscar E. Stuart to Bettie Stuart, 6 August 1861, Oscar J. E. Stuart and Family Papers, MDAH; William Anderson to Creek Anderson, 23 October 1861, William Anderson Papers, UVA.

34 Israel Shreve to Polly Shreve, 6 June 1776, Shreve Family Papers, Filson; William Henshaw to Phebe Henshaw, 30 January, 15 May 1776, Henshaw Family Papers, AAS; Otho Holland Williams to Mercy Stull, 11 April 1776, Otho Holland Williams Papers, MDHS.

35 Alexander McDougall to Nathanael Greene, 29 May 1780, Nathanael Greene Papers, WLCL; Samuel Blachley Webb to Joseph Barrell, 8 October 1782, *Correspondence and Journals of Samuel Blachley Webb*, vol. 1, coll. and ed. Worthington Chauncey Ford (New York: n.p., 1893; reprint, New York Times and Arno, 1969), 472. The emphasis and irony are from Webb.

36 Sharp Delany to Anthony Wayne, 21 December 1780, Anthony Wayne Papers, HSP; Wayne to William Irvine, 18 May 1784, Anthony Wayne Papers, HSP; Major Smith to James Stewart, 20 November 1777, Smith Letter, United States Revolution Collection, AAS; Timothy Pickering to Rebecca Pickering, 17 June 1783, Timothy Pickering Papers, MAHS. See Holly Mayer, *Belonging to the Army: Camp Followers and Community during the American Revolution* (Columbia: University of South Carolina Press, 1996) on the Continental army's broader community. Richard H. Kohn, "American Generals of the Revolution: Subordination and Restraint," in *Reconsiderations on the Revolutionary War: Selected Essays*, ed. Don Higginbotham (Westport, CT: Greenwood, 1978), 107, 109; Caroline Cox, *A Proper Sense of Honor: Service and Sacrifice in George Washington's Army* (Chapel Hill: University of North Carolina Press, 2004), 37, 40, 46–51.

37 Reid Mitchell, *The Vacant Chair: The Northern Soldier Leaves Home* (New York: Oxford University Press, 1993), xiii–xiv; 14, 21; William Harvey Lamb Wallace to Ann Dickey Wallace, 2 August 1861, Wallace-Dickey Family Papers, ILSL; James Callaway to Flanders and Jamimah Callaway, 9 August 1814, James Callaway

Papers, Joseph Maher Collection, MOHS; Daniel B. Holmes to Mr. and Mrs. B. Holmes, 8 September 1861, Daniel B. Holmes Papers, CHS.

38 R. Claire Snyder, *Citizen-Soldiers and Manly Warriors: Military Service and Gender in the Civic Republic Tradition* (Lanham, MD: Rowman and Littlefield, 1999), 1–2; 81, 85, 86–87; Amy S. Greenberg, *Manifest Manhood and the Antebellum American Empire* (New York: Cambridge University Press, 2005), 11–14; Lorien Foote, *Gentlemen and the Roughs: Violence, Honor, and Manhood in the Union Army* (New York: New York University Press, 2010), 1–4, 19, 77–78.

39 James Callaway to Flanders and Jamimah Callaway, 9 August 1814; Daniel B. Holmes to Mr. and Mrs. B. Holmes, 8 September 1861; William McCauley to John McCauley, 18 March 1814, Andrew McCauley Papers, SHC.

40 Timothy Pickering to Rebecca Pickering, 4 August 1778, Timothy Pickering Papers, MAHS; Gideon J. Pillow to Mary Pillow, September 1846, Gideon J. Pillow Papers, MOHS; John Avery Benbury to Harriet Armistead Ryan Benbury, 24 August 1861, Benbury and Haywood Family Papers, SHC; Edmund Kirby Smith to Cassie Selden Smith, 10 December 1861, Kirby-Smith Papers, SHC.

41 Nathaniel Henry Rhodes Dawson to Elodie Todd, 23 June, 11 July, 28 July, 14 December 1861, Nathaniel Henry Rhodes Dawson Papers, SHC; Elodie Todd to Nathaniel Henry Rhodes Dawson, 22 December 1861, Nathaniel Henry Rhodes Dawson Papers.

42 William Anderson to Creek Anderson, 23 October 1861, William Anderson Papers; William H. Dunham to William Odell, 15 November 1861, William H. Dunham Letters, Civil War Miscellaneous Collection, USAMHI.

43 James Griffin to Leila Griffin, 11 July 1861, James Griffin Letters, Civil War Times Illustrated Collection USAMHI; John W. Dodd to Eliza Dodd, 13 June 1847, John W. Dodd Papers, OHS.

44 Thomas Thomson Taylor to Antoinette Taylor, 23 May 1861, Thomas Thomson Taylor Papers, OHS. See Mary Beth Norton, *Liberty's Daughters: The Revolutionary Experience of American Women, 1750–1800* (Boston: Little, Brown, 1980) and Linda K. Kerber, *Women of the Republic: Intellect and Ideology in Revolutionary America* (Chapel Hill: University of North Carolina Press for the Institute of Early American History and Culture, 1980; reprint, New York: W. W. Norton, 1986) on republican motherhood.

45 Skelton, *An American Profession of Arms*, 200–201. The Scott-Gaines feud lasted nearly three decades, 1821–1849, while Twiggs's and Worth's dispute involved Scott, the Congress, and the president in 1847.

46 William Edwards, Brigade Orders for Camp at South Boston under the Command of William Edwards, 24 September 1814, Houghton; Winfield Scott, "Address to the Cherokee people, remaining in North Carolina, Georgia, Tennessee, and Alabama, 10 May 1838," Robert Anderson Papers, LC; Robert Anderson to Charles Anderson, 17 June 1840, Robert Anderson Collection, HEH; Selby Stephen Fish to Julia Maria Fish, 3 November 1861, Fish Family Papers, WLCL.

47 William Alexander McClintock, 2 November 1846, "Journal of a Soldier of the Second Kentucky Regiment: Trip Through Texas and Northern Mexico in 1846–1847," 55–56, CAH; Joseph H. Lamotte to Ellen Lamotte, 8 May 1846, Lamotte-Copinger Papers, MOHS.

48 Philip St. George Cooke, *Scenes and Adventures in the Army: Or, Romance of Military Life* (Philadelphia: Lindsay and Blakiston, 1859), 175–176.

49 John Francis Hamtramck to Nicholas Fish, 22 July 1785, Nicholas Fish Collection, WLCL; Jacob Jennings Brown to John Quincy Adams, 31 December 1825, Jacob Jennings Brown Papers, WLCL.

50 William Goodwyn Ridley to Elizabeth Norfleet Ridley Neely, 18 October 1861, Correspondence, Ridley Family Papers, VHS; William H. Ker to Mary S. Ker, 30 November 1861, William H. Ker Letters, Hill; Mason Gordon to Elizabeth L. Gordon, 28 May 1861 and 17 October 1861, Gordon Family Papers, UVA; Dexter F. Parker to Alonzo Hill, 30 June 1861, Letters to Rev. Alonzo Hill.

51 James Ewell Brown Stuart to Sons of Temperance, 22 February 1861, James Ewell Brown Stuart Papers, VHS; Roger Jones to Thomas Claiborne, 18 January 1861, Thomas Claiborne Papers, SHC.

52 George Gordon Meade to Joshua Barry, 7 September 1861, Meade Collection, HSP; William Chapman to Annie Chapman, 25 May 1861, Chapman-McCaskey Papers, USMA.

53 David H. Pierson to William H. Pierson, 22 April 1861, Hill.

54 Joseph Ward to Captain Hopkins, 24 March 1779, Joseph Ward Papers, NYPL.

55 Captain George Stubblefield, 19 March 1776, "Orderly Book of the Company of Captain George Stubblefield, Fifth Virginia Regiment, from March 3, 1776 to July 10, 1776," *Collections of the Virginia Historical Society: Miscellaneous Papers, 1672–1865*, n.s., 6 (1887): 151.

56 William W. Tompkins, *New York Military Magazine; Devoted to the Interests of the Militia Throughout the Union* 1, no. 5 (10 July 1841): 78; James L. Converse to Mary Converse, 7 September 1861, James L. Converse Letters, Civil War Letters, CHS; Henry Lord Page King to Florence Barclay King, 28 July 1861, King-Wilder Papers, GHS.

57 John Patton, General Orders, 18 July 1775, Orderly Book, Manuscripts of the American Revolution, BPL; Otho Holland Williams to Elie Williams, 12 June 1781, Otho Holland Williams Papers, MDHS.

58 Samuel Elbert, General Orders, Camp at Fort Howe, 21st May 1778, "Order Book of Samuel Elbert, Colonel and Brigadier General in the Continental Army, October 1776, to November 1778," *Collections of the Georgia Historical Society* 5, pt. 2 (1902): 146–147, 149–150.

59 John Taylor to William Woodford, 14 August 1776, Letter File, CHS; Royster, *A Revolutionary People at War*, 86–96, 197–201; James Kirby Martin and Mark Edward Lender, *A Respectable Army: The Military Origins of the Republic, 1763–1789*, 2nd ed. (Wheeling, IL: Harlan Davidson, 2006), 41–42, 104–108; Cox, *A Proper Sense of Honor*, 22–35, Francis Collins, 3 July 1848, "Journal of Francis

Collins: An Artillery Officer in the Mexican War," ed. Maria Clinton Collins, *Quarterly Publication of the Historical and Philosophical Society of Ohio* 10, no. 2 (April 1915): 101; "Journal of Francis Collins: An Artillery Officer in the Mexican War," ed. Maria Clinton Collins, *Quarterly Publication of the Historical and Philosophical Society of Ohio* 10, no. 3, (July 1915): 102.

60   Sidney Axinn, *A Moral Military* (Philadelphia: Temple University Press, 1989), 4; Royster, *Light-Horse Harry Lee*, 30, 34; Robert F. W. Allston, "Oration delivered by appointment of the Military & Citizens of Georgetown So Ca on the 22nd February 1841 in the Episcopal Church," R. F. W. Allston Papers, SCHS, 5, 8.

61   John Whitcomb to Massachusetts Provincial Congress, 21 March 1775, United States Revolution Collection, AAS; Bloomfield, *Citizen-Soldier*, 38.

62   Anthony Wayne to Mary Wayne, 7 June 1777, Anthony Wayne Papers, HSP; Wayne to Joseph Reed, 16 December 1780, Anthony Wayne Papers, HSP; Timothy Pickering to Rebecca Pickering, Timothy Pickering Papers, 6 June 1778, MAHS; George Washington to Joseph Jones, 13 August 1780, Nathanael Greene Papers, WLCL (photocopy; original in the Collection of Dr. Otto O. Fischer); George Weedon to John Page, 17 December 1777, George Weedon Papers, CHS.

63   William Goodwyn Ridley to Elizabeth Norfleet Ridley Neely, 1 November 1861, William Goodwyn Ridley Correspondence, Ridley Family Papers, UVA; David H. Pierson to William H. Pierson, 22 April 1861, David H. Pierson Letter, Hill.

64   Fred Anderson, *A People's Army: Massachusetts Soldiers and Society in the Seven Years' War* (Chapel Hill: University of North Carolina Press for the Institute of Early American History and Culture, 1984), 14, 16; Fred Anderson, *Crucible of War: The Seven Years' War and the Fate of Empire in British North America, 1754–1766* (New York: Alfred A. Knopf, 2000), 228–229, 317–320; Royster, *Light-Horse Harry Lee*, 122–123.

65   Don Higginbotham, *War and Society in Revolutionary America: The Wider Dimensions of Conflict* (Columbia: University of South Carolina Press, 1988), 97; Philip Van Cortlandt to Pierre Van Cortlandt, 23 March 1780, Van Cortlandt-Van Wyck Papers, NYPL.

66   Joseph Ward to Captain Hopkins, 24 March 1779, Joseph Ward Papers, NYPL (microfilm, CHS).

67   Ibid.; Samuel Tenny to Peter Turner, 12 June 1783, Letters from Dr. Peter Turner Relating to the Revolutionary War, Miscellaneous Bound Collection, WLCL; Philip Van Cortlandt to Pierre Van Cortlandt, 23 March 1780.

68   James Kirby Martin, "A 'Most Undisciplined, Profligate Crew': Protest and Defiance in the Continental Ranks, 1776–1783," in *Arms and Independence: The Military Character of the American Revolution*, ed. Ronald Hoffman and Peter J. Albert (Charlottesville: University Press of Virginia,, 1984), 119–140; Royster, *A Revolutionary People at War*, 68, 84, 92, 143, 195. See also Carl Van Doren, *Mutiny in January* . . . . (New York: Viking, 1943).

69   Robert Middlekauff, "Why Men Fought in the American Revolution," *Huntington Library Quarterly* 43, no. 2 (Spring 1980): 148; Nathanael Greene to Nicholas

Cooke, 4 July 1775, Greene to Christopher Greene, 29 January 1776, Nathanael Greene Papers, AAS; Edmund Kirby to Frances Kirby Smith, 12 September 1847, Edmund Kirby-Smith Papers, SHC.

70 John O'Brien to Mary Walker Tennyson, 23 September 1861, John O'Brien Letters, Civil War Miscellaneous Collection, USAMHI.

71 Nicholas Fish to Richard Varick, 16 May 1776, Nicholas Fish Collection, WLCL; Henry Dearborn, n.d., Diary of Campaigns, with Verse, Manuscripts of the American Revolution, BPL.

72 George Smith Avery to Elizabeth Little, 21, 29 April 1861, George Smith Avery Letters, Civil War Letters Collection, CHS; David Wyatt Aiken to Virginia Smith Aiken, 19 July 1861, David Wyatt Aiken Papers, SCL; William Preston Johnston to Rosa Duncan Johnston, 6 November 1861, Johnston Family, Filson.

73 Theodore Talbot to Adelaide Talbot, 10 March 1861, Theodore Talbot Papers, LC; Edward Murphy to W. H. Renaud, 16 August 1861, Murphy Family Papers, WRC; Nathaniel Henry Rhodes Dawson to Elodie Todd, 8 June 1861, Nathaniel Henry Rhodes Dawson Papers, SHC; William Ray Wells to Mary S. Hall, 6 July 1861, William Ray Wells Papers, SHC; John R. Hunt, Jr. to John R. Hunt, Sr., 28 April 1861, John Randolph Hunt, Jr. Letters, Northwest Corner Civil War Round Table Collection, USAMHI.

74 R. J. Stallings to Cousin Emma, 23 July 1861, Lucinda Sugg Moore Papers, SHC; Mason Gordon to Elizabeth L. Gordon, 4 August 1861, Gordon Family Papers, UVA; Louis Perrin Foster to Mrs. B. B. Foster, 5 August 1861, Louis Perrin Foster Letters, James Rion McKissick Papers, SCL; Rufus W. Cater to Fanny S. Cater, 20 September 1861, Douglas J. and Rufus W. Cater Letters, LC.

75 John Henry Stibbs to Mr. and Mrs. R. B. Stibbs, 21 April 1861, Stibbs Family Papers, Tulane; J. Mason Henry to Caleb Davis Bradlee, 19, 24 May 1861, Letters to Rev. Caleb Davis Bradlee, AAS.

76 Lloyd Powell to Charles L. Powell, 30 June 1861, Powell Family Papers, WMC.

77 Cunliffe, *Soldiers and Civilians*, 230; Drew Gilpin Faust, *This Republic of Suffering: Death and the American War* (New York: Alfred A. Knopf, 2008), 33–35, 54, 189; George C. Rable, *God's Almost Chosen Peoples: A Religious History of the American Civil War* (Chapel Hill: University of North Carolina Press, 2010), 52–53, 222–224.

78 Earl J. Hess, *Union Soldier: Enduring the Ordeal of Combat* (Lawrence: University Press of Kansas, 1997), 104, 108–109; Rable, *God's Almost Chosen Peoples*, 1, 2, 5; Robert Anderson to Sarah Marshall Anderson, 24 February 1840, Robert Anderson Collection, HEH. See also Faust, *This Republic of Suffering*.

79 Charles B. Fox, 21 October 1861, Journal, MAHS.

CHAPTER 2. PRESERVING, DEFENDING, AND CREATING THE POLITICAL ORDER

1 Portions of this chapter appeared in Ricardo A. Herrera, "Toward an American Army: U.S. Soldiers, the War of 1812, and National Identity," *Army History* 88 (Summer 2013): 42–57 and Ricardo A. Herrera, "A People and Its Soldiers: The

American Citizen as Soldier, 1775–1861," *International Bibliography of Military History* 33 (2013): 9–34; Charles Royster, "A Society and Its War," in *Adapting to Conditions: War and Society in the Eighteenth Century*, ed. Maarten Ultee (University: University of Alabama Press, 1986), 177; Israel Shreve to Polly, 6 June 1776, Shreve Family Papers, Filson; Louisiana Guard, *Constitution and By-Laws of the Louisiana Guard, Organized November 9, 1860* (New Orleans: H. P. Lathrop, 1861), 13.

2 Royster, "A Society and Its War," 187, 177; Stewart Lewis Gates, "Disorder and Social Organization: The Militia in Connecticut Public Life, 1660–1860" (PhD diss., University of Connecticut, 1975), 1.

3 Gordon S. Wood, *The Radicalism of the American Revolution* (New York: Knopf, 1992; reprint, Vintage Books, 1993), 104–105; Bernard Bailyn, *The Ideological Origins of the American Revolution*, enl. ed. (Cambridge, MA: Belknap Press of Harvard University Press, 1992), 77, 79, 188–189; Samuel Bixby, May 1775, Diary, AAS; George Washington to Henry Lee, 20 October 1794, Maryland Militia, General Orders, 21 October 1794, General Orders and Official Documents for the Direction and Government of the Army in the Suppression of Western Insurrection, 1794: Journals of Major Spear and Captain J[ohn] Machinheimer, HSP.

4 Mark Pitcavage, "An Equitable Burden: The Decline of the State Militias, 1783–1858" (PhD diss., Ohio State University, 1995), 1:358, 361; Gates, "Disorder and Social Organization," 169, 175, 176, 179.

5 Christopher Van Deventer, 27 December 1810, Christopher Van Deventer Papers, WLCL; Nathanael Greene to Thomas Jefferson, 20 November 1780, AAS; Tyler V. Johnson, *Devotion to the Adopted Country: U.S. Immigrant Volunteers in the Mexican War* (Columbia: University of Missouri Press, 2012), 2.

6 John K. Mahon, *History of the Militia and the National Guard* (New York: Macmillan, 1983), 83; R. Claire Snyder, *Citizen-Soldiers and Manly Warriors: Military Service and Gender in the Civic Republic Tradition* (Lanham, MD: Rowman and Littlefield, 1999), 85–89.

7 Mechanic Phalanx, *Constitution of the Mechanic Phalanx, Instituted at Chelmsford, Feb. 1, 1825* (East-Chelmsford, MA: William Baldwin, 1825), 4; Colonel [H.W.] Palfrey, "Grand Military Pageant," *Le Courrier De La Louisiane (New Orleans)*, 6 April 1852; Albert Tracy, *Annual Report of the Adjutant General of the State of Maine, 1853* (Augusta, ME: William T. Johnson, 1854), 7, 9; William W. Tompkins, *New York Military Magazine; Devoted to the Interests of the Militia Throughout the Union* 1, no. 10, (14 August 1841): 154; M. Grivot, *Report of the Adjutant General of the Louisiana Militia to the Legislature of the Legislature of the State of Louisiana, 1856* (New Orleans: John Claiborne, 1857), 1; Thomas Rodney to Caesar Rodney, 19 October 1781, *Letters to and From Caesar Rodney, 1756–1784* . . . , ed. George Herbert Ryden (Philadelphia: University of Pennsylvania Press for the Historical Society of Delaware, 1933), 381.

8 Robert Reinders "Militia and Public Order in Nineteenth-Century America,"
   Journal of American Studies 11, no. 1 (1977): 86; Marcus Cunliffe, *Soldiers and
   Civilians: The Martial Spirit in America, 1775-1865,* 2nd ed. (Boston: Little, Brown,
   1968; reprint, New York: Free Press, 1973), 215–216; John F. Kutolowski and
   Kathleen Smith Kutolowski, "Commissions and Canvasses: The Militia and
   Politics in Western New York, 1800-1845," *New York History* 63, no. 1 (1982): 7.

9 Brengle Home Guards, Proceedings of the Brengle Home Guards, Formed April
   1861 and Mustered into the 16th M M on Friday 26th Day April, Frederick Md,
   MDHS; John Watts De Peyster, *An Address to the Officers of the New York State
   Troops* . . . . (Poughkeepsie, NY: Platt and Schram, 1858), 1, 6, 23.

10 First California Guard, *By-Laws and Bill of Dress of the First California Guard,
   (Flying Artillery.) Instituted July 27th, 1849. Revised May 25th, 1852; Feb. 1st, 1855;
   July 27th, 1860* (San Francisco: Agnew and Deffebach, 1860), 3, 5, 7; Frank Soulé,
   John H. Gihon, and Frank Nisbet, *The Annals of San Francisco* . . . . (New York: D.
   Appleton, 1855), 227, 257 309, 472, 702-08; Carl Sifakis, "Hounds," in *Encyclopedia
   of American Crime,* 2nd ed. (New York: Facts On File, 2001), 437–38.

11 Cunliffe, *Soldiers and Civilians,* 215–216, 230; Kutolowski and Kutolowski,
   "Commissions and Canvasses," 7.

12 Kutolowski and Kutolowski, "Commissions and Canvasses," 12, 13.

13 Jedidiah Preble to John Hancock, 18 March 1775, United States Revolution
   Collection, AAS; Nathanael Greene to Ward, 14 July, 18 December 1775, Nathanael
   Greene Collection, HEH; Bailyn, *Origins,* 184–185; Wood, *Creation of the
   American Republic,* 293–294, 537–540; General Orders, George Washington to
   Thomas Gage, 4 July, 19 August 1775, *The Papers of George Washington,* ed. W. W.
   Abbot et al., Revolutionary War Series, *June-September 1775,* vol. 1, ed. Philander
   D. Chase (Charlottesville: University of Virginia Press, 1985), 54, 327. Washington
   recognized the change in the theory of sovereignty at an early date. In a letter to
   General Thomas Gage, Washington revealed his belief that the people, not the
   monarch, were the source of ultimate political power and legitimacy: "You affect,
   Sir, to despise all Rank not derived from the same Source with your own. I cannot
   conceive any more honourable, than that which flows from the uncorrupted
   Choice of a brave and free People—The purest Source and original Fountain of all
   Power. . . . [A] Mind of true Magnaminity, and enlarged Ideas would comprehend
   and respect it."

14 Royster, "A Society and Its War," 185–186; Caesar Rodney to William Killen, 27
   January 1777, Caesar Rodney, *Letters to and From Caesar Rodney,* 279; Benjamin
   Gilbert to Charles Bruce, 10 June 1783, Benjamin Gilbert, *Winding Down: The
   Revolutionary War Letters of Lieutenant Benjamin Gilbert of Massachusetts,
   1780-1783,* ed. John Shy (Ann Arbor: University of Michigan Press, 1989), 107;
   James McHenry, Testament, 29 July 1775, James McHenry Papers, LC.

15 Washington to the Massachusetts Provincial Congress, General Orders, General
   Orders, ca.4, ca.5 July, 10 August 1775, *Papers,* 1:59–60, 63, 281–282.

16 Christopher P. Yates, 16 July 1775, Enlistment Agreement, CHS; Samuel Blachley
    Webb, Agreement of the Wethersfield Company of Volunteers, Capt. Chester,
    April 23rd, 1775, *Correspondence and Journals of Samuel Blachley Webb*, coll. and
    ed. Worthington Chauncey Ford, vol. 1 (New York: n.p., 1893; reprint, New York
    Times and Arno, 1969), 55, 56; 21 July 1776, Isaac Bangs, *Journal of Lieutenant
    Isaac Bangs: April 1 to July 29, 1776*, ed. Edward Bangs (Cambridge, MA: John
    Wilson and Son, University Press, 1890; reprint, New York: New York Times and
    Arno, 1968), 64; Enos Hitchcock to John Low, 2 October 1778, "Diary of Enos
    Hitchcock, D.D., A Chaplain in the Revolutionary Army. With a Memoir," ed.
    William B. Weeden, *Publications of the Rhode Island Historical Society*, n.s., 7, no.
    2 (July 1899): 90.
17 Constitution of the Marblehead Light Infantry, 18 September 1814, Isaac Story
    Papers, WLCL; Christopher Van Deventer to Gustavus Loomis, 11 March 1814,
    Christopher Van Deventer Papers, WLCL.
18 Earl J. Hess, *The Union Soldier in Battle: Enduring the Ordeal of Combat*
    (Lawrence: University Press of Kansas, 1997), 97; Charles B. Fox, 1 October, 30
    November 1861, Journal, MAHS.
19 William Nelson Pendleton to Alfred Lee, 28 May 1861, William Nelson Pendleton
    Papers, SHC; Pendleton to Anzolette Elizabeth Page Pendleton, 31 May 1861,
    William Nelson Pendleton Papers; R. J. Stallings to Cousin Emma, 4 July 1861,
    Lucinda Sugg Moore Papers, SHC; John R. Jefferies to James Jefferies, 6 May 1861,
    Jefferies Family War Record, SCL; Eugene O. Williams to Beaufort T. Watts, 11
    June 1861, Watts Family Papers, SCL; Nathaniel Henry Rhodes Dawson to Elodie
    Todd, 2 July 1861, Nathaniel Henry Rhodes Dawson Papers, SHC.
20 James Daniel Webb to Justina Walton Webb, 19, 22 May 1861, Walton Family
    Papers, SHC. Presidents George Washington, Thomas Jefferson, James Madison,
    James Monroe, Andrew Jackson, John Tyler, James K. Polk, and Zachary Taylor
    had been slaveholders while serving in the presidency. William Preston Johnston
    to Rosa Duncan Johnston, 6 November 1861, Johnston Family Papers, Filson;
    Philip St. George Cocke to John Bowdoin Cocke, Broadside, 6 December 1860, 5
    May 1861, Philip St. George Cocke Papers, UVA.
21 Speech to the 5th Ward Mounted Rifles, July 1861, Clement Stanford Watson
    Family Papers, Tulane; William Preston Johnston to Rosa Duncan Johnston, 6
    November 1861, Johnston Family Papers, Filson. Local autonomy should not
    be confused with the inconsistently applied trope of states' rights, even as
    Southern politicians called for a stronger fugitive slave act and aggressive
    federal enforcement of it. They got this in the 1850 Fugitive Slave Act. The
    cases of runaway slaves Thomas Sims and Shadrach Minkins in 1851, Anthony
    Burns and Joshua Glover in 1854, and abolitionist Sherman Booth in 1854
    highlight the inconvenient truth and dissonance in states' rights. See Stanley
    W. Campbell, *The Slave Catchers: Enforcement of the Fugitive Slave Law,
    1850–1860* (Chapel Hill: University of North Carolina Press, 1970); Gary
    Collison, *Shadrach Minkins: From Fugitive Slave to Citizen* (Cambridge, MA:

Harvard University Press, 1997); Gordon S. Barker, *Imperfect Revolution: Anthony Burns and the Landscape of Race in Antebellum America* (Kent, OH: Kent State University Press, 2011); Gordon S. Barker, *Fugitive Slaves and the Unfinished American Revolution: Eight Cases, 1848–1856* (Jefferson, NC: McFarland, 2013); H. Robert Baker, *The Rescue of Joshua Glover: A Fugitive Slave, the Constitution and the Coming of the Civil War* (Athens: Ohio University Press, 2006).

22 Pamunkey Rifles, Petition to the Gov. John Letcher, 1861, VHS; Hannibal Paine to Virginia, 26 July, 26 November 1861, Paine Family Papers, TNSL; New Orleans *Daily Picayune*, 21 April 1861, quoted in James G. Hollandsworth Jr., *The Louisiana Native Guards : The Black Military Experience during the Civil War* (Baton Rouge: Louisiana State University Press, 1995), 2.

23 Hess, *Union Soldier in Battle*, 97, 98; Peter Warden to Mrs. Henry Vreeland, 29 September 1861, Warden Family, CHS; Samuel Nicoll Benjamin to father, 14 February 1860, Samuel Nicoll Benjamin Papers, USMA; Benjamin to mother, 21 March 1861, Samuel Nicoll Benjamin Papers; Davis Dwight to Howard Dwight, 23 April 1861, Dwight Family Papers, MAHS.

24 Dexter F. Parker to Alonzo Hill, 21 April 1861, Letters to Rev. Alonzo Hill, AAS; Benjamin Alvord to Solomon Foot, 16 September 1861, Benjamin Alvord, Frederick M. Dearborn Collection, Union Generals, Houghton.

25 Samuel Nicoll Benjamin to mother, 29 January 1861, Samuel Nicoll Benjamin Papers; Samuel S. Elder to Mrs. K. K. Peebles, 29 January 1861, Letters of Samuel S. Elder, NYPL.

26 Thomas Jefferson Jordan to Jane Jordan, 23 June 1861, Thomas Jefferson Jordan Civil War Letters, HSP; J. Mason Henry to Caleb Davis Bradlee, 19 May 1861, Letters to Rev. Caleb Davis Bradlee, AAS; J. Stewart Brown to Alonzo Hill, 1 May 1861, Letters to Rev. Alonzo Hill, AAS; Benjamin H. Grierson to Charlie Grierson, 17 July 1861, Benjamin H. Grierson Papers, ILSL.

27 Hess, *Union Soldier in Battle*, 124; Reid Mitchell, *The Vacant Chair: The Northern Soldier Leaves Home* (New York: Oxford University Press, 1993), 21–22; Amy S. Greenberg, *Manifest Manhood and the Antebellum American Empire* (New York: Cambridge University Press, 2005), 11–12; Ann M. Little, *Abraham in Arms: War and Gender in Colonial New England* (Philadelphia: University of Pennsylvania Press, 2007), 11.

28 William Harvey Lamb Wallace to Ann Dickey Wallace, 28 April 1861, Wallace-Dickey Family Papers, ILSL; George Smith Avery to Elizabeth Little, 6 May, 2 June 1861, George Smith Avery Letters, Civil War Letters Collection, CHS; William R. Williams to wife, 15 September 1861, William R. Williams Letters, Civil War Miscellaneous Collection, USAMHI.

29 John A. Quitman, *An Address on the Occasion of the Second Anniversary of the Palmetto Association, Delivered in Columbia, S. C., Tuesday, May 4th, 1858* (Columbia, SC: I. C. Morgan, 1858), 8; Israel Putnam, 12 October 1777, *General Orders Issued by Major-General Israel Putnam . . . .*, ed. Worthington Chauncey

Ford, (Brooklyn: Historical Printing Club, 1893; reprint, Boston: Gregg, 1972), 84; Davis Dwight to Howard Dwight, 23 April 1861, Dwight Family Papers.

30 Henry Sewall, 17 October 1779, Diary, MAHS; William Henry Harrison to Charles Scott, 10 March 1810, William Henry Harrison Correspondence, NYHS; Benjamin Alvord, *Address Before the Dialectic Society of the Corps of Cadets* . . . . (New York: Wiley and Putnam, 1839), 7; Cunliffe, *Soldiers and Civilians*, 50.

31 Soul of Soldiery, *Constitution of the Soul of Soldiery* (Boston: E. G. House, 1824), 3; James Mills, General Orders, 29 April 1813, Regimental Book for the 1st Regiment, 3rd Detachment of the Ohio Militia, Containing Orders Received and Issued by Colonel James Mills of Butler County and the State of Ohio, OHS; Philip St. George Cocke to John Bowdoin Cocke, 6 December 1860, Philip St. George Cocke Papers, UVA.

32 Samuel Nicoll Benjamin to mother, 5 January 1861, Samuel Nicoll Benjamin Papers; Mechanic Phalanx, Constitution, 4; Charlestown Light Infantry, 1821, Letterbook of the Charlestown Light Infantry, 1, AHAC; Putnam Phalanx *Excursion of the Putnam Phalanx to Mount Vernon, December 1860* (Hartford, CT: Charles G. Geer, 1861), 28.

33 Silas T. White to A. J. White, 18 April 1861, Silas T. White Papers, LC; John W. Ervin to John L. Manning, 4 January 1860, John L. Manning Papers, SCHS.

34 Erastus W. Everson to Salome B. Everson, 21 May 1861, Everson to grandmother, 15 September 1861, Erastus W. Everson Letters, BPL; Thomas Jefferson Jordan to Jane Jordan, 23 June 1861, Thomas Jefferson Jordan Civil War Letters, HSP; James Kirby Martin and Mark Edward Lender, *A Respectable Army: the Military Origins of the Republic, 1763–1789*, 2nd ed. (Arlington Heights, IL: Harlan Davidson, 2006), 207.

35 Charles Royster, "Founding a Nation in Blood: Military Conflict and American Nationality," in *Arms and Independence: The Military Character of the American Revolution*, ed. Ronald Hoffman and Peter J. Albert (Charlottesville: University Press of Virginia, 1984), 30; Nathanael Greene to Samuel Ward, 4 January 1776, Nathanael Greene Collection, HEH; Ethan Allen, *The Narrative of Colonel Ethan Allen* (Philadelphia: Robert Bell, 1779; reprint, New York: Corinth Books, 1961), 5.

36 Royster, "Founding a Nation in Blood," 45; Steven Rosswurm, *Arms, Country, and Class: The Philadelphia Militia and the "Lower Sort" During the American Revolution, 1775–1783* (New Brunswick, NJ: Rutgers University Press, 1987), 51, 252–53; Committee of Privates to the Privates of the several Battalions of Military Associators in the Province of Pennsylvania, 8 August 1776, Clymer Family Papers, HSP.

37 Copy of General Orders, 4 November 1813, Robert Carr, Journal and Letters, HSP.

38 Benjamin Franklin Butler, *The Military Profession in the United States* . . . . (New York: Samuel Colman, 1839), 14; Samuel Nicoll Benjamin to father, 14 February 1860, Samuel Nicoll Benjamin Papers.

39 S. E. Finer, *The Man on Horseback: The Role of the Military in Politics*, 2nd ed., enl., rev. and updated (Boulder, CO: Westview, 1962), 7, 29; George Blaney to

David Bates Douglass, 21 June 1816, David Bates Douglass Papers, WLCL; Andrew Jackson to Joseph Gardner Swift, 22 April 1817, Joseph Gardner Swift Papers, USMA.

40 Christopher Van Deventer to Samuel Cooper, 31 October 1813, Christopher Van Deventer Papers, WLCL; Lincoln Light Infantry, *Constitution, By-Laws, and Rules of Order, of the Lincoln Light Infantry* . . . . (Boston: Davis and Farmer, 1855), 3; Edward Fenno to James Fenno, 2 March 1820, Fenno-Hoffman Papers, WLCL; Fenno to Maria Fenno Hoffman, 9 February 1823, Fenno-Hoffman Papers.

41 Edward Fenno to Maria Fenno Hoffman, 9 February, 26 March, 8 April 1823, Fenno-Hoffman Papers; Boston National Guards, Orderly Book of the Boston National Guards, 10 January 1855, 17 January 1855, BPL; Cunliffe, *Soldiers and Civilians*, 230.

42 Maurice Matloff, "The Nature and Scope of Military History," in *New Dimensions in Military History: An Anthology*, ed. Russell F. Weigley (San Rafael, CA: Presidio, 1975), 390–391; New-York Hibernian Volunteers, 12 January 1796, Minute-Book.

43 Reinders, "Militia and Public Order in Nineteenth-Century America," 87; Cunliffe, *Soldiers and Civilians* 230; Mark Pitcavage, "An Equitable Burden," 1: 358, 361; Gates, "Disorder and Social Organization," 169, 175, 176, 179; Augustus P. Green, Autobiography, vol. 1, 17, 18, Augustus P. Green Collection, NYHS.

44 Roland Calhoun McConnell, *Negro Troops of Antebellum Louisiana: A History of the Battalion of Free Men of Color* (Baton Rouge: Louisiana State University Press, 1968), 35–6; Hollandsworth, *The Louisiana Native Guards*, 5, 8.

CHAPTER 3. FREE MEN IN UNIFORM

1 John Locke, *Second Treatise of Government*, ed. Samuel H. Beer and O. B. Hardison, Jr. (Arlington Heights, IL: Harlan Davidson, 1982), 3–10, 47–57. See also Fred Anderson, *A People's Army: Massachusetts Soldiers and Society in the Seven Years' War* (Chapel Hill: University of North Carolina Press for the Institute of Early American History and Culture, 1984); James Titus, *The Old Dominion at War: Society, Politics, and Warfare in Late Colonial Virginia* (Columbia: University of South Carolina Press, 1991); and Charles Patrick Neimeyer, *America Goes to War: A Social History of the Continental Army* (New York: New York University Press, 1996). Much of this chapter was originally published as Ricardo A. Herrera, "Self-Governance and the American Citizen as Soldier, 1775–1861," *Journal of Military History* 65, no. 1 (January 2001): 21–52.

2 Jerry Cooper, *The Rise of the National Guard: The Evolution of the American Militia, 1865–1920* (Lincoln: University of Nebraska Press, 1997), 13–17; Marilyn S. Blackwell and James S. Holway, "Reflections on Jacksonian Democracy and Militia Reform: The Waitsfield Militia Petition of 1836," *Vermont History: The Proceedings of the Vermont Historical Society* 55, no. 1 (Winter 1987): 5; Kenneth Otis McCreedy, "Palladium of Liberty: The American Militia System, 1815–1861" (PhD diss., University of California, Berkeley, 1991) and Mark Pitcavage, "An Equitable Burden: The Decline of the State Militias, 1783–1858" (PhD diss., Ohio

State University, 1995), examine widespread militia service and its decline and transformation against the backdrop of politics, continental expansion, citizenship, and individual military responsibility. Mary Ellen Rowe, *Bulwark of the Republic: The American Militia in [the] Antebellum West* (Westport, CT: Praeger, 2003), x, 8.

3   Don Higginbotham, *George Washiington and the American Military Tradition* (Athens: University of Georgia Press, 1985), 12.

4   Dean Paul Baker, "The Partridge Connection: Alden Partridge and Southern Military Education" (PhD diss., University of North Carolina, Chapel Hill, 1986); *The Eclaireur, a military journal* . . . . 3 vols., ed. John Watts De Peyster and Augustus T. Cowman (Hyde Park, NY: Platt and Schram, 1853–56); *The New York Military Magazine; Devoted to the Interests of the Militia Throughout the Union*, vol. 1, ed. William W. Tompkins (New York: Labree and Stockton, 1841).

5   Earl J. Hess, *Liberty, Virtue, and Progress: Northerners and Their War for the Union* (New York: New York University Press, 1988), 1, 2, 6, 7, 12; Earl J. Hess , *The Union Soldier in Battle: Enduring the Ordeal of Combat* (Lawrence: University Press of Kansas, 1997), 124, 142. See also R. Claire Snyder,*Citizen-Soldiers and Manly Warriors: Military Service and Gender in the Civic Republic Tradition* (Lanham, MD: Rowman and Littlefield, 1999).

6   Samuel McGowan, *An Address on the Occasion of the First Anniversary of the Palmetto Association, Delivered in Columbia, S. C., May 14th, A. D. 1857* (Columbia, SC: I.C. Morgan, 1857), 5, 6, 15; John Watts De Peyster, *An Address to the Officers of the New York State Troops* . . . . (Poughkeepsie, NY: Platt and Schram, 1858), 2; James Daniel Webb to Justina Walton Webb, 19 May 1861, Walton Family Papers, SHC; Benjamin W. Thompson, Recollections of War Times, Civil War Times Illustrated Collection, USAMHI; Nicole Eustace, *1812: War and the Passions of Patriotism* (Philadelphia: University of Philadelphia Press, 2012), 208.

7   John A. Logan, *The Volunteer Soldier, with Memoir of the Author and Military Reminiscences from General Logan's Private Journal* (Chicago: R. S. Peale, 1887), 90, 482; Marion Rifle Corps, *Constitution and By-Laws of the Marion Corps of Baltimore* (Baltimore: Sands and Neilson, 1831), 3; Albert Tracy, *Annual Report of the Adjutant General of the State of Maine, 1853* (Augusta, ME: William T. Johnson, 1854), 7, 9; Mechanic Phalanx, *Constitution of the Mechanic Phalanx, Instituted at Chelmsford, Feb. 1, 1825* (East-Chelmsford, MA: William Baldwin, 1825), 3,4.

8   Continental Rangers *Constitution and By-Laws of the Continental Rangers* (St. Louis, MO: Mantz, 1853), 3; Amy S. Greenberg, *Manifest Manhood and the Antebellum American Empire* (New York: Cambridge University Press, 2005), 8; Blackwell and Holway, "Reflections on Jacksonian Democracy and Militia Reform," 5, 6–8, 9, 11–14; Thomas R. Vardell, Address, on the Presentation of a Pair of Silver Pitchers by the Moultrie Guards . . . , Edward McCrady, Sr.

Collections, SCHS; J. Davidson, John Pool, and Thomas Mulligan "Temperance," *Army and Navy Chronicle* 1, no. 41 (8 October 1835): 321–322; James Ewell Brown Stuart, Address to the Military Order of Sons of Temperance, James Ewell Brown Stuart Papers, VHS; Robert Ruffin Ritchie to Thomas Ritchie, 20 May 1848, Ritchie-Harrison Papers, WMC.

9 Edward Murphy to Mr. W. H. Renaud, 16 August 1861, Murphy Family Papers, WRC; Anderson, *A People's Army*, viii, 39, 168; Ann M. Little, *Abraham in Arms: War and Gender in Colonial New England* (Philadelphia: University of Pennsylvania Press, 2007), 2, 5–7.

10 Frank A. Hardy to Mr. and Mrs. Amos Hardy, 11 November 1846, Frank A. Hardy Papers, OHS.

11 Anderson, *A People's Army*, 168; James Titus, *The Old Dominion at War: Society, Politics, and Warfare in Late Colonial Virginia* (Columbia: University of South Carolina Press, 1991), 148; George W. Chilton to Hezekiah William Rice, 10 June 1846, George W. Chilton Collection, HEH; Neimeyer, *America Goes to War*; Charles Royster, *A Revolutionary People at War: The Continental Army and American Character, 1775–1783* (Chapel Hill: University of North Carolina Press, 1979; reprint, New York: W. W. Norton for the Institute of Early American History and Culture, 1981), 195, 268, 373–278. See also Michael A. McDonnell, "Popular Mobilization and Political Culture in Revolutionary Virginia: The Failure of the Minutemen and the Revolution from Below," *Journal of American History* 85, no. 34 (December 1998): 946–981, for an analysis of the political and social background of Virginia's failure to recruit adequate numbers of volunteers in War for Independence.

12 Neimeyer, *America Goes to War*, xv; Royster, *A Revolutionary People at War*, 195, 268, 373–378.

13 Anderson, *A People's Army*, viii, 168. For treatments of the British army in North America see also John Shy, *Toward Lexington: The Role of the British Army in the Coming of the American Revolution* (Princeton, NJ: Princeton University Press, 1965); Douglas Edward Leach, *Arms for Empire: A Military History of the British Colonies, 1607–1763* (New York: Macmillan, 1973); Douglas Edward Leach, *Roots of Conflict: British Armed Forces and Colonial Americans, 1677–1783* (Chapel Hill: University of North Carolina Press, 1986); and Sylvia R. Frey, *The British Soldier in America: A Social History of Military Life in the Revolutionary Period* (Austin: University of Texas Press, 1981).

14 Robert Middlekauff, "Why Men Fought in the American Revolution," *Huntington Library Quarterly* 43, no. 2 (Spring 1980): 143–144, 148.

15 George Washington to John Hancock, 2 September 1776, *The Papers of George Washington*, ed. Dorothy Twohig et al., Revolutionary War Series, *August-October 1776*, vol. 6, ed. Frank E. Grizzard Jr. et al. (Charlottesville: University of Virginia Press, 1994), 199, 200; Royster, *A Revolutionary People at War*, 5, 7, 12.

16 Thomas T. Summers to Jacob and Stephen Summers, 28 July 1846, Thomas T. Summers Papers, Filson; Thomas T. Summers to Jacob and Stephen Summers, 13

February 1847, Thomas T. Summers Papers; John Claude to Dennis Claude, 22
March 1815, War of 1812 Collection, WLCL; Lewis Wallace to William Wallace, 26
July 1846, Lewis Wallace Papers, INHS; A.T. Traylor to mother, 24 June 1861,
Traylor and McLane Families, SCL.

17 George C. Furber, *The Twelve Months Volunteer* . . . . (Cincinnati, OH: J. A. and U.
P. James, 1850), 433; John Blount Robertson, *Reminiscences of a Campaign in
Mexico*. . . . (Nashville, TN: John York, 1849), 185; George Gordon Meade to
Margaret Meade, 27 May 1846, Meade Collection, HSP.

18 Robert Carr, General Orders, 23 August 1813, Journal and Letters, HSP. There is
no little irony in Wilkinson's call for officers' greater probity, given his treasonous
conduct as Spanish Agent 13.

19 Orders, 21 October 1794, General Orders and Official Documents for the
Direction and Government of the Army in the Suppression of Western
Insurrection, 1794: Journals of Major Spear and Captain J[ohn] Machinheimer,
HSP; Brigade Orders, 5 September 1838, Massachusetts Militia Order Book, U.S.
Army Miscellaneous Collection, vol. 1, USAMHI; Andrew Hynes to Tennessee
Volunteers, 14 November 1814, Andrew Hynes Papers, WMC.

20 General Orders, 7 October 1813 and 6 November 1813, Andrew Jackson, Orderly
Book, Frontier Wars Papers, SHSW; Augustus James Pleasonton, Diary, 8–10 June
1838, HSP.

21 Royster, *A Revolutionary People at War*, 60, 69, 74, 215, 236, 238, 244; Washington
to John Hancock, 2 September 1776, *Papers*, 6: 199, 200; Theodore J. Crackel, *Mr.
Jefferson's Army: Political and Social Reform of the Military Establishment,
1801–1809* (New York: New York University Press, 1987), 92; Edward M. Coffman,
The Old Army: A Portrait of the American Army in Peacetime, 1784–1898 (New
York: Oxford University Press, 1986), 33–34; Robert V. Remini; *Andrew Jackson
and the Course of American Empire, 1767–1821* (New York: Harper and Row, 1977),
150, 156, 160.

22 John Campbell to Alick Campbell, 21 October 1847, John Campbell, Civil War
Letters, UVA.

23 Don Higginbotham, *George Washington and the American Military Tradition*
(Athens: University of Georgia Press, 1985), 11, 12, 52; Robert Treat Paine to
Lavinia Paine, 19, 22 May, 25 July 1847, 6 July 1848, Robert Treat Paine Papers,
SHC.

24 Lucien B. Webster to Henry E. Davies, 9 June 1847, Smith-Kirby-Webster-Black-
Danner Family Papers, USAMHI; Greenberg, *Manifest Manhood*, 21–23, 26.

25 George Gordon Meade to Margaret Meade, 2 July 1846, 9 July 1846, and 2
December 1846, Meade Collection.

26 Daniel Harvey Hill, 31 July 1846, 2 August 1846, and 5 August 1846, Diary, SHC.

27 Robert Treat Paine to Lavinia Paine, 19 May 1847, 22 May 1847, 25 July 1847, and 6
July 1848, Paine Papers.

28 George Gordon Meade to Margaret Meade, 2 July 1846 and 2 December 1847,
Meade Collection; Daniel Harvey Hill, 28 November 1846, Diary, SHC; Zachary

Taylor to Thomas Butler, 19 June 1846, Pierce Butler Papers, Tulane; William H.
Ker to Mary S. Ker, 21 September 1861, John Ker and Family Papers, Louisiana and
Lower Mississippi Valley Collections, Hill.

29 George Gordon Meade to Margaret Meade, 12 October 1861, 24 November 1861,
and 28 November 1861, Meade Collection.

30 Lorien Foote, *Gentlemen and the Roughs: Violence, Honor, and Manhood in the
Union Army* (New York: New York University Press, 2010), 54–55, 121–122;
Andrew Hero Jr. to family, 27 August 1861, Andrew Jr. and George Hero Papers
Hill; Lyman Van Buren Furber to Judith and Louisa Furber, 6 November 1861,
Lyman Van Buren Furber Papers, Manuscripts, MDHS.

31 Nathaniel Henry Rhodes Dawson to Elodie Todd, 3 December 1861, Nathaniel
Henry Rhodes Dawson Papers, SHC; Frank Liddell Richardson to Francis
DuBose Richardson and Bethia Liddell Richardson, 4 September 1861, SHC;
Foote, *Gentlemen and the Roughs*, 78.

32 E. Wayne Carp, "The Problem of National Defense in the Early American
Republic," in *The American Revolution: Its Character and Limits*, ed. Jack P.
Greene (New York: New York University Press, 1987), 20; Alan C. Aimone and
Eric I. Manders, "A Note on New York City's Independent Companies, 1775–1776,"
New York History 63, no. 1 (January 1982): 59–73; Brunswick Guards, 7 December
1859, Minute Book, Brunswick Guards Papers, VHS.

33 John Adlum, Memoirs, 14–16, James S. Schoff Collection, WLCL; Robert
McCallen, Company Agreement, 7 December 1776, Robert McCallen Papers,
WLCL.

34 Association Agreement, Bristol, Mass., 10 April 1775, 14 April 1775, H. H. Edes
Papers, MAHS; Samuel Bixby, May 1775, Diary, AAS; Committee of Privates to
the Privates of the several Battalions of Military Associators in the Province of
Pennsylvania, 8 August 1776, Clymer Family Papers, HSP; Steven Rosswurm,
*Arms, Country, and Class: The Philadelphia Militia and the "Lower Sort" During
the American Revolution, 1775–1783* (New Brunswick, NJ: Rutgers University
Press, 1987), 51, 55, 252–553.

35 An Association of the Friends of the Union, ca. 1812, War of 1812 Collection,
WLCL; Constitution for the Marblehead Light Infantry, 18 September 1814,
Isaac Story Papers, WLCL; James Adger, Letterbook of James Adger,
Containing also the Constitution of the Charleston Independent Greens, SCL;
Baltimore Light Dragoons, Orderly Book, MDHS; Franklin Artillery Company,
Record Book, MDHS; Boston Sea Fencibles, *Constitution and Exercise of the
Boston Sea Fencibles, Instituted 11 September 1817* (Boston: Munroe and Francis,
1822); Soul of Soldiery, *Constitution of the Soul of Soldiery* (Boston: E. G.
House, 1824); Natchez Fencibles, *Constitution of the Natchez Fencibles: As
Adopted on the 21st Day of April, 1824 and Revised on the 11th Day of January
1827* (Natchez, MS: Ariel, 1827); First Northumberland Troop, Minute Book,
USAMHI; First Ward Guard, Minute Book, MDHS; Charleston Light
Dragoons, Records, SCL.

36 Hess, *Liberty, Virtue, and Progress*, 6, 7; Robert E. Shalhope, "The Armed Citizen in the Early Republic." *Law and Contemporary Politics* 49, no. 1 (Winter 1986): 126, 130, 132; Snyder, *Citizen-Soldiers and Manly Warriors*, 81.

37 Boston National Guards, Orderly Book, 10, 12, Manuscripts, BPL; Easton Infantry, Orderly Book, BPL; Mobile Rifle Company, *Constitution and By-Laws of the Mobile Rifle Company, Organized Feb. 22, 1836. Revised, July 12, 1837* (Mobile, AL: Dade and Thompson, 1842); Washington Light Infantry, Minutes, SCL; Independent Greys, Record Book, MDHS; Maryland Cadets and Maryland Guard, Records, MDHS; Irish Jasper Greens Papers, GHS; Lincoln Light Infantry, *Constitution, By-Laws, and Rules of Order, of the Lincoln Light Infantry . . . .* (Boston: Davis and Farmer, 1855); United Rifle Corps, Papers, HSP.

38 Crescent Blues, *Constitution and By-Laws of the Crescent Blues, Adopted April 4, 1861* (New Orleans: Clark and Brisbin, 1861), 5; First California Guard, *By-Laws and Bill of Dress of the First California Guard, (Flying Artillery.) Instituted July 27th, 1849. Revised May 25th, 1852; Feb. 1st, 1855; July 27th, 1860* (San Francisco: Agnew and Deffebach, 1860), 14; Saint Louis National Guard, *Constitution and By-Laws of the Corps of National Guard, Saint Louis, MO* (St. Louis, MO: Keemle and Hager, 1857); Mobile Cadets, *Constitution and By-Laws of the Mobile Cadets, Organized October* 1846 (Mobile, AL: J. Y. Thompson, 1858); Washington Artillery, *Constitution and By-Laws of the Washington Artillery, February 1, 1858: Organized Feb. 22, 1840* (New Orleans: Bulletin Book and Job Office, 1858); Maryland Guard, Record Book, MDHS; Amelia Troop Constitution and Bylaws, 1859, Irving Family Papers, VHS; Continental Rangers, Constitution, 3; Putnam Phalanx, *The Origin and First Parade of the Putnam Phalanx . . . .* (Hartford, CT: Case, Lockwood, 1860), 28; Louisiana Guard, *Constitution and By-Laws of the Louisiana Guard: Organized November 9, 1860* (New Orleans: H. P. Lathrop, 1861), 7, 13; St. Louis Grays, Records, MOHS; Divisionary Corps of Cadets, *Constitution of the Divisionary Corps of Cadets, First Division, M.V.M.* (Boston: n.p., 1860); Fay Light Guard, *By-Laws of the Fay Light Guard, Lancaster, Mass., Adopted May 1861* (Clinton, MA: Saturday Courant, 1861); St. Louis Montgomery Guards, Constitution and By-Laws, Records, MOHS; Washington Home Guard, Constitution and Records of the Washington Home Guard, Houghton; National Guards, Constitution and Bye Laws of the National Guards, HSP; Brengle Home Guards, Proceedings of the Brengle Home Guards, MDHS; Company D, 1st Regiment Gray Reserves Minute Book, HSP.

39 William Whiting and Mark Hopkins to Joseph Hawley, 7 February 1776, Elisha Porter Papers, MAHS.

40 Thomas Bailey, "Diary of the Mexican War," *Indiana Magazine of History* 14, no. 2 (1918): 145–146; William Orr to John Y. Sawyer, 1 July 1832, in *The Black Hawk War, 1831–1832*, vol. 2, comp. and ed. Ellen M. Whitney, Collection of the Illinois State Historical Library, ed. William K. Alderfer, no. 35 (Springfield: Illinois State Historical Library, 1970), 725; John W. Dodd to Eliza Dodd, 7 June 1847, John W.

Dodd Papers, OHS; Charles James Johnson to Lou Johnson, 7 August 1861, 8
August 1861, Charles James Johnson Papers, Hill.

41 William E. Mullin to A. Boyd Hamilton, 29 March 1847, Mexican War Collection,
WLCL; A. Davenport, 1 May, 5 September 1861, Letterbook, NYHS.

42 Otho Holland Williams to Nathanael Greene, 26 February 1781, Nathanael Greene
Papers, WLCL; William E. Mullin to A. Boyd Hamilton, 29 March 1847, Mexican
War Collection, WLCL; A. Davenport, , 1 May 1861 and 5 September 1861,
Letterbook, NYHS.

43 Donald R. Hickey, "New England's Defense Problem and the Genesis of the
Hartford Convention," *New England Quarterly* 50, no. 4 (December 1977): 595;
John Aspinwall Hadden, 13 December 1841, 12 February 1842, 25 April 1842, 30
April 1842, and 4 May 1842, Diary, NYPL; A. Beckley to John Buchanan Floyd, 30
August 1861, John Buchanan Floyd Papers, SHC.

44 Samuel Hamilton Walker, *Florida and Seminole Wars. Brief Observations on the
Conduct of the Officers, and on the Discipline of the Army of the United States*
(Washington, DC: n.p., 1840), 1, 10.

45 Petition to George Washington, 10 August 1775, *The Papers of George
Washington*, ed. W. W. Abbot et al., Revolutionary War Series, *June-September
1775*, vol.1, ed. Philander D. Chase (Charlottesville: University Press of Virginia,
1985), 285; Petition to Samuel Eugene Hunter, 24 May 1861, Hunter-Taylor Family
Papers, Hill; John Barrett Pendleton to Sallie Anne Meredith Pendleton, 4 June
1861 and 6 June 1861, Pendleton Family Papers, VHS; Petition to Maxcy Gregg,
1861, SCL.

46 William Davies to Nathanael Greene, 20 February 1781, Nathanael Greene Papers,
WLCL.

47 Petition to Anthony Wayne, Petition to Wayne, Wayne to Serjeants and Privates of
the Pennsylvania Line, 25 December 1780, 4 January 1781, and 7 January 1781,
Anthony Wayne Papers, HSP; Don Higginbotham, *The War for American
Independence: Military Attitudes, Policies, and Practice, 1763–1789* (New York:
Macmillan, 1971), 406, 403–405.

48 Petition to the Congress, ca.1846, Samuel Hamilton Walker Papers, TXSL; Ulysses
S. Grant to John W. Lowe, 26 June 1846, Grant to Julia Dent, 14 August 1846 and 1
February 1847, *The Papers of Ulysses S. Grant, 1837–1861*, vol. 1, ed. John Y. Simon
(Carbondale: Southern Illinois University Press, 1967), 97–98, 105; Richard Bruce
Winders, *Mr. Polk's Army: The American Military Experience in the Mexican War*
(College Station: Texas A&M University Press, 1997), 189, 192, 195.

49 Robert Treat Paine to Lavinia Paine, 13 August 1847, 16 August 1847, and 11 April
1848, Robert Treat Paine Papers, SHC; John J. Hardin to John E. Wool, 22
November 1846, Hardin Family Papers, CHS; Winders, *Mr. Polk's Army*, 128.

50 Company C, First Massachusetts Volunteer Infantry Regiment to Caleb Cushing,
n.d. February 1847, Caleb Cushing Papers, LC; Company C, First Massachusetts
Volunteer Infantry Regiment to Cushing, 27 February 1847, Cushing Papers, LC;
Stephen Curtis, Alfred W. Adams, and George W. Thompson to Cushing, 27

February 1847, Cushing Papers, LC; Company B, First Massachusetts Volunteer Infantry Regiment to Cushing, 21 February 1847, Cushing Papers, LC; Companies C, E, and F, First Massachusetts Volunteer Infantry Regiment to Cushing, n.d. [February] 1847; Thomas Reid to Cushing, n.d. February 1847, Cushing Papers, LC.

51 Field Officers of the Connecticut Light Horse to George Washington, Washington to the Field Officers of the Connecticut Light Horse 16 July 1776, *The Papers of George Washington*, ed. W. W. Abbot et al., Revolutionary War Series, *June-August 1776*, vol. 5, ed. Philander D. Chase (Charlottesville: University Press of Virginia, 1993), 336.

52 Royster, *A Revolutionary People at War*, 5, 7; Royster, "A Society and Its War," 175, 176.

CHAPTER 4. A PROVIDENTIALLY ORDAINED REPUBLIC

1 Anders Stephanson, *Manifest Destiny: American Expansion and the Empire of Right* (New York: Hill and Wang, 1995), xiii, xiv, 3, 5. Stephanson provides a brief and very useful account of the origins and development of what he terms "chosenness." John F. Berens, *Providence and Patriotism in Early America, 1640–1815* (Charlottesville: University Press of Virginia, 1978), ix, 2–4. See also Hans Kohn, *The Idea of Nationalism: A Study in its Origins and Background* (1944; repr., New York: Collier Books, 1960); Frederick Merk, *Manifest Destiny and Mission in American History: A Reinterpretation* (New York: Alfred A. Knopf, 1963); Reginald Horsman, *Race and Manifest Destiny: The Origins of American Racial Anglo-Saxonism* (Cambridge, MA: Harvard University Press, 1981); Thomas R. Hietala, *Manifest Destiny: Anxious Aggrandizement in Late Jacksonian America* (Ithaca, NY: Cornell University Press, 1985); and William Earl Weeks, *Building the Continental Empire: American Expansion from the Revolution to the Civil War* (Chicago: Ivan R. Dee, 1996). John M. Murrin, "The Jeffersonian Triumph and American Exceptionalism," *Journal of the Early Republic* 20, no. 1 (Spring 2000): 2. Martin Brückner, *The Geographic Revolution in America: Maps, Literacy, and National Identity* (Chapel Hill: University of North Carolina Press for the Omohundro Institute of Early American History and Culture, 2006), examines the intersection between geography, expansion, and identity.

2 Stephanson, *Manifest Destiny*, 3–6, 28; Berens, *Providence and Patriotism*, 14–31; George C. Rable, *God's Almost Chosen Peoples: A Religious History of the American Civil War* (Chapel Hill: University of North Carolina Press, 2010), 1, 2, 5; James P. Byrd, *Sacred Scripture, Sacred War: The Bible and the American Revolution* (New York: Oxford University Press, 2013), 1–3; 5–7, 10–13. See David Hackett Fischer, *Albion's Seed: Four British Folkways in America* (New York: Oxford University Press, 1989) on the threads of English cultural continuity in North America.

3 Stephanson, *Manifest Destiny*, 3–6, 28; John L. O'Sullivan, "Annexation," *United States Magazine and Democratic Review* 17, no.1 (July-August 1845): 6; Berens, *Providence and Patriotism*, 14–31.

4 Stephanson, *Manifest Destiny*, xiv, 6; Fred Anderson, *A People's Army: Massachusetts Soldiers and Society in the Seven Years' War* (Chapel Hill: University of North Carolina Press for the Institute of Early American History and Culture, 1984), 196; Kohn, *The Idea of Nationalism*, 291, 323; Hietala, *Manifest Destiny*, vii-ix, 133, 255; Merk, *Manifest Destiny and Mission in American History*, viii-ix, 33; Israel Putnam, 12 October 1777, *General Orders Issued by Major-General Israel Putnam when in Command of the Highlands, in the Summer and Fall of 1777*, ed. Worthington Chauncey Ford (Brooklyn: Historical Printing Club, 1893; reprint, Boston: Gregg, 1972), 84; Berens, *Providence and Patriotism*, 71-2.

5 Francis Paul Prucha, *The Sword of the Republic: The United States Army on the Frontier, 1783-1846* (New York: Macmillan, 1969), xvii, 331; Richard H. Immerman, *Empire for Liberty: A History of American Imperialism from Benjamin Franklin to Paul Wolfowitz* (Princeton, NJ: Princeton University Press, 2010), 5-11; William H. Goetzmann, *Army Exploration in the American West, 1803-1863* (New Haven, CT: Yale University Press, 1959), 4. Eran Shalev, *American Zion: The Old Testament as a Political Text from the Revolution to the Civil War* (New Haven, CT: Yale University Press, 2013), examines the intersection of sacred text and American political belief.

6 Agreement of the Wethersfield Company of Volunteers, Capt. Chester, April 23rd 1775, Samuel Blachley Webb, *Correspondence and Journals of Samuel Blachley Webb*, vol. 1, coll. and ed. Worthington Chauncey Ford (New York: n.p., 1893; reprint, New York Times and Arno, 1969), 55-56; Isaac Bangs, 21 July 1776, *Journal of Lieutenant Isaac Bangs: April 1 to July 29, 1776*, ed. Edward Bangs (Cambridge, MA: John Wilson and Son, University Press, 1890; reprint, New York: New York Times and Arno, 1968), 64; Benjamin Gilbert to Daniel and Mary Goddard Kimball Gilbert, 8 October 1780, *Winding Down: The Revolutionary War Letters of Lieutenant Benjamin Gilbert of Massachusetts, 1780-1783*, ed. John Shy (Ann Arbor: University of Michigan Press, 1989), 22; Enos Hitchcock to John Low, 2 October 1778, "Diary of Enos Hitchcock, D.D., A Chaplain in the Revolutionary Army. With a Memoir," ed. William B. Weedon, *Publications of the Rhode Island Historical Society*, n.s., 7, no. 2 (July 1899): 90.

7 Charles Royster, *A Revolutionary People at War: The Continental Army and American Character, 1775-1783* (Chapel Hill: University of North Carolina Press, 1979; reprint, New York: W. W. Norton for the Institute of Early American History and Culture, 1981), 5, 13-15, 27.

8 The literature on religiously inspired or religiously fueled war in Europe is enormous; for a brief entrée to the secondary literature see Mack P. Holt, *The French Wars of Religion, 1562-1629*, 2nd ed. (New York: Cambridge University Press, 1995); James B. Wood, *The King's Army: Warfare, Soldiers and Society during the Wars of Religion in France, 1562-76* (New York: Cambridge University Press, 1996); Peter H. Wilson, *The Thirty Years War: Europe's Tragedy* (Cambridge, MA: Belknap Press of Harvard University Press, 2009). Iverson Lea Graves to Sarah Dutton Graves, 3 June 1836, Graves Family Papers, SHC.

9   L. L. Allen to editor, 26 June 1846, 27 June 1846, and 11 August 1846, *Pencillings of Scenes Upon the Rio Grande: Originally Published in the Saint Louis American*, 2d ed. (New York: n.p., 1848), 11, 17; Robert Armstrong to Mariane P. Longfellow, 13 February 1848, Mexican War Collection, UTA.

10 Robert W. Johannsen, *To the Halls of the Montezumas: The Mexican War in the American Imagination* (New York: Oxford University Press, 1985), 49.

11 Berens, *Providence and Patriotism*, 170; Louis Perrin Foster to Mrs. B. B. Foster, 5 August 1861, Louis Perrin Foster Letters, James Rion McKissick Papers, SCL; Samuel Nicoll Benjamin to mother, 8 April 1861, Samuel Nicoll Benjamin Papers, USMA; Joseph Roswell Hawley to Hattie Hawley, 1 June 1861, Joseph Roswell Hawley Papers, LC; George Smith Avery to Elizabeth Little, 2 July 1861, George Smith Avery Letters, Civil War Letters Collection, CHS; Gerald F. Linderman, *Embattled Courage: The Experience of Combat in the American Civil War* (New York: Free Press, 1987), 2–3, 7.

12 John Q. Winfield to Sallie Winfield, 2 September 1861, John Q. Winfield Letters, SHC; William Nelson Pendleton, 1 May 1861, Papers, SHC.

13 Earl J. Hess, *The Union Soldier in Battle: Enduring the Ordeal of Combat* (Lawrence: University Press of Kansas, 1997), 102; William Harvey Lamb Wallace to Ann Dickey Wallace, 30 August 1861, Wallace-Dickey Family Papers, ILSL; Caleb J. Allen to Matilda T. Allen, 4 September 1861, Samuel T. Allen Papers, CAH; William R. Williams to wife, 15 September 1861, William R. Williams Letters, Civil War Miscellaneous Collection, USAMHI; Peter Warden to Elizabeth Vreeland, 22 September 1861, Warden Family, CHS; Hess, *The Union Soldier in Battle*, 104.

14 Hitchcock, "A Devout Soldier: A Sermon Preached at West Point, June 23, 1782; At Providence, February 2, 1783," in "Diary of Enos Hitchcock," 104–106.

15 Harvey Brown, 10 June 1846, Journal of Campaigns Under Genls Taylor and Scott in Mexico during the Years 1846, 1847, and 1848, HEH; Reid Mitchell, *The Vacant Chair: The Northern Soldier Leaves Home* (New York: Oxford University Press, 1993), 4, 7, 26–27; Ann M. Little, *Abraham in Arms: War and Gender in Colonial New England* (Philadelphia: University of Pennsylvania Press, 2007), 6–7, 24–25; Lorien Foote, *Gentlemen and the Roughs: Violence, Honor, and Manhood in the Union Army* (New York: New York University Press, 2010), 4.

16 Richard Varick to Archibald Laidley, 16 August 1776, Richard Varick Papers, NYHS; Thomas Rodney, 15 December 1776, Journal of Campaign, 1776–1777, NYPL. See Drew Gilpin Faust, *This Republic of Suffering: Death and the American Civil War* (New York: Alfred A. Knopf, 2008), on death in mid-nineteenth-century American culture.

17 William Henry Tatum to Belle Tatum, 20 July 1861, William Henry Tatum Papers, VHS; Tristram Lowther Skinner to Eliza Fisk Harwood Skinner, 12 September 1861, Skinner Family Papers, SHC; Mason Gordon to Lucy Robertson, 18 August 1861, Gordon Family Papers, UVA.

18 Nathanael Greene to Samuel Ward, 4 January 1776, Nathanael Greene Collection, HEH; Immerman, *Empire for Liberty*, 8–11, 106; Amy S. Greenberg, *Manifest Manhood and the Antebellum American Empire* (New York: Cambridge University Press, 2005), 3, 4, 6, 14, 21–23.

19 "American" is used in the sense of a sovereign and independent people. Although independence was not declared until 1776, the military and political activities of American colonists in 1775, especially the open state of hostilities, were demonstrative of courses of action pursued by an independent people. Royster, *A Revolutionary People at War*, 152, 157, 164; James Allen, 6 July 1775, HSP; James McHenry, Testament, 29 July 1775, James McHenry Papers, LC.

20 [Anthony Wayne?] to Tom Robinson, 11 April 1776, Anthony Wayne Papers, HSP; Anthony Wayne to James Moore, 2 January 1777, Anthony Wayne Papers, HSP.

21 [Anthony Wayne?] to Tom Robinson, 11 April 1776, Anthony Wayne Papers; Anthony Wayne to James Moore, 2 January 1777, Anthony Wayne Papers.

22 Nathanael Greene to Samuel Ward, 18 December 1775, Nathanael Greene Papers, WLCL; Moses Greenleaf, 18 January 1779, West Point Orderly Book, MAHS; General Orders, 10 August 1775, John Patton Orderly Book, Manuscripts of the American Revolution, BPL.

23 Weeks, *Building the Continental Empire*, x, 31, 61–64; Merk, *Manifest Destiny and Mission*, 33, 227; Edward Larkin, "Nation and Empire in the Early US," *American Literary History* 22, no. 3 (Fall 2010): 501–526.

24 Immerman, *Empire for Liberty*, 5–11; Greenberg, *Manifest Manhood*, 20.

25 Peter Silver, *Our Savage Neighbors: How Indian War Transformed Early America* (New York: W. W. Norton, 2008), 118–119, 120, 121, 133, 264–296; Little, *Abraham in Arms*, 3, 5; Horsman, *Race and Manifest Destiny*, 1, 27.

26 Horsman, *Race and Manifest Destiny*, 1, 27.

27 Ibid. George Bancroft, *History of the United States of America, from the Discovery of the American Continent*, 10 vols. (Boston: Charles Bowen, 1834–1837, vols. 1–2; Boston: Little, Brown, 1842–1874, vols. 3–10), went through some twenty-five editions.

28 Horsman, *Race and Manifest Destiny*, 1, 6; Weeks, *Building the Continental Empire*, 62–64.

29 Prucha, *Sword of the Republic*, 331.

30 Benjamin Alvord, *Address Before the Dialectic Society of the Corps of Cadets . . . .* (New York: Wiley and Putnam, 1839), 20–21.

31 Johannsen, *To the Halls of the Montezumas*, 51, 170, 171; Henry Smith Lane to Samuel Stone, 5 November 1846, Henry Smith Lane Papers, Filson; Robert E. May, *Manifest Destiny's Underworld: Filibustering in Antebellum America* (Chapel Hill: University of North Carolina Press, 2002), 14.

32 Johannsen, *To the Halls of the Montezumas*, 281, 289–290, 291, 292.

33 Joseph H. Lamotte to Ellen Lamotte, 5 October 1846 and 16 April 1848, Lamotte-Copinger Papers, MOHS.

34 James Willoughby Anderson to Ellen Anderson, 1 May 1847 and 5 May 1847, James Willoughby Anderson Papers, USMA.

35 Joseph H. Lamotte to Ellen Lamotte, 16 April 1848, Lamotte-Copinger Papers.

36 J. Jacob Oswandel to Frederick Oswandel, 17 April 1847, *Notes on the Mexican War, 1846–47–48 . . .*, rev. ed. (Philadelphia: n.p., 1885), 571; James Wall Schureman, 1 February 1848, Diary, UVA; Johannsen, *To the Halls of the Montezumas*, 298–99.

37 Schureman, 1 February 1848, Diary.

38 John A. Quitman to Louisa Quitman, 4 January 1847, Quitman Family Papers, SHC; John A. Quitman to Eliza Quitman, 29 April 1847, Quitman Family Papers; Samuel H. Walker to Jonathan T. Walker, 4 August 1847 and 5 October 1847, Samuel Hamilton Walker Papers, TXSL.

39 John A. Quitman to H. S. Foote, 15 October 1847, Quitman Family Papers; Robert E. May, *John A. Quitman: Old South Crusader* (Baton Rouge: Louisiana State University Press, 1984), 197, 199; May, *Manifest Destiny's Underworld*, 14, 86–89.

40 Samuel H. Walker to Jonathan T. Walker, 4 August, 5 October 1847, Samuel Hamilton Walker Papers.

41 James M. McCaffrey, *Army of Manifest Destiny: The American Soldier in the Mexican War, 1846–1848* (New York: New York University Press, 1992); Johannsen, *To the Halls of the Montezumas*, 289, 297; Samuel H. Walker to Jonathan T. Walker, 5 October 1847, Samuel Hamilton Walker Papers.

42 Robert E. May, "Young American Males and Filibustering in the Age of Manifest Destiny: The United States Army as a Cultural Mirror," *Journal of American History* 7, no. 3 (December 1991): 862, 876, 881, 886.

43 Ibid, 876.

44 Edward Ashley Bowen Phelps to Samuel M. Phelps, 3 April 1847, 16 April 1848, Edward Ashley Bowen Phelps Letters, NYPL.

45 Edward Ashley Bowen Phelps to Samuel M. Phelps, 29 January 1848 and 9 February 1848, Edward Ashley Bowen Phelps Letters.

46 Edward Ashley Bowen Phelps to Samuel M. Phelps, 29 January 1848 and 9 February 1848, Edward Ashley Bowen Phelps Letters.

47 Edward Phelps to Samuel Phelps, 9 February 1848, Edward Ashley Bowen Phelps Letters.

48 Edward Phelps to Samuel Phelps, 24 February 1848, Edward Ashley Bowen Phelps Letters; Greenberg, *Manifest Manhood*, 26, 45.

49 Greenberg, *Manifest Manhood*, 26, 45, 89, 91.

CHAPTER 5. QUESTING FOR PERSONAL DISTINCTION

1 George Washington introduced the Purple Heart to recognize military valor during the War for Independence. It did not reappear until the twentieth century. The Medal of Honor was not awarded until after 1861.

2 E. Wayne Carp, *To Starve the Army at Pleasure: Continental Army Administration and American Political Culture, 1775–1783* (Chapel Hill: University of North

Carolina Press, 1984), 163, 164; Edward M. Coffman, *The Old Army: A Portrait of the American Army in Peacetime, 1784–1898* (New York: Oxford University Press, 1986), 66, 67, 90.

3 Douglass Adair, "Fame and the Founding Fathers," in *Fame and the Founding Fathers: Essays by Douglass Adair*, ed. Trevor Colbourn (New York: W. W. Norton for the Institute of Early American History and Culture, 1974), 9.

4 Thomas C. Linn, "Ethics Versus Self-Interest in How We Fight," in *Moral Obligation and the Military: Collected Essays* (Washington, DC: National Defense University Press, 1988), 220–22.

5 Adair, "Fame and the Founding Fathers," 8; Carp, *To Starve the Army at Pleasure*, 164, 167.

6 Carp, *To Starve the Army at Pleasure*, 159, 161, 163, 164, 167; Coffman, *The Old Army*, 66, 67, 90. See also William B. Skelton, *An American Profession of Arms: The Army Officer Corps, 1784–1861* (Lawrence: University Press of Kansas, 1992).

7 Carp, *To Starve the Army at Pleasure*, 163, 164, 167; Adair, "Fame and the Founding Fathers," 24.

8 Adair, "Fame and the Founding Fathers," 7–9; Carp, *To Starve the Army at Pleasure*, 164, 167; Earl J. Hess, *The Union Soldier in Battle: Enduring the Ordeal of Combat* (Lawrence: University Press of Kansas, 1997), 2, 46, 51, 74, 95–97; Charles Royster, "Founding a Nation in Blood: Military Conflict and American Nationality," in *Arms and Independence: The Military Character of the American Revolution*, ed. Ronald Hoffman and Peter J. Albert (Charlottesville: University Press of Virginia, 1984), 45; Charles Royster, "A Society and Its War," in *Adapting to Conditions: War and Society in the Eighteenth Century*, ed. Maarten Ultee (University: University of Alabama Press, 1986), 181.

9 George Washington to Burwell Bassett, General Orders, 19 June, 7 July 1775, *The Papers of George Washington*, ed. W. W. Abbot et al., Revolutionary War Series, *June-September 1775*, vol. 1, ed. Philander D. Chase (Charlottesville: University Press of Virginia, 1985), 13, 71–72; Washington to Rudolphus Ritzema, 14 July 1776, *The Papers of George Washington*, ed. W. W. Abbot et al., Revolutionary War Series, *June-August 1776*, vol. 5, ed. Philander D. Chase (Charlottesville: University Press of Virginia, 1993), 316.

10 Leo Braudy, *The Frenzy of Renown: Fame and Its History* (New York: Oxford University Press, 1986), 7. See also John F. Berens, *Providence and Patriotism in Early America, 1640–1815* (Charlottesville: University Press of Virginia, 1978) for an understanding of Americans' belief in God in their affairs.

11 Joseph Ward to Captain Hopkins, 24 March 1779, Joseph Ward Papers, NYPL (microfilm, CHS); Anthony Wayne to Thomas Wharton, 22 November 1777, Anthony Wayne Papers, WLCL; Thomas Fanning, "A War Song," n.d., Notebook, AAS; Benjamin Gilbert to Charles Bruce, 10 June 1783, Benjamin Gilbert, *Winding Down: The Revolutionary War Letters of Lieutenant Benjamin Gilbert of Massachusetts, 1780–1783*, ed. John Shy (Ann Arbor: University of Michigan Press, 1989), 107; Thomas Rodney to Caesar Rodney, 14 January 1777, *Letters to and From*

Caesar Rodney, 1756–1784 . . . , ed. George Ryden Herbert (Philadelphia: University of Pennsylvania Press for the Historical Society of Delaware, 1933), 154. Pennsylvania's first constitution vested "supreme executive power" in the president and council. In 1790 the new Constitution abolished the council and replaced the president with a governor. See 1776 PA Const. § 3, and 1790 PA Const. art. II, § 1.

12 Alexander Scammell to Otho Holland Williams, 25 February 1781, Otho Holland Williams Papers, MDHS.

13 James Mills, 21 July 1813, Regimental Book for the 1st Regiment, 3rd Detachment of the Ohio Militia, Containing Orders Received and Issued by Colonel James Mills of Butler County and the State of Ohio, OHS, 100; James Callaway to Flanders and Jamimah Callaway, 9 August 1814, James Callaway Papers, Joseph Maher Collection, MOHS; George Armistead to Louisa Armistead, 10 September 1814, War of 1812 Collection, MDHS; Nicole Eustace, *1812: War and the Passions of Patriotism* (Philadelphia: University of Philadelphia Press, 2012), 143.

14 Frank A. Hardy to Mr. and Mrs. Amos Hardy, 11 November 1846, Frank A. Hardy Papers, OHS; Robert E. May, *John A. Quitman: Old South Crusader* (Baton Rouge: Louisiana State University Press, 1984), 146, 162–163, 166; Isaac Bowen to Katie Bowen, 24 August 1846, Isaac Bowen Papers, USAMHI.

15 J. Mason Henry to Rev. Caleb Davis Bradlee, 30 May 1861, Letters to Rev. Caleb Davis Bradlee, AAS.

16 Royster, "A Society and Its War," 181; W. M. Blackmore to Peter H. Martin, 7 January 1847, W.M. Blackmore Correspondence, TNSL; Drew Gilpin Faust, *This Republic of Suffering: Death and American Civil War* (New York: Alfred A. Knopf, 2008), 6–17; Mark S. Schantz, *Awaiting the Heavenly Country: The Civil War and America's Culture of Death* (Ithaca, NY: Cornell University Press, 2008), 2, 19, 67, 69; Richard F. Miller, "Brahmin Janissaries: John A. Andrew Mobilizes Massachusetts' Upper Class for the Civil War," *New England Quarterly* 75, no. 2 (June 2002): 210.

17 Adair, "Fame and the Founding Fathers," 10; William F. Gordon to Elizabeth Lindsay Gordon, 31 August 1814, Gordon Family Papers, UVA.

18 Morris Janowitz, *The Professional Soldier: A Social and Political Portrait* (New York: Free Press, 1960), 137; R. Claire Snyder, *Citizen-Soldiers and Manly Warriors: Military Service and Gender in the Civic Republic Tradition* (Lanham, MD: Rowman and Littlefield, 1999), 85–87.

19 Otho Holland Williams to Elie Williams, 24 February 1779, Otho Holland Williams Papers.

20 George W. Melvin to Asa B. Sizer, 6 February 1814, Sizer Family Papers, Tulane; John McCarty and David Foot to Asa B. Sizer, 6 February 1814, Sizer Family Papers; S. Johnson to Christopher Quarles Tompkins, 11 September 1845, Tompkins Family Papers, VHS.

21 Royster, "Founding a Nation in Blood," 25, 30; Charles Royster, *A Revolutionary People at War: The Continental Army and American Character, 1775–1783* (Chapel Hill: University of North Carolina Press, 1979; reprint, New York: W. W. Norton

for the Institute of Early American History and Culture, 1981), 88, 207; K. Jack Bauer, *The Mexican War, 1846–1848* (New York: Macmillan Publishing, 1974), 149, 150; Amy S. Greenberg, *Manifest Manhood and the Antebellum American Empire* (New York: Cambridge University Press, 2005), 12; Lorien Foote, *Gentlemen and the Roughs: Violence, Honor, and Manhood in the Union Army*. New York: New York University Press, 2010), 77–79; John J. Hardin to John E. Wool, 22 November 1846, Hardin Family Papers, CHS.

22   John J. Hardin to John E. Wool, 22 November 1846, Hardin Family Papers.

23   Alexis de Tocqueville, *Democracy in America*, ed. J. P. Mayer, trans. George Lawrence (New York: Harper and Row Perennial Library, 1966), 488–489, 567–571, 612–14, 647–48; Bertram Wyatt-Brown, "Andrew Jackson's Honor," *Journal of the Early Republic* 17, no. 1 (Spring 1997): 1, 4, 15, 20.

24   Robert Middlekauff, "Why Men Fought in the American Revolution," *Huntington Library Quarterly* 42, no. 2 (Spring 1980): 142–143, 147–148.

25   Joseph Bloomfield, *Citizen-Soldier: The Revolutionary War Journal of Joseph Bloomfield*, ed. Mark E. Lender and James Kirby Martin (Newark: New Jersey Historical Society, 1982), 3 May 1776, 41–2; Washington to Martha Washington, 18 June 1775, *Papers*, 1: 4.

26   Philip Gooch Ferguson, *Marching with the Army of the West, 1846–1848 . . .* , ed. Ralph P. Bieber (Glendale, CA: Arthur H. Clark, 1936), 28; Carnot Posey to George Gordon, 19 February 1847, Carnot Posey and Family Papers, MDAH; Charles R. Adams to Isabella A. Adams, 24 September 1859, Simeon Roe Adams and Family Papers, MDAH.

27   Roger Jones to Thomas Claiborne, 18 January 1861, Thomas Claiborne Papers, SHC.

28   John S. R. Miller to Elisha P. Miller, 5 February 1861, John S. R. Miller Papers, SHC.

29   Albert Sidney Johnston to Dr. Johnston, 14 April 1861, Frederick M. Dearborn Collection, Confederate Generals, Houghton; George Gordon Meade to Margaret Meade, 12 October 1861, Meade Collection, HSP.

30   Richard Ackerman to Mr. and Mrs. Abraham Ackerman, 28 August 1861, Richard Ackerman Papers, MOHS; Richard Ackerman to Abraham Ackerman, 4 September 1861, Richard Ackerman Papers; Richard Ackerman to Abraham Ackerman, 16 October 1861, Richard Ackerman Papers; Holmes Conrad to Elizabeth Whiting Powell Conrad, 10 November 1861, Holmes Conrad Papers, VHS; Robert Lewis Dabney to Lavinia Morrison Dabney, 5 September 1861, Charles William Dabney Papers, SHC.

31   Thomas Corwin Honnell to Benjamin Epler, 21 May 1861, Thomas Corwin Honnell Papers, OHS; William Augustin M. Larue to Eliza Cornelia Grantham, 8 May 1861, Larue Family Papers, VHS.

32   Anthony Wayne to Mary Wayne, 1 April 1777, Anthony Wayne Papers, HSP.

33   Gideon J. Pillow to Gideon J. Pillow, Jr., 14 September 1846 and 11 January 1848, Gideon J. Pillow Papers, MOHS; J. Jacob Oswandel to Frederick Oswandel, 17

April 1847, *Notes on the Mexican War, 1846–47–48* . . . . , rev. ed. (Philadelphia: n.p., 1885), 121.

34 Andrew McCollam, Jr. to Andrew McCollam, Sr., 1 May 1861, Andrew McCollam Papers, SHC; Hannibal Paine to Virginia, 26 July 1861, Paine Family Collection, TNSL; James Trooper Armstrong to Ladie Armstrong James Trooper Armstrong Papers, 5 August 1861, SHC; William Anderson to Creek Anderson, 23 October 1861, William Anderson Papers, UVA; James S. Colwell to Annie Colwell, 23 June 1861, James S. Colwell Letters, Civil War Miscellaneous Collection, USAMHI; James P. Stewart to brother, 3 November 1861, James P. Stewart Letters, Civil War Times Illustrated Collection, USAMHI; Samuel J. Alexander to Agnes G. Alexander, 1 September 1861, Samuel J. Alexander, Correspondence, Civil War Miscellaneous Collection, USAMHI; William Preston Johnston to Rosa Duncan Johnston, Johnston Family Papers, 6 November 1861, Filson.

35 *Webster's American Military Biographies* (1978), s.v. "Harmar, Josiah," "St. Clair, Arthur;" David Eggenberger, *An Encyclopedia of Battles: Accounts of Over 1,560 Battles from 1479 B.C. to the Present* (New York: Dover, 1985), 150, 152; Anthony Wayne to Henry Knox, 23 October 1793 and 14 August 1794, Anthony Wayne Letterbooks, WLCL.

36 Stephen Watts Kearny to Ethan Allen Hitchcock, 6 May 1841, Hitchcock Family Papers, MOHS; Francis Paul Prucha, *The Sword of the Republic: The United States Army on the Frontier, 1783–1846* (New York: Macmillan, 1969), 269; Samuel J. Watson, *Peacekeepers and Conquerors: The Army Officer Corps on the American Frontier, 1821–1846* (Lawrence: University Press of Kansas, 205–208; Samuel J. Watson, e-mail message to author, 2 April 2014.

37 William Austine to cousin, 25 July 1848, William Austine Letters, SHC.

38 Isaac Bowen to Katie Bowen, 25 October 1846, Isaac Bowen Papers, USAMHI; Daniel Harvey Hill, 21 November 1846, Diary, SHC. Carp, *To Starve the Army at Pleasure*, Theodore J. Crackel, *Mr. Jefferson's Army: Political and Social Reform of the Military Establishment, 1801–1809* (New York: New York University Press, 1987) and Lawrence Delbert Cress, *Citizens in Arms: The Army and the Militia in American Society to the War of 1812* (Chapel Hill: University of North Carolina Press, 1982) are excellent starting points in any examination of American opposition to standing armies.

39 William A. De Palo, *The Mexican National Army, 1822–1852* (College Station: Texas A&M University Press, 1997) 100–102; William Chetwood De Hart to Charles Ferguson Smith, 27 May 1846, USMA.

40 George Stubblefield, General Orders, 19 March 1776, "Orderly Book of the Company of Captain George Stubblefield, Fifth Virginia Regiment, from March 3, 1776 to July 10, 1776," *Collections of the Virginia Historical Society: Miscellaneous Papers, 1672–1865*, n.s., 6 (1887): 151; Samuel Elbert, Regimental Orders, 13 April 1777, General Orders, 8 May 1777, "Order Book of Samuel Elbert, Colonel and Brigadier General in the Continental Army, October 1776, to November 1778,"

Collections of the Georgia Historical Society 5, part 2 (1902):16, 60; Thomas Sidney Jesup, Detachment Orders, 2 August 1813, Thomas Sidney Jesup Papers, LC.

41 Andrew Hynes to Tennessee Volunteers, 14 November 1814, Andrew Hynes Papers, Tulane.

42 Robert Carr, Copy of General Orders, 4 November 1813, Journal and Letters, HSP; For the most recent biography of Wilkinson, see Andro Linklater, *An Artist in Treason: The Extraordinary Double Life of General James Wilkinson* (New York: Walker, 2009).

43 Howell O. Tatum, 8 January 1815, Journal, War of 1812 Series, Tulane; Thomas J. Barclay, 19 May 1847, Journal, Mexican War Collection, WLCL.

44 Dennis Hart Mahan to James Birdseye McPherson, 28 July 1852, James Birdseye McPherson Papers, LC.

45 Henry C. McCook to John C. Kelton, 21 December 1861, Charles Ferguson Smith Papers, USMA.

46 Adair, "Fame and the Founding Fathers," 11, 12, 19; Royster, *A Revolutionary People at War*, 5, 204.

47 Braudy, *The Frenzy of Renown*, 7, 15, 393, 399.

48 Nathanael Greene to Samuel Ward, 14 July 1775, Nathanael Greene Collection, HEH; Nathanael Greene to Samuel Ward, 14 July 1775, Nathanael Greene Papers, WLCL; Marie Paul Joseph Roch Yves Gilbert du Motier, Marquis de Lafayette to George Washington, 14 October, 31 December 1777, *The Letters of Lafayette to Washington, 1777–1799*, ed. and rev. Louis Gottschalk and Shirley A. Bill (New York: H.. F. Hubbard, 1944; reprint, Philadelphia: American Philosophical Society, 1976), 4, 17.

49 Hess, *The Union Soldier in Battle*, 2; Thomas Fanning, "A War Song," Notebook, AAS.

50 Benjamin Smead to John M. McNeil, 21 August 1814, Benham-McNeil Family Papers, LC.

51 Thomas S. Jesup to Joseph Gardner Swift, Joseph Gardner Swift Papers, 4 September 1820, USMA.

52 Philip St. George Cooke, *Scenes and Adventures in the Army: Or, Romance of Military Life* (Philadelphia: Lindsay and Blakiston, 1859), 175–176.

53 Ethan Allen Hitchcock to Richard Bache, 10 August 1827, Hitchcock Family Papers, MOHS; Robert Anderson to W. Gates, 13 May 1846, Robert Anderson Papers, LC; Ulysses S. Grant to John Garland, [August 1846], *The Papers of Ulysses S. Grant, 1837–1861*, vol. 1, ed. John Y. Simon (Carbondale, IL: Southern Illinois University Press, 1967), 106–107; George Brinton McClellan, *The Mexican War Diary of George B. McClellan*, ed. William Starr Myers (Princeton, NJ: Princeton University Press, 1917), 16–17. In his *Memoirs*, Grant wrote of the war with Mexico as "one of the most unjust ever waged by a stronger against a weaker nation." As a lieutenant, however, Grant did not question the war or its propriety in any of his letters from 1844–1848. See Grant, *Papers*, 1:23–169; Ulysses S. Grant, *Personal Memoirs of U.S. Grant*, vol. 1 (New York: Charles L. Webster, 1885), 22–24.

54 William E. Mullin to A. Boyd Hamilton, 29 March 1847, Mexican War Collection, WLCL; Henry Clay Jr. to Henry Clay, Sr., 12 February 1847, *Papers of Henry Clay: Candidate, Compromiser, Elder Statesman, January 1, 1844-June 29, 1852*, vol. 10, ed. Melba Porter Hay and Carol Reardon (Lexington: University Press of Kentucky, 1991), 305.

55 Robert E. May, "Young American Males and Filibustering in the Age of Manifest Destiny: The United States Army as a Cultural Mirror," *Journal of American History* 7, no. 3 (December 1991): 861, 862, 874, 876; Robert E. May *Manifest Destiny's Underworld: Filibustering in Antebellum America* (Chapel Hill: University of North Carolina Press, 2002), 101–103, 111–112.

56 Thomas Sumter to Nathanael Greene, 29 January 1781, Civil War Collection, HEH.

57 John A. Quitman, *An Address on the Occasion of the Second Anniversary of the Palmetto Association, delivered in Columbia, S.C., Tuesday, May 4th, 1858* (Columbia, SC: I.C. Morgan, 1858), 7, 8, 9.

58 Otho Holland Williams to Edward Giles, 23 September 1781, Otho Holland Williams Papers, MDHS.

59 Instructions for Colonel Webb, November 1782, *Correspondence and Journals of Samuel Blachley Webb*, vol. 2, coll. and ed. Worthington Chauncey Ford (New York: n.p., 1893; reprint, New York Times and Arno, 1969), 433, 434; John Gooch to Nathanael Greene, 26 September 1780, Nathanael Greene Papers, WLCL.

60 William Atherton, *Scenes of the Late War* . . . . (Frankfort, KY: A. G. Hodges, 1842), 3; Louis P. Towles, *A World Turned Upside Down: The Palmers of South Santee, 1818-1881* (Columbia: University of South Carolina Press, 1996), 987–988; William E. Mikell, *Oration Delivered Before the Washington Light Infantry, on Their Fifty-second Anniversary, at the Institute Hall, February 22, 1859* (Charleston, SC: Walker, Evans, 1859), 5.

EPILOGUE

1 James McPherson, *Battle Cry of Freedom: The Civil War Era* (New York: Oxford University Press, 1988), 234–237, 264, 276–284, 318.

2 Ibid., 306,

3 John Pelham to [Elizabeth Pelham], 9 March 1861, John Pelham Letter, ADAH.

4 George Smith Avery to Elizabeth Little, 21 April 1861, 29 April 1861,and 6 May 1861, George Smith Avery Letters, Civil War Letters Collection, CHS.

5 Charles Royster, "Founding a Nation in Blood: Military Conflict and American Nationality," in *Arms and Independence: The Military Character of the American Revolution*, ed. Ronald Hoffman and Peter J. Albert (Charlottesville: University Press of Virginia, 1984), 45.

6 Mark Grimsley, "The American Civil War and Civic Virtue," *Foreign Policy Research Institute Footnotes: The Newsletter of the Wachman Center* 13, no. 11 (November 2008): 1–4.

BIBLIOGRAPHY

MANUSCRIPT AND ARCHIVAL SOURCES

Alabama Department of Archives and History
Pelham, John. Letters.

American Antiquarian Society
Anderson, John E. Reminiscences. Civil War Collection, 1861–1868.
Ballard, Franklin E. Miscellaneous. Correspondence.
Baker, Henry W. Letters.
Bixby, Samuel. Diary.
Bradlee, Caleb Davis. Letters.
Corthell, William P. Letters.
Fanning, Thomas. Notebook.
Greene, Nathanael. Papers.
Henshaw Family. Papers.
Hill, Alonzo. Letters.
Joslin, Henry L. Letters.
United States Revolution Collection.
    New Stamford, New Hampshire. Petition.
    Preble, Jedidiah. Letter.
    Whitcomb, John. Letter.
    Smith. Letter.

Ancient and Honorable Artillery Company
Charlestown Light Infantry. Letterbook.
Columbian Guards. Orderly Book.

Bancroft Library, University of California, Berkeley
Dimmick, Kimball Hale. Correspondance and Papers.

Boston Public Library
Boston National Guards. Orderly Book.
Easton Infantry. Orderly Book.
Everson, Erastus W. Letters.
Manuscripts of the American Revolution.
    Dearborn, Henry. Diary of Campaigns, with Verse.

Lee, Charles. Letter.
Patton, John. Orderly Book.
Suffolk Guards. Records.

Center for American History, University of Texas, Austin
Allen, Samuel T. Papers.
Bryan, James Lecompte. Papers.
Crutcher-Shannon Family. Papers.
    Crutcher, William O. Correspondence.
    Morris, Howard. Correspondence.
Curry, Wilmot Walter. Papers.
Holland, James K. Papers.
McClintock, William Alexander. Journal of a Soldier of the Second Kentucky Regiment: Trip through Texas and Northern Mexico in 1846–1847.
Walker, John B. Letter. Philpott Texana Collection.

Chicago Historical Society
Barnum, Ephraim K. Letter.
Civil War Letters. Collection.
    Avery, George Smith. Letters.
    Converse, James L. Letters.
Ellsworth, Elmer Ephraim. Collection.
Hardin Family. Papers.
Holmes, Daniel B. Papers.
Taylor, John. Letter. Letter File.
Wallace, William Harvey Lamb. Papers.
Ward, Joseph. Papers (New York Public Library microfilm).
Warden Family. Papers.
Weedon, George. Papers.
Yates, Christopher P. Papers.
Yell, Archibald. Papers.

William L. Clements Library, University of Michigan
Barclay, Thomas J. Journal.
Brown, Jacob Jennings. Papers.
Douglass, David Bates. Papers.
Fenno-Hoffman Family. Papers.
Fish, Nicholas. Collection.
Fish Family. Papers.
Greene, Nathanael. Papers.
Jesup, Thomas Sidney. Papers.
McCallen, Robert. Papers.
McHenry, James. Papers.

Mexican War. Collection.
    Meginnes, John Franklin. Sketch of a Tour in Mexico.
    Mullin, William E. Letter.
Orderly Book. Collection.
    Howe, Robert. Orderly Book.
    Polley, John. Orderly Book.
Schoff, James S. Revolutionary War Collection.
    Adlum, John. Memoirs.
    Wayne, Anthony. Letter.
Story, Isaac. Papers.
Turner, Peter. Letters from Dr. Peter Turner Relating to the Revolutionary War
    Miscellaneous Bound. Collection.
Van Deventer, Christopher. Papers.
War of 1812. Collection
    Chandler, J. Letter.
    Claude, John. Letter.
    Fairfield, Connecticut Volunteers. Proposed rules for a Company of Musquetry
        (Volunteers).
    Grant, Asa. Letter.
    New Gloucester, Maine. An Association of the Friends of the Union.
Wayne, Anthony. Letterbooks.
Wayne, Anthony. Papers.

The Filson Club
Johnston Family. Papers.
Lane, Henry Smith. Papers.
Shreve, Family. Papers.
Summers, Thomas T. Papers.

Jenkins Garrett Library, University of Texas, Arlington
Armstrong, Robert. Letter. Mexican War. Collection.

Georgia Historical Society
Irish Jasper Greens. Papers.
King-Wilder Family. Papers.
Oglethorpe Light Infantry. Papers.
Screven, Richard Bedon. Papers.

Hill Memorial Library, Louisiana State University
Duffell, Edward. Papers.
Flournoy, Alfred. Papers.
Foster, James. Papers.
Hero, Andrew, Jr. and George. Papers.

Hunter-Taylor Family. Papers.
Johnson, Charles James. Papers.
Ker, John and Family. Papers.
Ker, William H. Letters.
Mandeville, Henry D. and Family. Papers.
Pierson, David H. Letter.
White, Silas T. Papers.

Historical Society of Pennsylvania
Allen, James. Diary.
Carr, Robert. Papers.
Clymer Family. Papers.
Company D, 1st Regiment Gray Reserves Minute Book.
Johnson, Jesse. Diary.
Jordan, Thomas Jefferson. Civil War. Letters.
Maryland Militia. Papers.
Meade. Collection.
National Guards. Constitution and Bye Laws.
Pleasonton, Augustus James. Diary.
United Rifle Corps. Papers.
Wayne, Anthony. Papers.
Young, William. Journal, 1776–1777.

Houghton Library, Harvard University
Alvord, Benjamin. Letter. Frederick M. Dearborn Collection. Union Generals.
Bidwell, Daniel D. Letter. Frederick M. Dearborn Collection. Union Generals.
Edwards, William. Brigade Orders for Camp at South Boston under the Command of
    William Edwards.
Johnston, Albert Sidney. Letter. Frederick M. Dearborn Collection. Confederate Generals.
Knox, Henry. Letter. Frederick M. Dearborn Collection. Revolutionary Generals.
Washington Home Guard. Constitution and Records.

Howard-Tilton Memorial Library, Tulane University
Butler, Pierce. Papers.
Hynes, Andrew. Papers.
Sizer Family. Papers.
Stibbs Family. Papers.
Tatum, Howell O. Journal. War of 1812. Series.
Watson, Clement Stanford Family. Papers.

Henry E. Huntington Library
Anderson, Robert. Collection.

Brown, Harvey. Journal of Campaigns under Genls Taylor and Scott in Mexico during the years 1846, 1847, and 1848.
Greene, Nathanael. Collection.
Merrill, Hamilton Wilcox. Collection.
Chilton, George W. Collection.
Civil War. Collection.
    Sherman, William Tecumseh. Collection.
    Sumter, Thomas. Collection.
Wayne, Anthony. Brigade Orderly Book.

Illinois State Historical Library
Grierson, Benjamin H. Papers.
Mahon, James and Family. Papers.
Wallace-Dickey Family. Papers.

Indiana Historical Society
Wallace, Lewis. Papers.

Indiana State Library
Lasselle Family. Papers.

Library of Congress
Anderson, Robert. Papers.
Benham-McNeil Family. Papers.
Cater, Douglas J. and Rufus W. Letters.
Clinton, James and George. Papers.
Cushing, Caleb. Papers.
Fish, Nicholas. Papers.
Foster, Isaac, Family. Papers.
Hatch, John Porter. Papers.
Hawley, Joseph Roswell. Papers.
Jesup, Thomas Sidney. Papers.
King, Benjamin. Papers.
McHenry, James. Papers.
McPherson, James Birdseye. Papers.
Talbot, Theodore. Papers.

Maryland Historical Society
Archer, James J. Collection.
Armistead, George. Letter. War of 1812. Collection.
Baltimore Light Dragoons. Record Book.
Bayard. Papers.

Brengle Home Guards. Proceedings of the Brengle Home Guards, Formed April 1861 and Mustered into the 16th M M on Friday 26th Day April, Frederick Md.
First Ward Guard. Minute Book.
Franklin Artillery Company. Record Book.
Furber, Lyman Van Buren. Papers.
Independent Greys. Record Book.
Maryland Cadets and Maryland Guard. Records.
Maryland Guard. Record Book.
Williams, Otho Holland. Papers.

Massachusetts Historical Society
Colman, Dudley. Papers.
Crowninshield, Caspar. Papers.
Cushman, Thomas. Diary.
Dwight Family. Papers.
Edes, H. H. Papers.
Fox, Charles B. Journal.
Greenleaf, Moses. West Point Orderly Book.
Pickering, Timothy. Papers.
Porter, Elisha. Papers.
Sewall, Henry. Diary.

Mississippi Department of Archives and History
Adams, Simeon Roe and Family. Papers.
Posey, Carnot and Family. Papers.
Stuart, Oscar J. E. and Family. Papers.

Missouri Historical Society
Ackerman, Richard. Papers.
Callaway, James. Papers. Joseph Maher. Collection.
Hitchcock Family. Papers.
Lamotte-Copinger Family. Papers.
Pillow, Gideon J. Papers.
St. Louis Grays. Records.
St. Louis Montgomery Guards. Records.

New-York Historical Society
Davenport, A. Letterbooks.
George Mitchell. Letters.
Green, Augustus P. Autobiography.
Harrison, William Henry. Correspondence.
New-York Hibernian Vollunteers. Minute-Book.
Pickering, Timothy. Manuscripts.

Varick, Richard. Papers.
Webb, Samuel Blatchley. Manuscripts.

New York Public Library
Dearborn, Henry. Papers.
Elder, Samuel S. Letters.
Hadden, John Aspinwall. Diary.
Norris, James. Journal.
Phelps, Edward Ashley Bowen. Letters.
Rodney, Thomas. Journal.
Van Cortlandt-Van Wyck Family. Papers.
Wainwright Family of Rhinebeck, New York and of New York City. Papers.

Ohio Historical Society
Denny, James. Papers.
Dodd, John W. Papers.
Hardy, Frank A. Letters.
Honnell, Thomas Corwin. Papers.
Loudon, DeWitt Clinton. Papers.
Mills, James. Regimental Book for the 1st Regiment, 3rd Detachment of the Ohio Militia, Containing Orders Received and Issued by Colonel James Mills of Butler County and the State of Ohio.
Newsom, Nathan. A Short Summary of a Journey Taken by Volunteers from Gallia County for the Purpose of Destroying Indians and the Invasion of Canada.
Taylor, Thomas Thomson. Papers.

South Carolina Historical Society
Allston, R. F. W. Papers.
Bratton, John. Letters.
Manning, John L. Papers.
McCrady, Edward, Sr. Collections.

South Caroliniana Library, University of South Carolina
Adams, Cicero. Letter.
Adger, James. Letterbook.
Aiken, David Wyatt. Papers.
Charleston Light Dragoons. Records.
First Regiment, South Carolina Volunteers. Papers.
Foster, Louis Perrin. Letters. James Rion McKissick. Papers.
Jefferies Family. War Record.
Traylor and McLane Families. Papers.
Washington Light Infantry. Minutes of the Washington Light Infantry.
Watts Family. Papers.

Southern Historical Collection, Wilson Library, University of North Carolina, Chapel Hill
Alcorn, James Lusk. Papers.
Alexander, Edward Porter. Papers.
Armstrong, James Trooper. Papers.
Austine, William. Letters.
Benbury and Haywood Family. Papers.
Boykin Family. Papers.
Claiborne, Thomas. Papers.
Dabney, Charles William. Papers.
Dawson, Nathaniel Henry Rhodes. Papers.
Govan, Daniel Chevilette. Papers.
Graham, William Alexander Graham. Papers.
Graves Family. Papers.
Haskell, Alexander Cheves. Papers.
Hill, Daniel Harvey. Diary.
Kendrick, H. C. Letters.
Kirby-Smith, Edmund. Papers.
Lenoir Family. Papers.
Mackay and Stiles Family. Papers.
Manning, John L. Papers.
McCauley, Andrew. Papers.
McCollam, Andrew. Papers.
McLaws, Lafayette. Papers.
Miller, John S. R. Papers.
Moore, Lucinda Sugg. Papers.
Mordecai Family. Papers.
Paine, Robert Treat. Papers.
Pendleton, William Nelson. Papers.
Quitman Family. Papers.
Richardson, Frank Liddell. Papers.
Skinner Family. Papers.
Walton Family. Papers.
Wells, William Ray. Papers.
Winfield, John Q. Letters.

Special Collections, Earl Gregg Swem Library, College of William and Mary
Brock Family. Papers.
Calfee Family. Papers.
Floyd, John Buchanan. Papers.
Powell Family. Papers.
Ritchie-Harrison Family. Papers.

Taliaferro, William Booth. Papers.
Tucker-Coleman Family. Papers.

Special Collections, University of Texas at Arlington Library
Armstrong, Robert. Letter. Mexican War Collection.

Special Collections, University of Virginia Library
Anderson, William. Papers.
Campbell, John. Letters.
Cocke, Philip St. George. Papers.
Gordon Family. Papers.
Randall Family. Papers.
Schureman, James Wall. Diary.

Special Collections and Archives, United States Military Academy Library
Anderson, James Willoughby. Papers.
Arnold, Isaac Jr. Papers.
Barbour, Philip Nordbourne. Papers.
Benjamin, Samuel Nicoll. Papers.
Chapman-McCaskey Family. Papers.
Dana, Napoleon Jackson Tecumseh. Papers.
Duncan, James. Papers.
Halleck, Henry Wager. Papers.
Lyford, Stephen Carr Jr. Papers.
Mansfield, Joseph King Fenno. Papers.
Smith, Charles Ferguson. Papers.
Swift, Joseph Gardner. Papers.

State Historical Society of Wisconsin
Jackson, Andrew. Orderly Book. Frontier Wars Papers. Lyman Copeland Draper.
    Manuscripts.
Wood, Eleazar D. Papers.

Tennessee State Library and Archives
Blackmore, W. M. Correspondence.
Lillard Family. Papers.
Paine Family. Papers.

Texas State Library and Archives
Walker, Samuel Hamilton. Papers.

United States Army Military History Institute, Carlisle Barracks
Beardsley, Harrison. Correspondence. Dawson Flinchbaugh. Collection.

Bliss, Zenas R. Papers.
Bowen, Isaac. Papers.
Brooks, William T. H. Papers.
Civil War Miscellaneous. Collection.
   Alexander, Samuel J. Correspondence.
   Boucher, John Vincent. Letters.
   Browne, Robert A. Letters.
   Colwell, James S. Letters.
   Dunham, William H. Letters.
   Kibbee, Amos W. Letters.
   O'Brien, John. Letters.
   Walling, William Henry. Letters.
   Watson, Richard H. Letters.
   Williams, William R. Letters.
Civil War Times Illustrated. Collection.
   Griffin, James. Letters.
   McClintock, Andrew. "Waterbury goes to War: The Civil War Letters of Andrew
      McClintock, Color Sergeant, First Connecticut Infantry." Edited by Frederick W.
      Chesson. 1989. Frederick W. Chesson. Collection.
   Stewart, James P. Letters.
   Thompson, Benjamin W. Recollections of War Times.
Fynn, John. Papers.
Lantzy, Philip A. Letters. Harrisburg Civil War Round Table. Collection.
Massachusetts Militia. Order Book. U.S. Army Miscellaneous. Collection.
Northumberland, First Troop. Papers.
Northwest Corner Civil War Round Table. Collection.
   Hunt, John Randolph, Jr. Letters.
   Wells, Frank. Papers.
Peckham, James. Letters. Wiley Sword. Papers.
Smith-Kirby-Webster-Black-Danner Family. Papers.
Sparks, David Rhodes. Memoirs and Letters. Curtis J. Herrick. Papers.
Wagner, Levi. Recollections of an Enlistee, 1861–1864: Levi Wagner, Pvt., Company A,
   First Ohio Volunteer Infantry.

Virginia Historical Society
Amelia Troop. Constitution and Bylaws. Irving Family. Papers.
Brunswick Guards. Papers.
Conrad, Holmes. Papers.
Keith Family. Papers.
Larue Family. Papers.
Pamunkey Rifles. Petition to the Governor of Virginia, 1861. New Kent County
   Collection.
Pendleton Family. Papers.

Ridley, William Goodwyn. Correspondence. Ridley Family. Papers.

Scott, Alfred Lewis. Memoir of Service in the Confederate Army.

Stuart, James Ewell Brown. Papers.

Tatum, William Henry. Papers.

Tompkins Family. Papers.

Williams Research Center of the Historic New Orleans Collection
Murphy Family. Papers.

Ruggles, Francis Dunbar. Papers.

Walton-Glenny Family. Papers.

PUBLISHED PRIMARY SOURCES

Allen, Ethan. *The Narrative of Colonel Ethan Allen*. Philadelphia: Robert Bell, 1779.
    Reprint, New York: Corinth Books, 1961.

Allen, L. L. *Pencillings of Scenes Upon the Rio Grande: Originally Published in the Saint Louis American*. 2d ed. New York: n.p., 1848.

Alvord, Benjamin. *Address before the Dialectic Society of the Corps of Cadets . . . .* New York: Wiley and Putnam, 1839.

Atherton, William. *Scenes of the Late War, Narrative of the Suffering & Defeat of the North-Western Army Under General Winchester . . . .* Frankfort, KY: A.G. Hodges, 1842.

Bailey, Thomas. "Diary of the Mexican War." *Indiana Magazine of History* 14, no. 2 (1918): 134–147.

Ballentine, George. *Autobiography and an English Soldier in the United States Army*. Edited by William H. Goetzmann. New York: Stringer and Townsend, 1853. Reprint, Chicago: R. R. Donnelly and Sons Lakeside Classics, 1986.

Bangs, Isaac. *Journal of Lieutenant Isaac Bangs: April 1 to July 29, 1776*. Edited by Edward Bangs. Cambridge, MA: John Wilson and Son, University Press, 1890. Reprint, New York: New York Times and Arno, 1968.

Beall, John Bramblett. *In Barrack and Field: Poems and Sketches of Army Life*. Nashville: Smith and Lamar, 1906.

Bennett, James A. *Forts and Forays: A Dragoon in New Mexico, 1850–1856*. Edited by Clinton E. Brooks and Frank D. Reeve. Albuquerque: University of New Mexico Press, 1948.

Bieber, Ralph P., ed. *Marching with the Army of the West, 1846–1848*, by Abraham Robinson Johnston, Marcellus Ball, and Philip Gooch Ferguson. Glendale, CA: Arthur H. Clark, 1936.

Bloomfield, Joseph. *Citizen-Soldier: The Revolutionary War Journal of Joseph Bloomfield*. Edited by Mark E. Lender and James Kirby Martin. Newark: New Jersey Historical Society, 1982.

Boston Sea Fencibles. *Constitution and Exercise of the Boston Sea Fencibles, Instituted 11 September 1817*. Boston: Munroe and Francis, 1822.

Butler, Benjamin Franklin. *The Military Profession in the United States . . . .* New York: Samuel Colman, 1839.

Captain of Infantry. *Hints Bearing on the United States Army, with an Aim at the Adaptation, Availability, Efficiency and Economy Thereof.* Philadelphia: Henry B. Ashmead, 1858.

Chamberlain, Samuel E. *My Confession: The Reflections of a Rogue.* Edited by Roger Butterfield. New York: Harper and Bros., 1956.

Clay, Henry. *The Papers of Henry Clay: Candidate, Compromiser, Elder Statesman, January 1, 1844-June 29, 1852.* Vol. 10. Edited by Melba Porter Hay and Carol Reardon. Lexington: University Press of Kentucky, 1991.

Cohen, M[eyer]. M. *Notices of Florida and the Campaigns.* Charleston: Burges and Honour, 1836.

Collins, Francis. "Journal of Francis Collins: An Artillery Officer in the Mexican War." Edited by Maria Clinton Collins. *Quarterly Publication of the Historical and Philosophical Society of Ohio* 10, no. 2 (April 1915): 37–70; no. 3 (July 1915): 71–109.

Continental Rangers. *Constitution and By-Laws of the Continental Rangers.* St. Louis: Mantz, 1853.

Cooke, Philip St. George. *Scenes and Adventures in the Army: Or, Romance of Military Life.* Philadelphia: Lindsay and Blakiston, 1859.

Crescent Blues. *Constitution and By-Laws of the Crescent Blues, Adopted April 4, 1861.* New Orleans: Clark and Brisbin, 1861.

Davidson, J., John Pool, and Thomas Mulligan. "Temperance." *Army and Navy Chronicle* 1, no. 41 (8 October 1835): 321–22.

De Peyster, John Watts. *An Address to the Officers of the New York State Troops . . . .* Poughkeepsie, NY: Platt and Schram, 1858.

Divisionary Corps of Cadets. *Constitution of the Divisionary Corps of Cadets, First Division, M.V.M.* Boston: Printed for the Cadets, 1860.

The Eclaireur, a military journal . . . . 3 vols. Edited by John Watts De Peyster and Augustus T. Cowman. Hyde Park, NY: Platt and Schram, 1853–56.

Elbert, Samuel. "Order Book of Samuel Elbert, Colonel and Brigadier General in the Continental Army, October 1776, to November 1778." *Collections of the Georgia Historical Society* 5, pt. 2 (1902): 5–191.

Elderkin, James D. *Biographical Sketches and Anecdotes of a Soldier of Three Wars . . . .* Detroit: James D. Elderkin, 1899.

Fay Light Guard. *By-Laws of the Fay Light Guard, Lancaster, Mass., Adopted May 1861.* Clinton, MA: Saturday Courant, 1861.

First California Guard. *By-Laws and Bill of Dress of the First California Guard, (Flying Artillery.) . . . .* San Francisco: Agnew and Deffebach, 1860.

Ford, Worthington Chauncey. *Journals of the Continental Congress.* Vol. 2, *10 May-20 September 1775.* Washington, DC: Government Printing Office, 1905.

Furber, George C. *The Twelve Months Volunteer . . . .* Cincinnati: J. A. and U. P. James, 1850.

Gilbert, Benjamin. *Winding Down: The Revolutionary War Letters of Lieutenant Benjamin Gilbert of Massachusetts, 1780–1783.* Edited by John Shy. Ann Arbor: University of Michigan Press, 1989.

Goree, Thomas J. *Longstreet's Aide: The Civil War Letters of Major Thomas J. Goree.* Edited by Thomas W. Cutrer. Charlottesville: University Press of Virginia, 1995.

Grant, Ulysses S. *The Papers of Ulysses S. Grant, 1837-61.* Vols.1-2. Edited by John Y. Simon. Carbondale: IL: Southern Illinois University Press, 1967-1969.

———. *Personal Memoirs of U. S. Grant.* Vol. 1. New York: Charles L. Webster, 1885.

Grivot, M. *Annual Report of the Adjutant General to the Legislature of the State of Louisiana, 1859.* Baton Rouge: J. M. Taylor, 1860.

———. *Report of the Adjutant General of the Louisiana Militia to the Legislature of the Legislature of the State of Louisiana, 1856.* New Orleans: John Claiborne, 1857.

Higginson, Thomas Wentworth. *Massachusetts in the Army and the Navy during the War of 1861-1865.* Vol. 2. Boston: Wright and Potter, 1895.

Hitchcock, Enos. "Diary of Enos Hitchcock, D. D., A Chaplain in the Revolutionary Army. With a Memoir." *Publications of the Rhode Island Historical Society,* n.s., 7, no. 2 (July 1899): 87-134.

Hopkins, Frederick W. *Discourses at Norwich, Vermont, During the Obsequies of Truman B. Ransom, Colonel of the New England Regiment, February Twenty-second, 1848.* Hanover, NH: Dartmouth and Journal, 1848.

Jackson, Andrew. *The Papers of Andrew Jackson. 1804-1813.* Vol. 2. Edited by Harold D. Moser and Sharon MacPherson. Knoxville: University of Tennessee Press, 1984.

Lafayette, Marie Paul Joseph Roch Yves Gilbert du Motier, Marquis de. *The Letters of Lafayette to Washington, 1777-1799.* Edited and revised by Louis Gottschalk and Shirley A. Bill. New York: H. F. Hubbard, 1944. Reprint, Philadelphia: American Philosophical Society, 1976.

Lane, Henry S. "The Mexican War Journal of Henry S. Lane." Edited by Graham A. Barringer. *Indiana Magazine of History* 53, no. 4 (1957): 383-434.

Laurens, John. *The Army Correspondence of Colonel John Laurens in the Years 1777-8.* New York: n.p., 1867. Reprint, New York: New York Times and Arno, 1969.

Lincoln Light Infantry. *Constitution, By-Laws, and Rules of Order, of the Lincoln Light Infantry . . . .* Boston: Davis and Farmer, 1855.

Locke, John. *Second Treatise of Government: An Essay Concerning the True Original, Extent and End of Civil Government.* Edited by Richard H. Cox. Arlington Heights, IL: Harlan Davidson, 1982.

Logan, John A. *The Volunteer Soldier of America, with Memoir of the Author and Military Reminiscences from General Logan's Private Journal.* Chicago: R. S. Peale, 1887.

Louisiana Guard. *Constitution and By-Laws of the Louisiana Guard: Organized November 9, 1860.* New Orleans: H. P. Lathrop, 1861.

Marcy, Randolph Barnes. *Border Reminiscences.* New York: Harper and Bros., 1872.

Marion Rifle Corps. *Constitution and By-Laws of the Marion Corps of Baltimore.* Baltimore: Sands and Neilson, 1831.

Martin, Joseph Plumb. *Private Yankee Doodle: Being a Narrative of Some of the Adventures, Dangers and Sufferings of a Revolutionary Soldier.* Edited by George F. Scheer. New York: New York Times and Arno, 1968.

McClellan, George Brinton. *The Mexican War Diary of George B. McClellan.* Edited by William Starr Myers. Princeton, NJ: Princeton University Press, 1917.

McGowan, Samuel. *An Address on the Occasion of the First Anniversary of the Palmetto Association, Delivered in Columbia, S. C., May 14th, A. D. 1857.* Columbia, SC: I. C. Morgan, 1857.

McIntosh, David Gregg. *Reminiscences of Early Life in South Carolina.* Edited by Horace Fraser Rudisill. Florence, SC: St. David's Society, 1985.

Mechanic Phalanx. *Constitution of the Mechanic Phalanx, Instituted at Chelmsford, Feb. 1, 1825.* East-Chelmsford, MA: William Baldwin, 1825.

———. *Constitution of the Mechanic Phalanx, Instituted at Chelmsford, Feb. 1, 1825, with the Amendment in 1831.* Lowell, MA: John S. C. Knowlton, 1831.

Mikell, William E. *Oration Delivered Before the Washington Light Infantry, on Their Fifty-second Anniversary, at the Institute Hall, February 22, 1859.* Charleston, SC: Walker, Evans, 1859.

Mobile Cadets. *Constitution and By-Laws of the Mobile Cadets, Organized October 1846.* Mobile, AL: J. Y. Thompson, 1858.

Mobile Rifle Company. *Constitution and By-Laws of the Mobile Rifle Company, Organized Feb. 22, 1836. Revised, July 12, 1837.* Mobile, AL: Dade and Thompson, 1842.

Natchez Fencibles. *Constitution of the Natchez Fencibles: As Adopted on the 21st Day of April, 1824 and Revised on the 11th Day of January 1827.* Natchez, MS: Ariel, 1827.

New York Military Magazine; Devoted to the Interests of the Militia Throughout the Union, vol. 1. Edited by William W. Tompkins. New York: Labree and Stockton, 1841.

O'Sullivan, John L. "Annexation." *United States Magazine and Democratic Review* 17, no.1 (July-August 1845): 5–10.

Oswandel, J. Jacob. *Notes on the Mexican War, 1846–47–48 . . . .* Rev. ed. Philadelphia: n.p., 1885.

Palfrey, [H.W.] "Grand Military Pageant." *Le Courrier De La Louisiane (New Orleans).* 6 April 1852.

Pennsylvania. Constitution. 1776.

———. Constitution. 1790.

Putnam, Israel. *General Orders Issued by Major-General Israel Putnam When in Command of the Highlands, in the Summer and Fall of 1777.* Edited by Worthington Chauncey Ford. Brooklyn: Historical Printing Club, 1893. Reprint, Boston: Gregg, 1972.

Putnam Phalanx. *Excursion of the Putnam Phalanx to Mount Vernon, December 1860.* Hartford, CT: Charles G. Geer, 1861.

———. *The Origin and First Parade of the Putnam Phalanx . . . .* Hartford, CT: Case, Lockwood, 1860.

Quitman, John A. *An Address on the Occasion of the Second Anniversary of the Palmetto Association, Delivered in Columbia, S. C., Tuesday, May 4th, 1858.* Columbia, SC: I. C. Morgan, 1858.

Robertson, John Blount. *Reminiscences of a Campaign in Mexico* . . . . Nashville: John York, 1849.

Rodney, Caesar. *Letters to and From Caesar Rodney, 1756–1784* . . . . Edited by George Herbert Ryden. Philadelphia: University of Pennsylvania Press for the Historical Society of Delaware, 1933.

Saint Louis National Guard. *Constitution and By-Laws of the Corps of National Guard, Saint Louis, MO*. St. Louis: Keemle and Hager, 1857.

Smith, Ashbel. *Addresses Delivered in the Chapel at West Point* . . . . New York: W. L. Burroughs, 1848.

Soulé, Frank, John H. Gihon, and Frank Nisbet. *The Annals of San Francisco* . . . . New York: D. Appleton, 1855.

Soul of Soldiery. *Constitution of the Soul of Soldiery*. Boston: E. G. House, 1824.

Stubblefield, George. "Orderly Book of the Company of Captain George Stubblefield, Fifth Virginia Regiment, from March 3, 1776 to July 10, 1776. *Collections of the Virginia Historical Society: Miscellaneous Papers, 1672–1865*. n.s., 6 (1887): 141–91.

Tocqueville, Alexis de. *Democracy in America*. Edited by J. P. Mayer. Translated by George Lawrence. New York: Harper and Row, Perennial Library, 1966.

Tracy, Albert. *Annual Report of the Adjutant General of the State of Maine, 1853*. Augusta, ME: William T. Johnson, 1854.

Walker, E. T. *The Citizen Soldier: An Address in Commemoration of the 28th of June, 1776, to Have Been Delivered Before the Moultrie and Palmetto Guards*. Charleston: A. J. Burke, 1858.

Walker, Samuel Hamilton. *Florida and Seminole Wars. Brief Observations on the Conduct of the Officers, and on the Discipline of the Army of the United States*. Washington, DC: n.p., 1840.

Washington, George. *The Papers of George Washington: Revolutionary War Series*. June 1775–October 1776. Vols. 1–6. Edited by Philander D. Chase, et al. Charlottesville: University Press of Virginia, 1985–1994.

Washington Artillery. *Constitution and By-Laws of the Washington Artillery* . . . . New Orleans: Bulletin Book and Job Office, 1858.

Webb, Samuel Blachley. *Correspondence and Journals of Samuel Blachley Webb*. 3 vols. Collected and edited by Worthington Chauncey Ford. New York: n.p., 1893. Reprint, New York: New York Times and Arno, 1969.

Whitney, Ellen M., comp. and ed. *The Black Hawk War, 1831–1832*. 3 vols. Springfield: Illinois State Historical Library, 1970–1975.

Zeh, Frederick. *An Immigrant Soldier in the Mexican War*. Translated by William J. Orr. Edited by William J. Orr and Robert Ryal Miller. College Station: Texas A&M University Press, 1995.

PUBLISHED SECONDARY SOURCES

Adams, Michael C. C. *Our Masters the Rebels: A Speculation on Union Military Failure in the East, 1861–1865*. Cambridge, MA: Harvard University Press, 1978.

Ahearn, Marie. *The Rhetoric of War: Training Day, the Militia, and the Military Sermon.* New York: Greenwood, 1989.

Aimone, Alan C., and Eric I. Manders. "A Note on New York City's Independent Companies, 1775–1776." *New York History* 63, no.1 (January 1982): 59–73.

Anderson, Fred. *Crucible of War: The Seven Years' War and the Fate of Empire in British North America, 1754–1766.* New York: Alfred A. Knopf, 2000.

———. *A People's Army: Massachusetts Soldiers and Society in the Seven Years' War.* Chapel Hill: University of North Carolina Press for the Institute of Early American History and Culture, 1984.

Appleby, Joyce. *Liberalism and Republicanism in the Historical Imagination.* Cambridge, MA: Harvard University Press, 1992.

———. "Republicanism in Old and New Contexts." *William and Mary Quarterly,* 3rd ser., 43, no. 1 (January 1986): 20–34.

———, ed. "Republicanism in the History and Historiography of the United States." Special Issue. *American Quarterly* 37, no. 4 (Autumn 1985).

Axinn, Sidney. *A Moral Military.* Philadelphia: Temple University Press, 1989.

Bacevich, Andrew J. *The New American Militarism: How Americans Are Seduced by War.* New York: Oxford University Press, 2005.

Bailyn, Bernard. *The Ideological Origins of the American Revolution.* Enlarged Edition. Cambridge, MA: Belknap Press of Harvard University Press, 1992.

Baker, H. Robert. *The Rescue of Joshua Glover: A Fugitive Slave, the Constitution and the Coming of the Civil War.* Athens: Ohio University Press, 2006.

Baker, Jean. "From Belief into Culture: Republicanism in the Antebellum North," *American Quarterly* 37, no. 4 (Autumn 1985): 532–550.

Ball, Durwood. *Army Regulars on the Frontier, 1848–1861.* Norman: University of Oklahoma Press, 2001.

Bancroft, George. *History of the United States of America, from the Discovery of the American Continent.* 10 vols. Vols. 1–2. Boston: Charles Bowen, 1834–1837. Vols. 3–10. Boston: Little, Brown, 1842–1874.

Banning, Lance. *The Jeffersonian Persuasion: Evolution of a Party Ideology.* Ithaca, NY: Cornell University Press, 1978.

Barker, Gordon S. *Fugitive Slaves and the Unfinished American Revolution: Eight Cases, 1848–1856.* Jefferson, NC: McFarland, 2013.

———. *Imperfect Revolution: Anthony Burns and the Landscape of Race in Antebellum America.* Kent, OH: Kent State University Press, 2011.

Bauer, K. Jack. *The Mexican War, 1846–1848.* New York: Macmillan, 1974.

Berens, John F. *Providence and Patriotism in Early America, 1640–1815.* Charlottesville: University Press of Virginia, 1978.

Beringer, Richard E. "Confederate Identity and the Will to Fight." In *On the Road to Total War: The American Civil War and the German Wars of Unification, 1861–1871,* edited by Stig Förster and Jörg Nagler, 75–100. Cambridge: Cambridge University Press, 1997.

Bickham, Troy. *The Weight of Vengeance: The United States, the British Empire, and the War of 1812*. New York: Oxford University Press, 2012.

Black, Jeremy. *War and the Cultural Turn*. Malden, MA: Polity, 2012.

Blackwell, Marilyn S., and James S. Holway. "Reflections on Jacksonian Democracy and Militia Reform: The Waitsfield Militia Petition of 1836." *Vermont History: The Proceedings of the Vermont Historical Society* 55, no.1 (Winter 1987): 5–15.

Boynton, Lindsay. *The Elizabethan Militia, 1588–1638*. London: Routledge and Kegan Paul, 1967.

Braudy, Leo. *The Frenzy of Renown: Fame and Its History*. New York: Oxford University Press, 1986.

Brooks, Charles E. "The Social and Cultural Dynamics of Soldiering in Hood's Texas Brigade." *Journal of Southern History* 67, no. 3 (August 2001): 535–72.

Brückner, Martin. *The Geographic Revolution in America: Maps, Literacy, and National Identity*. Chapel Hill: University of North Carolina Press for the Omohundro Institute of Early American History and Culture, 2006.

Butler, Jon. *Becoming America: The Revolution before 1776*. Cambridge, MA: Harvard University Press, 2000.

Byrd, James P. *Sacred Scripture, Sacred War: The Bible and the American Revolution*. New York: Oxford University Press, 2013.

Caldwell, Norman W. "The Frontier Army Officer, 1794–1814." *Mid-America: An Historical Review* 37 (April 1955): 101–28.

Campbell, Stanley W. *The Slave Catchers: Enforcement of the Fugitive Slave Law, 1850–1860*. Chapel Hill: University of North Carolina Press, 1970.

Carp, E. Wayne. *To Starve the Army at Pleasure: Continental Army Administration and American Political Culture, 1775–1783*. Chapel Hill: University of North Carolina Press, 1984.

Coffman, Edward M. "The Duality of the American Military Tradition: A Commentary." *Journal of Military History* 64, no. 4 (October 2000): 967–980.

———. *The Old Army: A Portrait of the American Army in Peacetime, 1784–1898*. New York: Oxford University Press, 1986.

Cohen, Eliot A. *Supreme Command: Soldiers, Statesmen, and Leadership in Wartime*. New York: Anchor Books, 2003.

Colbourn, Trevor, ed. *Fame and the Founding Fathers: Essays by Douglass Adair*. New York: W. W. Norton for the Institute of Early American History and Culture, 1974.

Collison, Gary. *Shadrach Minkins: From Fugitive Slave to Citizen*. Cambridge, MA: Harvard University Press, 1997.

Cooper, Jerry. *The Rise of the National Guard: The Evolution of the American Militia, 1865–1920*. Lincoln: University of Nebraska Press, 1997.

Corvisier, André. *Armies and Societies in Europe, 1494–1789*. Translated by Abigail T. Siddall. Bloomington: Indiana University Press, 1979. Originally published as *Armées et sociétés en Europe de 1494 à 1789* (Paris: Presses Universitaires de France, 1976).

Cox, Caroline. *A Proper Sense of Honor: Service and Sacrifice in George Washington's Army*. Chapel Hill: University of North Carolina Press, 2004.

Crackel, Theodore J. "The Founding of West Point: Thomas Jefferson and the Politics of Security." *Armed Forces and Society* 12, no. 4 (Summer 1981): 529–543.

——. "Jefferson, Politics, and the Army: An Examination of the Military Peace Establishment Act of 1802." *Journal of the Early Republic* 2 (1982): 21–38.

——. *Mr. Jefferson's Army: Political and Social Reform of the Military Establishment, 1801–1809*. New York: New York University Press, 1987.

Cress, Lawrence Delbert. *Citizens in Arms: The Army and the Militia in American Society to the War of 1812*. Chapel Hill: University of North Carolina Press, 1982.

Cunliffe, Marcus. *Soldiers and Civilians: The Martial Spirit in America, 1775–1865*. 2nd ed. Boston: Little, Brown, 1968. Reprint, New York: Macmillan, 1973.

De Palo, William A., Jr. *The Mexican National Army, 1822–1852*. College Station: Texas A&M University Press, 1997.

Doolen, Andy. "Early American Civics: Rehistoricizing the Power of Republicanism." *American Literary History* 19, no. 1 (Spring 2007): 120–140.

Doubler, Michael D. *Civilian in Peace, Soldier in War: The Army National Guard, 1636–2000*. Lawrence: University Press of Kansas, 2003.

Eames, Steven C. *Rustic Warriors: Warfare and the Provincial Soldier on the New England Frontier, 1689–1748*. New York: New York University Press, 2011.

Edwards, Mackubin Thomas. *US Civil-Military Relations After 9/11: Renegotiating the Civil-Military Bargain*. New York: Continuum, 2011.

Eggenberger, David. *An Encyclopedia of Battles: Accounts of Over 1,560 Battles from 1479 B.C. to the Present*. New York: Dover, 1985.

Ericson, David F. "The Nullification Crisis, American Republicanism, and the Force Bill Debate." *Journal of Southern History* 61, no. 2 (May 1995): 249–270.

Eustace, Nicole. *1812: War and the Passions of Patriotism*. Philadelphia: University of Philadelphia Press, 2012.

Faust, Drew Gilpin. *This Republic of Suffering: Death and the American War*. New York: Alfred A. Knopf, 2008.

Ferling, John E. *A Wilderness of Miseries: War and Warriors in Early America*. Westport, CT: Greenwood, 1980.

Finer, S. E. *The Man on Horseback: The Role of the Military in Politics*. 2nd ed., rev., enl., and updated. Boulder, CO: Westview, 1988.

Fischer, David Hackett. *Albion's Seed: Four British Folkways in America*. New York: Oxford University Press, 1989.

Foos, Paul. *A Short, Offhand, Killing Affair: Soldiers and Social Conflict in the Mexican-American War*. Chapel Hill: University of North Carolina Press, 2002.

Foote, Lorien. *Gentlemen and the Roughs: Violence, Honor, and Manhood in the Union Army*. New York: New York University Press, 2010.

Frank, Joseph Allan. *With Ballot and Bayonet: The Political Socialization of American Civil War Soldiers*. Athens: University of Georgia Press, 1998.

Frank, Joseph Allan, and Barbara Duteau. "Measuring the Political Articulateness of United States Civil War Soldiers: The Wisconsin Militia." *Journal of Military History* 64, no. 1 (January 2000): 53–77.

Franklin, John Hope. *The Militant South, 1800–1861*. (Cambridge, MA: Harvard University Press, 1956.

Frey, Sylvia R. *The British Soldier in America: A Social History of Military Life in the Revolutionary Period*. Austin: University of Texas Press, 1981.

Gaines, William H. "The Forgotten Army: Recruiting for a National Emergency (1799–1800)." *Virginia Magazine of History and Biography* 56 (1948): 267–279.

Goetzmann, William H. *Army Exploration in the American West, 1803–1863*. New Haven, CT: Yale University Press, 1959.

Gough, Robert. "Officering the American Army, 1798." *William and Mary Quarterly*, 3rd ser., 43, no. 3 (July 1986): 460–71.

Greenberg, Amy S. *Manifest Manhood and the Antebellum American Empire*. New York: Cambridge University Press, 2005.

Greene, Jack P. *The American Revolution: Its Character and Limits*. New York: New York University Press, 1987.

Greiss, Thomas E., and Jay Luvaas, ed. *Reconsiderations on the Revolutionary War: Selected Essays*. Westport, CT: Greenwood, 1978.

Grenier, John. *The First Way of War: American War Making on the Frontier*. New York: Cambridge University Press, 2005.

Grimsley, Mark. "The American Civil War and Civic Virtue," *Foreign Policy Research Institute Footnotes: The Newsletter of the Wachman Center* 13, no. 11 (November 2008): 1–4.

Gross, Robert A. *The Minutemen and Their World*. New York: Hill and Wang, 1976.

Hagan, Kenneth J., and William R. Roberts, ed. *Against All Enemies: Interpretations of American Military History from Colonial Time to the Present*. New York: Greenwood, 1986.

Heitman, Francis B. *Historical Register and Dictionary of the United States Army, from Its Organization, September 29, 1789, to March 2, 1903*. 2 vols. Washington, DC: Government Printing Office, 1903.

Herrera, Ricardo A. "A People and Its Soldiers: The American Citizen as Soldier, 1775–1861." *International Bibliography of Military History* 33 (2013): 9–34.

———. "Self-Governance and the American Citizen as Soldier, 1775–1861." *Journal of Military History* 65, no. 1 (January 2001): 21–52.

———. "Toward an American Army: U.S. Soldiers, the War of 1812, and National Identity." *Army History* 88 (Summer 2013): 42–57.

Hess, Earl J. *Liberty, Virtue, and Progress: Northerners and Their War for the Union*. New York: New York University Press, 1988.

———. *The Union Soldier in Battle: Enduring the Ordeal of Combat*. Lawrence: University Press of Kansas, 1997.

Hickey, Donald R. "New England's Defense Problem and the Genesis of the Hartford Convention." *New England Quarterly* 50, no. 4 (December 1977): 587–604.

――――. *The War of 1812: A Forgotten Conflict.* Urbana: University of Illinois Press, 1989.

Hietala, Thomas R. *Manifest Destiny: Anxious Aggrandizement in Late Jacksonian America.* Ithaca, NY: Cornell University Press, 1985.

Higginbotham, Don. "The Early American Way of War: Reconnaissance and Appraisal." *William and Mary Quarterly,* 3d ser., 44, no. 2 (April 1987): 230–73.

――――. *George Washington and the American Military Tradition.* Athens: University of Georgia Press, 1985.

――――. *War and Society in Revolutionary America: The Wider Dimensions of Conflict.* Columbia: University of South Carolina Press, 1988.

――――. *The War for American Independence: Military Attitudes, Policies, and Practice, 1763–1789.* New York: Macmillan, 1971.

Hill, Jim Dan. *The Minute Man in War and Peace: A History of the National Guard.* Harrisburg, PA: Stackpole, 1964.

Hoffman, Ronald, and Peter J. Albert, eds. *Arms and Independence: The Military Character of the American Revolution.* Charlottesville: University Press of Virginia, 1984.

Hollandsworth, James G. Jr. *The Louisiana Native Guards: The Black Military Experience During the Civil War.* Baton Rouge: Louisiana State University Press, 1995.

Holt, Mack P. *The French Wars of Religion, 1562–1629.* 2nd ed. New York: Cambridge University Press, 1995.

Horsman, Reginald. *Race and Manifest Destiny: The Origins of American Racial Anglo-Saxonism.* Cambridge, MA: Harvard University Press, 1981.

Huntington, Samuel P. *The Soldier and the State: The Theory and the State of Civil-Military Relations.* Cambridge, MA: Belknap Press of Harvard University Press, 1957.

Immerman, Richard H. *Empire for Liberty: A History of American Imperialism from Benjamin Franklin to Paul Wolfowitz.* Princeton, NJ: Princeton University Press, 2010.

Janowitz, Morris. *The Professional Soldier: A Social and Political Portrait.* New York: Free Press, 1971.

Johannsen, Robert W. *To the Halls of the Montezumas: The Mexican War in the American Imagination.* New York: Oxford University Press, 1985.

Johnson, Tyler V. *Devotion to the Adopted Country: U.S. Immigrant Volunteers in the Mexican War.* Columbia: University of Missouri Press, 2012.

Kammen, Michael. *People of Paradox: An Inquiry Concerning the Origins of American Civilization.* New York: Knopf, 1972. Reprint, Ithaca, NY: Cornell University Press, 1980.

Kerber, Linda K. *Women of the Republic: Intellect and Ideology in Revolutionary America.* New York: W. W. Norton, 1986.

Kloppenberg, James T. "The Virtues of Liberalism: Christianity, Republicanism, and Ethics in American Political Discourse." *Journal of American History* 74, no. 1 (June 1987): 9–33.

Knouff, Gregory T. *The Soldiers' Revolution: Pennsylvanians in Arms and the Forging of American Identity.* University Park: Pennsylvania State University Press, 2003.

Kohn, Hans. *The Idea of Nationalism: A Study in Its Origins and Background.* New York: Macmillan, 1944. Reprint, New York: Collier Books, 1960.

Kohn, Richard H. *Eagle and Sword: The Federalists and the Creation of the Military Establishment in America, 1783–1802.* New York: Free Press, 1975.

———. "The Social History of the American Soldier: A Review and Prospectus for Research." *American Historical Review* 86, no. 3, (June 1981): 553–567.

———, ed. *The United States Military under the Constitution of the United States, 1789–1989.* New York: New York University Press, 1991.

Kortenhof, Kurt Daniel. "Republican Ideology and Wartime Reality: Thomas Mifflin's Struggle as the First Quartermaster General of the Continental Army, 1775–1778." *Pennsylvania Magazine of History and Biography* 122, no. 3 (July 1998): 179–210

Kramnick, Isaac. *Bolingbroke and His Circle: The Politics of Nostalgia in the Age of Walpole.* Cambridge, MA: Harvard University Press, 1968.

———. *Republicanism and Bourgeois Radicalism: Political Ideology in Late-Eighteenth Century England and America.* Ithaca, NY: Cornell University Press, 1990.

Kruman, Marc W. "The Second American Party System and the Transformation of Revolutionary Republicanism." *Journal of the Early Republic* 12 (1992): 509–537.

Kutolowski, John F., and Kathleen Smith Kutolowski. "Commissions and Canvasses: The Militia and Politics in Western New York, 1800–1845." *New York History* 63, no. 1 (January 1982): 5–38.

Langston, Thomas S. *Uneasy Balance: Civil-Military Relations in Peacetime America since 1783.* Baltimore: Johns Hopkins University Press, 2003.

Larkin, Edward. "Nation and Empire in the Early US." *American Literary History* 22, no. 3 (Fall 2010): 501–526.

Laver, Harry S. *Citizens more than Soldiers: The Kentucky Militia and Society in the Early Republic.* Lincoln: University of Nebraska Press, 2007.

Leach, Douglas Edward. *Arms for Empire: A Military History of the British Colonies in North America, 1607–1763.* New York: Macmillan, 1973.

———. *Roots of Conflict: British Armed Forces and Colonial Americans, 1677–1783.* Chapel Hill: University of North Carolina Press, 1986.

Lee, Wayne E. *Barbarians and Brothers: Anglo-American Warfare, 1500–1865.* New York: Oxford University Press, 2011.

———. "Mind and Matter—Cultural Analysis in American Military History: A Look at the State of the Field." *Journal of American History* 93, no. 4 (March 2007): 1116–1142.

Linderman, Gerald F. *Embattled Courage: The Experience of Combat in the American Civil War.* New York: Free Press, 1987.

Linenthal, Edward Tabor. *Sacred Ground: Americans and Their Battlefields, Lexington and Concord, The Alamo, Gettysburg, The Little Bighorn, Pearl Harbor* Champaign: University of Illinois Press, 1991.

Linklater, Andro. *An Artist in Treason: The Extraordinary Double Life of General James Wilkinson.* New York: Walker, 2009.

Linn, Thomas C. "Ethics Versus Self-Interest in How We Fight." In *Moral Obligation and the Military: Collected Essays*, 219–233. Washington, DC: National Defense University Press, 1988.

Little, Ann M. *Abraham in Arms: War and Gender in Colonial New England*. Philadelphia: University of Pennsylvania Press, 2007.

Magra, Christopher P. "'Soldiers . . . Bred to the Sea': Maritime Marblehead, Massachusetts, and the Origins and Progress of the American Revolution." *New England Quarterly* 77, no. 4 (December 2004): 531–562.

Mahon, John K. *History of the Militia and the National Guard*. New York: Macmillan, 1983.

Mahon, John K., and Roman Danysh. *Infantry*, pt. 1, *Regular Army*. Washington, DC: Office of the Chief of Military History, 1972.

Martin, James Kirby, and Mark Edward Lender. *A Respectable Army: The Military Origins of the Republic, 1763–1789*. 2nd ed. Arlington Heights, IL: Harlan Davidson, 2006.

Matloff, Maurice. "The Nature and Scope of Military History." In *New Dimensions in Military History: An Anthology*, edited by Russell F. Weigley, 387–410. San Rafael, CA: Presidio, 1975.

May, Robert E. "Invisible Men: Blacks and the U.S. Army in the Mexican War." *Historian* 49, no. 4 (Fall 1987): 463–477.

———. *John A. Quitman: Old South Crusader*. Baton Rouge: Louisiana State University Press, 1984.

———. *Manifest Destiny's Underworld: Filibustering in Antebellum America*. Chapel Hill: University of North Carolina Press, 2002.

———. "Young American Males and Filibustering in the Age of Manifest Destiny: The United States Army as a Cultural Mirror." *Journal of American History* 7, no. 3 (December 1991): 857–886.

Mayer, Holly A. *Belonging to the Army: Camp Followers and Community during the American Revolution*. Columbia: University of South Carolina Press, 1996.

McCaffrey, James M. *Army of Manifest Destiny: The American Soldier in the Mexican War, 1846–1848*. New York: New York University Press, 1992.

McConnell, Roland C. *Negro Troops of Antebellum Louisiana: A History of the Battalion of Free Men of Color*. Baton Rouge: Louisiana State University Press, 1968.

McCoy, Drew R. *The Elusive Republic: Political Economy in Jeffersonian America*. Chapel Hill: University of North Carolina Press, 1980.

McDonnell, Michael A. "Popular Mobilization and Political Culture in Revolutionary Virginia: The Failure of the Minutemen and the Revolution from Below." *Journal of American History* 85, no. 3 (December 1998): 946–981.

McHenry, Robert, ed. *Webster's American Military Biographies*. Springfield, MA: Merriam, 1978.

McPherson, James M. *Battle Cry of Freedom: The Civil War Era*. New York: Oxford University Press, 1988.

———. *For Cause and Comrades: Why Men Fought in the Civil War.* New York: Oxford University Press, 1997.

McRandle, James H. *The Antique Drums of War.* College Station: Texas A&M University Press, 1994.

Merk, Frederick. *Manifest Destiny and Mission in American History: A Reinterpretation.* New York: Alfred A. Knopf, 1963.

Middlekauff, Robert. "Why Men Fought in the American Revolution." *Huntington Library Quarterly* 43, no. 2 (Spring 1980): 135–148.

Miller, Richard F. "Brahmin Janissaries: John A. Andrew Mobilizes Massachusetts' Upper Class for the Civil War." *New England Quarterly* 75, no. 2 (June 2002): 204–234.

Millett, Allan R. "'The Constitution and the Citizen-Soldier." In *The United States Military Under the Constitution, 1789–1989,* edited by Richard H. Kohn, 97–119. New York: New York University Press, 1991.

Millis, Walter. *Arms and Men: A Study in American Military History.* New York: G. P. Putnam's Sons, 1956.

Milner, Marc. "In Search of the American Way of War: The Need for a Wider National and International Context." *Journal of American History* 93, no. 4 (March 2007): 1151–1153.

Mitchell, Reid. *Civil War Soldiers: Their Expectations and Their Experiences.* New York: Viking Penguin, 1988. Reprint, New York: Touchstone, 1989.

———. *The Vacant Chair: The Northern Soldier Leaves Home.* New York: Oxford University Press, 1993.

Morgan, Edmund S. *Inventing the People: The Rise of Popular Sovereignty in England and America.* New York: W. W. Norton, 1988.

Myers, Minor, Jr. *Liberty without Anarchy: A History of the Society of the Cincinnati.* Charlottesville: University Press of Virginia, 1983.

Neilson, Suzanne C., and Don M. Snider, eds. *American Civil-Military Relations: The Soldier and the State in a New Era.* Baltimore: Johns Hopkins University Press, 2009.

Neimeyer, Charles Patrick. *America Goes to War: A Social History of the Continental Army.* New York: New York University Press, 1996.

Norton, Mary Beth. *Liberty's Daughters: The Revolutionary Experience of American Women, 1750–1800.* Boston: Little, Brown, 1980.

Oakes, James. "From Republicanism to Liberalism: Ideological Change and the Crisis of the Old South." *American Quarterly* 37, no. 4 (Autumn 1985): 551–571.

Papenfuse, Edward C., and Gregory A. Stiverson. "General Smallwood's Recruits: The Peacetime Career of the Revolutionary War Private." *William and Mary Quarterly,* 3rd ser., 30 (1973): 117–132.

Pinheiro, John C. *Manifest Ambition: James K. Polk and Civil-Military Relations during the Mexican War.* Santa Barbara, CA: ABC-Clio, 2007.

Pitcavage, Mark. "Ropes of Sand: Territorial Militias, 1801–1812." *Journal of the Early Republic* 13, no. 4 (Winter 1993): 481–500.

Pocock, J. G. A. "Between Gog and Magog: The Republican Thesis and the *Ideologia Americana*," *Journal of the History of Ideas* 48, no. 2 (April–June 1987): 325–46.
——. *The Machiavellian Moment: Florentine Political Thought and the Atlantic Republican Tradition*. Princeton, NJ: Princeton University Press, 1975.
Probasco, Nate. "The Role of Commoners and Print in Elizabethan England's Acceptance of Firearms." *Journal of Military History* 76, no. 2 (April 2012): 343–372.
Prucha, Francis Paul. *Broadax and Bayonet: The Role of the United States Army in the Development of the Northwest, 1815–1860*. Madison: State Historical Society of Wisconsin, 1953.
——. *The Sword of the Republic: The United States Army on the Frontier, 1783–1846*. New York: Macmillan, 1969.
Purcell, Sarah J. *Sealed with Blood: War, Sacrifice, and Memory in Revolutionary America*. Philadelphia: University of Pennsylvania Press, 2002.
Rable, George C. *God's Almost Chosen Peoples: A Religious History of the American Civil War*. Chapel Hill: University of North Carolina Press, 2010.
Rahe, Paul A. *Republics Ancient and Modern: Classical Republicanism and the American Revolution*. Chapel Hill: University of North Carolina Press, 1992.
Reinders, Robert. "Militia and Public Order in Nineteenth-Century America." *Journal of American Studies* 11, no. 1 (1977): 81–101.
Remini, Robert V. *Andrew Jackson and the Course of American Empire, 1767–1821*. New York: Harper and Row, 1977.
Renner, Richard Wilson. "Ye Kort Martial: A Tale of Chicago Politics, Theatre, Journalism, and Militia." *Journal of the Illinois State Historical Society* 66, no. 4 (Winter 1973): 376–386.
Resch, John. *Suffering Soldiers: Revolutionary War Veterans, Moral Sentiment, and Political Culture in the Early Republic*. Amherst: University of Massachusetts Press, 1999.
Resch, John, and Walter Sargent, eds. *War and Society in the American Revolution*. DeKalb: Northern Illinois University Press, 2007.
Roberts, Keith. *Cromwell's War Machine: The New Model Army, 1646–1660*. Barnsley, UK: Pen and Sword, 2005
Roberts, Rita. "Patriotism and Political Criticism: The Evolution of Political Consciousness in the Mind of a Black Revolutionary Soldier." In "African-American Culture in the Eighteenth-Century," edited by Rose Zimbardo and Benilde Montgomery, special issue, *Eighteenth-Century Studies* 27, no. 4 (Summer 1994): 569–588.
Rodgers, Daniel T. "Republicanism: The Career of a Concept," *Journal of American History* 79, no. 1 (June 1992): 11–38.
Rodgers, Thomas E. "Billy Yank and G.I. Joe: An Exploratory Essay on the Sociopolitical Dimensions of Soldier Motivation." *Journal of Military History* 69, no. 1 (January 2005): 93–121.
Rosswurm, Steven. *Arms, Country, and Class: The Philadelphia Militia and the "Lower Sort" During the American Revolution, 1775–1783*. New Brunswick, NJ: Rutgers University Press, 1987.

Rowe, Mary Ellen. *Bulwark of the Republic: The American Militia in [the] Antebellum West*. Westport, CT: Praeger, 2003.

Royster, Charles. *Light-Horse Harry Lee and the Legacy of the American Revolution*. New York: Knopf, 1981. Reprint, Baton Rouge: Louisiana State University Press, 1994.

———. *A Revolutionary People at War: The Continental Army and American Character, 1775–1783*. Chapel Hill: University of North Carolina Press, 1979. Reprint, New York: W. W. Norton for the Institute of Early American History and Culture, 1981.

Rozbicki, Michal Jan. *Culture and Liberty in the Age of the American Revolution*. Charlottesville: University of Virginia Press, 2011.

Ryan, Garry D., and Timothy K. Nenninger, eds. *Soldiers and Civilians: The U. S. Army and the American People*. Washington, DC: National Archives and Records Administration, 1987.

Schantz, Mark S. *Awaiting the Heavenly Country: The Civil War and America's Culture of Death*. Ithaca, NY: Cornell University Press, 2008.

Seidule, James Tyrus. "'Treason is Treason': Civil War Memory at West Point, 1861–1902." *Journal of Military History* 76, no. 2 (April 2012): 427–452.

Shalev, Eran. *American Zion: The Old Testament as a Political Text from the Revolution to the Civil War*. New Haven, CT: Yale University Press, 2013.

Shalhope, Robert. "The Armed Citizen in the Early Republic." *Law and Contemporary Politics* 49, no. 1 (Winter 1986): 125–141.

———. "Republicanism and Early American Historiography." *William and Mary Quarterly*, 3d ser., 39, no. 2 (April 1982): 334–356.

———. "Toward a Republican Synthesis: The Emergence of an Understanding of Republicanism in American Historiography." *William and Mary Quarterly*, 3rd ser., 29 (January 1972): 49–80.

Shy, John. "The Cultural Approach to the History of War." *Journal of Military History* 57, no. 5 (October 1993): 13–26.

———. *A People Numerous and Armed: Reflections on the Military Struggle for American Independence*. Rev. ed. Ann Arbor: University of Michigan Press / Ann Arbor Paperbacks, 1990.

———. *Toward Lexington: The Role of the British Army in the Coming of the American Revolution*. Princeton, NJ: Princeton University Press, 1965.

Sifakis, Carl. "Hounds." In *The Encyclopedia of American Crime*. 2nd ed. New York: Facts On File, 2001), 437–438.

Silver, Peter. *Our Savage Neighbors: How Indian War Transformed Early America*. New York: W. W. Norton, 2008.

Skelton, William B. *An American Profession of Arms: The Army Officer Corps, 1784–1861*. Lawrence: University Press of Kansas, 1992.

———. "The Army in the Age of the Common Man, 1815–1845." In *Against All Enemies: Interpretations of American Military History from Colonial Times to the Present*, edited by Kenneth J. Hagan and William R. Roberts, 91–112. New York: Greenwood, 1986.

Smith, Joshua M. "The Yankee Soldier's Might: The District of Maine and the Reputation of the Massachusetts Militia, 1800–1812." *New England Quarterly* 84, no. 2 (June 2011): 234–264.

Snyder, R. Claire. *Citizen-Soldiers and Manly Warriors: Military Service and Gender in the Civic Republican Tradition*. Lanham, MD: Rowman and Littlefield, 1999.

Stagg, J.C.A. "Soldiers in Peace and War: Comparative Perspectives on the Recruitment of the United States Army, 1802–1815." *William and Mary Quarterly*, 3rd ser., 57, no. 1 (January 2000): 79–120.

———. *The War of 1812: Conflict for a Continent*. New York: Cambridge University Press, 2012.

Stephanson, Anders. *Manifest Destiny: American Expansion and the Empire of Right*. New York: Hill and Wang, 1995.

Stuart, Reginald C. *Civil-Military Relations during the War of 1812*. Santa Barbara, CA: ABC-Clio, 2009.

———. *War and American Thought: From the Revolution to the Monroe Doctrine*. Kent, OH: Kent State University Press, 1982.

Summers, Mark Wahlgren. "'Freedom and Law Must Die Ere They Sever': The North." In *Why the Civil War Came*, edited by Gabor Boritt, 177–200. New York: Oxford University Press, 1996.

Tate, Michael L. *The Frontier Army in the Settlement of the West*. Norman: University of Oklahoma Press, 1999.

———. "The Multi-Purpose Army on the Frontier: A Call for Further Research." In *The American West: Essays in Honor of W. Eugene Hollon*, edited by Ronald Lora, 171–208. Toledo, OH: University of Toledo Press, 1980.

Taylor, Alan. *The Civil War of 1812: American Citizens, British Subjects, Irish Rebels, & Indian Allies*. New York: Alfred A. Knopf, 2010.

Taylor, Paul, ed. *The Military-Civilian Gap: War and Sacrifice in the Post 9/11 Era*. Washington, DC: Pew Research Center, 2011.

Titus, James. *The Old Dominion at War: Society, Politics, and Warfare in Late Colonial Virginia*. Columbia: University of South Carolina Press, 1991.

Towles, Louis P. *A World Turned Upside Down: The Palmers of South Santee, 1818–1881*. Columbia: University of South Carolina Press, 1996.

Tucker, Phillip C. "Ho, for Kansas: The Southwest Expedition of 1860." *Missouri Historical Review* 86, no. 1 (October 1991): 22–36.

Ultee, Maarten, ed. *Adapting to Conditions: War and Society in the Eighteenth Century*. University: University of Alabama Press, 1986.

Utley, Robert M. *Frontiersmen in Blue: The United States Army and the Indian, 1848–1865*. New York: Macmillan, 1967.

Van Doren, Carl. *Mutiny in January: The Story of a Crisis in the Continental Army Now for the First Time Fully Told from Many Hitherto Unknown or Neglected Sources, Both American and British*. New York: Viking, 1943.

Warner, Ezra J. *Generals in Gray: Lives of the Confederate Commanders*. Baton Rouge: Louisiana State University Press, 1959.

Watson, Samuel J. "Developing 'Republican Machines': West Point and the Struggle to Render the Officer Corps Safe for America." In *Thomas Jefferson's Military Academy: Founding West Point*, edited by Robert M.S. McDonald, 154–81. Charlottesville: University of Virginia Press, 2004.

———. *Jackson's Sword: The Army Officer Corps on the American Frontier, 1810–1821*. Lawrence: University Press of Kansas, 2012.

———. "Manifest Destiny and Military Professionalism: Junior U. S. Army Officers' Attitudes Toward War with Mexico, 1844–1846." *Southwestern Historical Quarterly* 99, no. 4 (April 1996): 466–498.

———. *Peacekeepers and Conquerors: The Army Officer Corps on the American Frontier, 1821–1846*. Lawrence: University Press of Kansas, 2013.

———. "Religion and Combat Motivation in the Confederate Armies." *Journal of Military History* 58, no. 1 (January 1994): 29–55.

Weeks, William Earl. *Building the Continental Empire: American Expansion from the Revolution to the Civil War*. Chicago: Ivan R. Dee, 1996.

Weigley, Russell F. *History of the United States Army*. New York: Macmillan, 1967.

Weitz, Mark A. "Drill, Training, and the Combat Performance of the Civil War Soldier: Dispelling the Myth of the Poor Soldier, Great Fighter." *Journal of Military History* 62, no. 2 (April 1998): 263–829.

Western, J. R. *The English Militia in the Eighteenth Century: The Story of a Political Issue, 1660–1802*. London: Routledge and Kegan Paul, 1967.

Wettemann, Robert P., Jr. "A Part or Apart: The Alleged Isolation of Antebellum U.S. Army Officers." *American Nineteenth Century History* 7, no. 2 (June 2006): 193–217.

———. *Privilege vs. Equality: Civil-Military Relations in the Jacksonian Era, 1815–1845*. Santa Barbara, CA: ABC-Clio, 2009.

Wiley, Bell Irvin. *The Life of Billy Yank: The Common Soldier of the Union*. Baton Rouge: Louisiana State University Press, 1952.

———. *The Life of Johnny Reb: The Common Soldier of the Civil War*. Baton Rouge: Louisiana State University Press, 1943.

Wilson, Major L. "The 'Country' versus the 'Court': A Republican Consensus and Party Debate in the Bank War." *Journal of the Early Republic* 15 (1995): 619–647.

———. "Republicanism and the Idea of Party in the Jacksonian Period." *Journal of the Early Republic* 8 (1988): 419–432.

Wilson, Peter H. *The Thirty Years War: Europe's Tragedy*. Cambridge, MA: Belknap Press of Harvard University Press, 2009.

Winders, Richard Bruce. *Mr. Polk's Army: The American Military Experience in the Mexican War*. College Station: Texas A&M University Press, 1997.

Wood, Gordon S. *The Creation of the American Republic, 1776–1787*. Chapel Hill: University of North Carolina Press, 1969. Reprint, New York: W. W. Norton for the Institute of Early American History and Culture, 1972.

———. *The Radicalism of the American Revolution* New York: Random House, Vintage Books, 1993.

Wood, James B. *The King's Army: Warfare, Soldiers and Society during the Wars of Religion in France, 1562–76*. New York: Cambridge University Press, 1996.

Wooster, Robert. *The American Military Frontiers: The United States Army in the West, 1783–1900*. Albuquerque: University of New Mexico Press, 2009.

Wright, James. *Those Who Have Borne the Battle: A History of America's Wars and Those Who Fought Them*. New York: Public Affairs, 2012.

Wright, Robert K. Jr. *The Continental Army*. Washington, DC: United States Army Center of Military History, 1983.

Wyatt-Brown, Bertram. "Andrew Jackson's Honor." *Journal of the Early Republic* 17, no. 1 (Spring 1997): 1–36.

Zelner, Kyle F. *A Rabble in Arms: Massachusetts Towns and Militiamen in King Philip's War*. New York: New York University Press, 2009.

DISSERTATIONS

Baker, Dean Paul. "The Partridge Connection: Alden Partridge and Southern Military Education." PhD diss., University of North Carolina, Chapel Hill, 1986.

Fowle, Barry Windsor. "The Maryland Militia during the Revolutionary War: A Revolutionary Organization." PhD diss., University of Maryland, 1982.

Gates, Stewart Lewis. "Disorder and Social Organization: The Militia in Connecticut Public Life, 1660–1860." PhD diss., University of Connecticut, 1975.

Kindred, Marilyn Anne. "The Army Officer Corps and the Arts: Artistic Patronage and Practice in America, 1820–85." PhD diss., University of Kansas, 1981.

McCreedy, Kenneth Otis. "Palladium of Liberty: The American Militia System, 1815–1861." PhD diss., University of California, Berkeley, 1991.

Pitcavage, Mark. "An Equitable Burden: The Decline of the State Militias, 1783–1858." PhD diss., Ohio State University, 1995.

Steinhauer, Dale Richard. "'Sogers:' Enlisted Men in the U. S. Army, 1815–1860." PhD diss., University of North Carolina, Chapel Hill, 1992.

White, John Todd. "Standing Armies in Time of War: Republican Theory and Military Practice during the American Revolution." PhD diss., George Washington University, 1978.

INDEX

monarchy, 4, 28, 93

Mormon War, 40

musters, 11, 68, 85, 89, role of as public theater, 69

mutiny, 13, 91; by First Massachusetts Volunteers, 96; by soldiers of the Pennsylvania Line, 108

Napoleonic wars, 17

national heritage, 75

national legitimacy, 81

national mission, x, 127, 130; American faith in, 113, 134–35, 144; American sense of predestination and, 119; racially tinged spirit of, 125

nationalism, 123

nativity, 82, 88

natural rights, 65

New England, 9, 10, 14; militiamen in, 30; revolutionary volunteers from, 114; theocratic elite in, 113; warfare in colonial, 123

New York Military Magazine, 52

Old Dominion, 74, 90, 113

Old World, the, 112, 132

Ordnance of Secession, 51

O'Sullivan, John L., 113

Paine, Colonel Robert Treat, 38, 39, 96, 98–99

parades, 3; role as public theater, 69

patriotism, 59; bellicose form of, 3; doubts over militiamen's, 87; military service and, 88; soldiering as, 25; volunteers' doubt over regulars', 93

Patton, Colonel John, 53, 121

Phelps, Edward A. B. 131–33

Pickering, Colonel Timothy, 43, 55

Pillow, General Gideon J., 45, 150

Polk, James K., 21. 108–9

predestination, American sense of, 119, 124

Protestants, 20, 127

Prucha, Francis Paul, 22, 124

Pugh, Colonel Isaac, 155

Puritans, 10, 77, 112

Quitman, General John A., 129, 160

race, 123, 124, 125, 127, 129, 131, 133; European understanding of, 123; and miscegenation, 127; and "Revolutionary republicanism," 126; and slavery, 75

racial superiority, 121, 123, 133

Ransom, Colonel Truman B., 36

Regiment of Mounted Rifles, 21, 109, 131, 147. *See also* Third Cavalry Regiment

religion, 28, 54, 68, 76, 117, 120; monopoly of, 128

religious pluralism, 128

republican culture, 15, 18, 19, 24

republicanism, 5–6, 12, 14, 20, 31, 67, 69, 87, 128, 180n11; American, 57, 85, 113, 124, 133–34, 136; ancient, 77; ideology of, 16; liberal, 5; military ethos of, x, xii, 1, 10, 18, 24, 26, 27, 162–63, 165–66; military service and, 25; red and black, 74; revolutionary, 19, 21, 126

Revolution, American, the, 4, 14–16, 24–25, 45, 59, 70, 75, 78, 79, 83, 94, 112, 121, 122, 129, 130, 139, 172n6

rights, 11, 27, 70, 74, 114, 119, 121, 134, 164; American, 22, 26, 35, 61, 71; of citizen-soldiers, 14, 72, 88, 100, 111; defense of traditional, 2, 64, 102, 166; free trade and sailors', 17; individual, 12, 20, 65, 87, 91, 93–94, 113; of property, 73; of states, 190n21

Roman Catholic Church, 127

Roman Catholicism, 97, 128

Roman Catholics, 19, 20, 126, 128. *See also* Roman Catholicism

Rosswurm, Steven J., 80

Royster, Charles, 15, 31, 56, 59, 64, 166

Rozbicki, Michal Jan, 4, 25

ABOUT THE AUTHOR

Ricardo A. Herrera is Associate Professor of Military History at the School of Advanced Military Studies, U.S. Army Command and General Staff College. He is a graduate of Marquette University and the University of California, Los Angeles.